The Perception of Time

Using a concise question and answer format, *The Perception of Time: Your Questions Answered* examines basic temporal processes and the ways in which our perception of time can be altered.

Divided into three parts, the book provides a contemporary overview of the study of the temporal mind. It begins by introducing the fundamental processes of time perception: how it can be measured, how it can be hindered, and to what extent it can be enhanced. It proceeds to explain how cognitive and psychological disorders, such as schizophrenia, ADHD, and anxiety can be linked to temporal dysfunction, and answers common questions that face us all: why does time seem to go faster as we age? How do our emotions affect our perception of time? How does our relationship with time differ from others?

Providing comprehensive answers to the most pertinent questions of time perception, this book is an ideal companion for advanced students and researchers interested in the psychology of time.

Simon Grondin is Professor of Psychology at Université Laval, Québec, Canada.

"This book is pedagogic and synthetic, and covers an impressive amount of easy-to-grasp information"
—**Anne Giersch, French National Institute of Health and Medical Research, Strasbourg, France**

"This book will appeal to both the intelligent layperson and the advanced undergraduate or graduate"
—**Vincent Walsh, Professor of Human Brain Research, University College London, UK**

The Perception of Time
Your Questions Answered

Simon Grondin

NEW YORK AND LONDON

First published 2020
by Routledge
52 Vanderbilt Avenue, New York, NY 10017

and by Routledge
2 Park Square, Milton Park, Abingdon, Oxon, OX14 4RN

Routledge is an imprint of the Taylor & Francis Group, an informa business

© 2020 Taylor & Francis

The right of Simon Grondin to be identified as author of this work has been asserted by him in accordance with sections 77 and 78 of the Copyright, Designs and Patents Act 1988.

All rights reserved. No part of this book may be reprinted or reproduced or utilised in any form or by any electronic, mechanical, or other means, now known or hereafter invented, including photocopying and recording, or in any information storage or retrieval system, without permission in writing from the publishers.

Trademark notice: Product or corporate names may be trademarks or registered trademarks, and are used only for identification and explanation without intent to infringe.

Library of Congress Cataloging-in-Publication Data
A catalog record for this book has been requested

ISBN: 978-0-367-43164-8 (hbk)
ISBN: 978-0-367-43163-1 (pbk)
ISBN: 978-1-003-00163-8 (ebk)

Typeset in Goudy
by Apex CoVantage, LLC

Contents

Foreword   xi

PART 1
Basic Temporal Processes   1

1 How Are Timing and Time Perception Studied?   3

General Distinctions 3
Specific Investigation Methods 4
Methods Based on Comparison 5
Comparisons With an Implicit Standard 7
Other Methods or Performance Indexes 7
Conclusion 8
References 8

2 Do Psychophysical Laws Hold for Time Perception?   10

The Psychophysical Law 10
Weber's Law 11
Law of Vierordt 13
Conclusion 13
References 14

3 Is Psychological Time Punctuated With Critical Durations?   16

Nature of Temporal Experiences 16
Around Time 0 17
Psychological Moment 17
Automatic Processing 18
Maximum Sensitivity 18
One Second as a Transition Point 19
Psychological Present 20

Conclusion 20
References 21

4 Do We Have an Internal Clock? 23

Types of Mechanisms 23
Pacemaker-Counter Device 24
An Information Processing Version 25
Conclusion 26
References 27

5 Which Parts of the Brain Are Involved in the Processing of Temporal Information? 30

Positioning of the Problem 31
Noncentral Timing 31
Cortical Areas 32
Subcortical Structures 33
Cerebellum 34
Conclusion 34
References 35

6 Is Temporal Information Processing Based on Rhythm? 38

Number of Intervals and Their Role 38
Unique Intervals vs. Rhythm 39
Attending, Attention, and Entrainment 40
Regularity, Cognitive Efficiency, and Brain 41
Conclusion 42
References 42

7 Does the Perception of Time Emerge From Our Senses? 44

Senses for Addressing the Internal Clock Issue 44
Intramodal Processing of Duration 45
Conclusion 47
References 47

8 Can We Improve the Processing of Temporal Information? 50

Training and Intramodal Transfer 50
Training and Intermodal Transfer 51
Transfer Towards Other Types of Activity 53
Conclusion 54
References 54

9 What Is the Influence of Attention on Time Perception?   56

Retrospective Judgments 56
Prospective Judgments 57
With or Without an Internal Clock 58
Conclusion 59
References 59

10 How Does Space Affect Time Judgments?   61

Kappa Effect 61
Influence of Movement 63
Conclusion 64
References 64

11 What Factors Cause Temporal Distortions?   67

Perceptual Effects 67
Cognitive Effects 68
Body Effects 69
Conclusion 71
References 71

PART 2
Time and Pathologies   75

12 What Experience of Time Do People With Schizophrenia Have?   77

Continuity and Order of Sensory Events 77
Explicit Judgments on Duration 78
Neuroscience Data 79
Conclusion 80
References 80

13 What Relation to Time Do Autistic People Have?   82

Temporal Rigidity 82
Performances With Classical Temporal Tasks 83
Conclusion 84
References 85

14 How Is ADHD Linked to Temporal Problems?   86

Deficits in the Processing of Temporal Information 86
Neurological Bases of Temporal Disorders in ADHD 87

Aversion to Delays 88
Conclusion 89
References 89

15 Does a Depressive State Affect Time Perception? 91

Classical Temporal Tasks 91
Temporal Orientation and Impression 92
Conclusion 93
References 94

16 Does Anxiety Affect Time Perception? 96

Classical Temporal Tasks 96
Temporal Orientation 98
Conclusion 99
References 99

17 How Is Parkinson's Disease Related to the Processing of Temporal Information? 100

Temporal Tasks Involving Motor Skills 100
Perceptual Temporal Tasks 101
Emotions 102
Conclusion 103
References 103

18 Do People With Traumatic Brain Injury Have Temporal Dysfunctions? 105

Perceived Duration 105
Variability 106
Links With Other Neuropsychological Tasks 106
Conclusion 107
References 108

19 Are Language and Reading Impairments Caused by Temporal Information Processing Problems? 109

Speech and Language Impairments 109
Reading Impairments 110
Conclusion 111
References 112

20 Can Time and Rhythm Be Useful in Physical Rehabilitation? 114

Rhythmic Training 114
The Case of Stuttering 115
Temporal Equivalence 116
Conclusion 116
References 117

PART 3
Personal and Social Time 119

21 Are Musicians Better at Perceiving Time? 121

Some Facts 121
Resistance to Certain Effects and Difficulty Levels 122
Generalization of the Competence 123
Conclusion 124
References 125

22 What Place Does Synchronization Have in Relationships Between People? 127

Synchronization of Gestures 127
Speech Pace 128
In Therapy 129
Conclusion 130
References 130

23 How Does Emotion Affect Time Perception? 132

Retrospective Judgments 132
Prospective Judgments 134
Conclusion 135
References 136

24 What Knowledge Do Children Have of Time? 138

Piagetian Approach 138
Temporal Estimations 139
Temporal Representations on a Larger Scale 140
Conclusion 141
References 141

25 Does Time Perception Differ According to Sex? 143

Prospective Judgments 143
Retrospective Judgments 144
Emotions 144
Conclusion 145
References 146

26 How Do People Differ in Their Relationship to Time? 148

Assessment of Individual Differences 148
Cultural Differences 150
Conclusion 151
References 151

27 Do We Correctly Estimate the Time It Takes to Do a Task? 153

Retrospective Judgments 153
Planning Fallacy 154
Conclusion 156
References 156

28 How Do We Remember When an Event Occurred? 158

Theoretical Proposals 158
Some Facts 159
Memory Encoding Troubles 160
Conclusion 161
References 161

29 Why Does Time Seem to Go Faster as We Get Older? 163

Some Classical Interpretations or Hypotheses 163
Study of Temporal Acceleration 165
Conclusion and Ad Lib 166
References 167

Index 169

Foreword[1]

Because my main professional activity is to do research on the perception of time, I have often been asked, for more than three decades, questions about psychological time. These questions indeed take all kinds of forms. Even if it is not possible here to provide answers to each one, it is the will to provide some elements of answer and avenues of reflection related to some of these questions which motivates the writing of this work and justifies the chosen format.

A difficulty encountered during the writing was the final choice of the questions and their order of presentation. Some questions were needed because they often come to people's mind, others were needed because they touch on some important contemporary research avenues in the field of time perception and psychological time. The order was sometimes difficult to establish, but was mainly aimed at reducing the redundancy of certain pieces of information. Because of the relevance of some of these elements in different places, the reader is sometimes referred to different chapters during reading.

Beyond the questions themselves, it was also necessary to sort out the sources of information and determine the content of each answer. Of course, the fact of having already worked on many of the themes tints the book; spontaneously, I first tried to turn to what I knew most. But the field of psychological time is a vast ocean, with a long tradition of scientific research enriched by the results of a huge wave of recent work conducted around the world. There are inevitably relevant questions and important sources of information that have escaped my attention, or that it would not have been possible to integrate into the content of the book.

The book has three main parts. Because it is more abstract and theoretical, I suspect that the first part, devoted to fundamental temporal processes, will be a little more difficult to read. The reading of the other two parts should be facilitated by reading the first part, and in particular by reading the first chapter. The second part should appeal to readers who are particularly interested in cognitive, neurological, or psychiatric problems. The third part is probably the one that comes closest to the daily questioning of people about psychological time because it touches on themes such as emotion, time in children, and individual differences. Ultimately, this book is an invitation to travel in the universe of psychological time. It aims to make readers understand the extent of the temporal mind and how we constantly have to deal, under one form or another, with that obscure creature that is time.

In closing, I would like to acknowledge the contribution of the Natural Sciences and Engineering Research Council of Canada, which since 1991 has been financially supporting my work on the fundamental processes involved in time perception. The Social Sciences and Humanities Research Council of Canada has also contributed to the financial support of numerous works on psychological time conducted under my direction.

Simon Grondin

Note

1. This book is the translation of a book in French entitled *Le temps psychologique en questions* published in Canada by Presses de l'Université Laval, and in France by Éditions Hermann. This foreword is contained in the French version of the book. I would like to thank Jamie McArthur for her careful reading of the English version.

Part 1
Basic Temporal Processes

1 How Are Timing and Time Perception Studied?

Because the idea of perceiving time, or taking it into account, may take several forms, there are numerous ways of studying it. The following methods presented are classical ones in the field of time perception and should prove useful in the reading of the present work, especially during the first parts. In the third and final part, different tools such as questionnaires were also used for collecting information about psychological time. The following presentation of the methods, therefore, is not exhaustive, the specificity of the questions addressed often requiring methodological adjustments.

Before listing some of the most classical or most often used methods, it is relevant to proceed with some simple distinctions, particularly between two types of experiments and between two types of dependent variables.

General Distinctions

When the participants of an experiment are asked to make explicit judgments about time, these judgments belong to one of two categories: *prospective* or *retrospective* (Hicks, Miller, & Kinsbourne, 1976; Tobin, Bisson, & Grondin, 2010). When participants judge duration in a retrospective way, it means that they did not know in advance that they were going to have to estimate the duration of an event or an activity (Bisson, Tobin, & Grondin, 2009; Boltz, 1995, 2005; Eisler, Eisler, & Montgomery, 2004; Grondin & Plourde, 2007). Prospective judgments rather refer to conditions where the participants are informed beforehand by an experimenter that time (the duration of an interval, defined in some way) must be estimated (Brown & Stubbs, 1988; Predebon, 1996; Zakay, 1993). Most of the time, within the framework of retrospective judgments, the intervals to be judged will be long, whereas, in conditions of prospective judgments, the intervals will be very short (from tens of milliseconds to a few seconds).

In order to understand the literature on time perception, it is also important to keep in mind on which of two types of dependent variables the emphasis is put. We could classify these types as being related to the average estimations, by opposition to the variability of these estimations. Suppose that you want to know the efficiency of a person who claims to be able to give you the right time. You ask this person to estimate one minute two different times. The first time, this person indicates that a minute has passed after 59 seconds, and the second time, after 61 seconds. This person's average timing will be perfect (60 seconds), i.e., on the target. Another person makes similar estimations and indicates that a minute has passed after 55 and 65 seconds; the estimations will also be, on average, on the target, but this second person will exhibit a much larger variability than the first person. When extracting information about duration in the literature, it will thus be necessary to verify if it is about the quality that allows staying on average near the target (the central tendency, or perceived duration) or about the capacity to minimize the gap between the various time estimations (variability).

Specific Investigation Methods

Cognitive psychology researchers interested in the study of psychological time often distinguish four important categories of methods (Bindra & Waksberg, 1956; Wallace & Rabin, 1960; see Block, Grondin, & Zakay, 2018; Grondin, 2008). The first one is called *verbal estimation*. It first requires the presentation of a target interval to a participant who then has to provide verbally, by means of known chronometric units (second or minutes), an estimation of the aforementioned interval. In a second method, said of *production*, an experimenter indicates a time interval (duration) to a participant, by means of chronometric units. This participant then has to produce this same interval, usually by using two digital keystrokes (on the space bar of a computer keyboard for example) in order to mark the beginning and the end of the interval, or by pressing a button for duration considered equivalent to the target interval.

A third method, said of *reproduction*, requires a presentation by an experimenter of a target interval. This interval can be marked by a sound or a continuous visual stimulus, or by two brief signals determining the beginning and the end of the interval to reproduce. There are various ways to make this reproduction. A participant could either have to press a button only at the end of the target interval, following a signal (brief sound or flash) indicating the beginning of the interval to be reproduced, or to press it twice to indicate the beginning and the end of the reproduced interval, or to press it in a continuous way during the duration of the interval to reproduce. The precision turns out to be greater when it is necessary to press the button twice to indicate the beginning and the end of the interval, but the variability is lower when using the method involving a continuous key press during the interval (Mioni, Stablum, McClintock, & Grondin, 2014).

It is worth mentioning that when investigations include retrospective judgments, methods of verbal estimation or of interval reproduction will be used. With the prospective judgments, these three methods can be used, as well as the fourth described in the following text (see Figure 1.1).

Clearly, it is possible to study the perceived duration during prospective judgments by means of the three methods described up to here; it is also

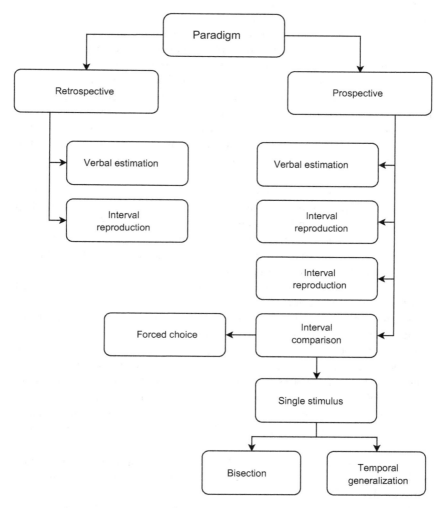

Figure 1.1 Summary of the main methods for investigating the mechanisms involved in the processing of temporal information (Grondin, 2010).

possible to study variability by multiplying trials, since interval production and reproduction methods lend themselves better than verbal estimation to an analysis of the variability.

Methods Based on Comparison

The fourth way of investigating time perception is known as the comparison method. It can sometimes be considered as a discrimination task. This method brings us closer to some traditional methods used in psychophysics and since it is often used, in one way or another, in numerous works, it is relevant to describe it in detail and in its various forms. Most of the time, this method contains a comparison between two intervals presented in succession. These intervals to be compared may consist of two continuous sounds or two continuous flashes (which are called filled), the length of which varies; or may consist of a duration between two brief sounds or between two brief flashes (an empty interval) that must be compared with the duration between two other brief sounds or two other brief flashes. Regardless of whether the intervals are empty or filled, most of the time, the participant has to indicate, by pressing the appropriate button, if the second interval is shorter or longer than the first one; therefore, the participant is forced to make a choice between two possibilities.

In psychophysics, we often use a standard and a comparison interval, with the length of this comparison interval being likely to change from trial to trial. When the standard is always presented first, the method is referred to as a reminder task, but when the order of the standard and comparison intervals randomly varies from trial to trial, the method is called roving (Macmillan & Creelman, 1991). Temporal interval discrimination turns out to be much better when the standard, which always keeps the same value, is always presented first (Grondin & McAuley, 2009).

By preselecting a series of comparison intervals (generally from six to eight), some longer and some shorter than the standard, as is done with the constant method—a traditional one in psychophysics—it becomes possible to build psychometric functions. We can extract from these functions two relevant indexes of performance: one about perceived duration and the other about variability. The comparison intervals are randomly presented from trial to trial, every interval being presented several times. The psychometric function contains on the x axis the values of the comparison intervals, in ascending order, and, on the y axis, the probability that the participant answered that the standard interval is greater than the comparison interval. According to the chosen intervals, it usually results in a monotonous ascending function, with the shape of an ogive.

Various models can be adopted to draw with precision the function on which both indexes of interest can be identified: These indexes are the point on the x axis corresponding to 50% of "standard > comparison" responses and the distance on the x axis corresponding to 25% and 75% of "standard > comparison" responses. It is necessary to understand that 25% and 75% represent middle points between a response that is always correct (0% and 100%) and the incapacity to respond (random level: 50%). The 50% value is called the point of subjective equality and provides information on the perceived duration of the second interval compared with the first one. In the second case, the value of the distance between 25% and 75%, divided by 2, will provide a measure of the difference threshold, which is the value from which the participant can give a correct response more than 50% of the time (i.e., above threshold). In fact, this value provides information about the sensitivity of the participant, a smaller value of the threshold indicating a higher sensitivity (or a smaller variability).

It is also possible to extract threshold values on the basis of a series of trials containing a standard and a comparison stimulus, without using the constant method. For instance, an adaptive method can be adopted. In such a case, the comparison intervals are not determined beforehand, but adapted to the fact that a correct or an incorrect response was given by the participant. There are various functioning rules that allow a convergence toward a stimulus value that will be operationally considered as the one reflecting the difference threshold (Grassi & Soranzo, 2009; Kearnbach, 1991).

Comparisons With an Implicit Standard

Some experimental procedures do not require the presentation of a standard presentation on every trial (single stimulus procedure). Strictly speaking, these are categorization procedures, rather than discrimination procedures. In some cases, the task of a participant is to assign the presented interval to one of two categories: "short intervals" vs. "long intervals". Over the course of trials, the participant develops an implicit standard (Allan, 1979; Morgan, Watamaniuk, & McKee, 2000).

There are, in the psychological time literature, classical variants of the use of the procedure based on the presentation of a single stimulus in each trial. These variants were developed by researchers interested in animal behavior. One is called *temporal bisection* and is now often used in human timing studies. It consists in a presentation, several times at the beginning of the experience, of the shortest and of the longest intervals (referred to as standards, or anchors) of a series of predetermined intervals. Then, the task consists in determining, on each trial, if the presented interval is closer to the short or the long standard. A psychometric function as that described previously can then be drawn. Another procedure is called *temporal generalization*. In this case, the interval (standard) representing the middle point of the retained series of intervals for the experiment is first presented several times. The participant then has to indicate, on each trial, whether the presented interval was or was not of the same duration as the standard.

Other Methods or Performance Indexes

Sometimes, for expressing performances about the relative length of intervals (discrimination or categorization), we may simply use the percentage of correct responses for quantifying sensitivity, and the probability of responding more or less often "short" (or "long") for quantifying perceived duration. We may also express performance levels on the basis of the signal detection theory; for example, the d' index (pronounced "dee prime") would indicate the sensitivity level.

In parallel to all these methods, Kuroda and Hasuo (2014) suggest using another classical psychophysical method, called *adjustment*, for studying time perception. With this method, a participant is successively presented with a standard and a comparison interval. The participant has to adjust the duration of the comparison interval until it seems equal to the duration of the standard. After a series of trials, it becomes possible to obtain a point of subjective equality, which indicates the perceived duration of the comparison interval, and the variability of the various adjustments (standard deviation), which can be interpreted as a value of the difference threshold.

Conclusion

To study time, it is necessary to identify the nature of what we are trying to know: retrospective vs. prospective judgments, and mean vs. variability of the estimations. Also, the length of the time interval of interest might help to determine which method is appropriate. For example, with very long intervals, it would be preferable to avoid the method of reproduction, and with very short intervals, one might want to avoid using motor skills for delineating intervals.

References

Allan, L. G. (1979). The perception of time. *Perception & Psychophysics, 26,* 340–354.

Bindra, D., & Waksberg, H. (1956). Methods and terminology in the studies of time estimation. *Psychological Bulletin, 53,* 155–159.

Bisson, N., Tobin, S., & Grondin, S. (2009). Remembering the duration of joyful and sad musical excerpts. *NeuroQuantology, 7,* 46–57.

Block, R. A., Grondin, S., & Zakay, D. (2018). Prospective and retrospective timing processes: Theories, methods, and findings. In D. A. Vatakis, F. Balci, M. Di Luca, & A. Correa (Eds.), *Timing and time perception: Procedures, measures, and applications* (pp. 32–51). Leiden, The Netherlands: Brill.

Boltz, M. G. (1995). Effects of event structure on retrospective duration judgments. *Perception & Psychophysics, 57,* 1080–1096.

Boltz, M. G. (2005). Duration judgments of naturalistic events in the auditory and visual modalities. *Perception & Psychophysics, 67,* 1362–1375.

Brown, S. W., & Stubbs, D. A. (1988). The psychophysics of retrospective and prospective timing. *Perception, 17,* 297–310.

Eisler, A., Eisler, H., & Montgomery, H. (2004). A quantitative model for retrospective subjective duration. *NeuroQuantology, 4,* 263–291.

Grassi, M., & Soranzo, A. (2009). MLP: A MATLAB toolbox for rapid and reliable auditory threshold estimation. *Behavior Research Methods, 41,* 20–28.

Grondin, S. (2008). Methods for studying psychological time. In S. Grondin (Ed.), *Psychology of time* (pp. 51–74). Bingley, UK: Emerald Group Publishing.

Grondin, S. (2010). Timing and time perception: A review of recent behavioral and neuroscience findings and theoretical directions. *Attention, Perception & Psychophysics, 72,* 561–582.

Grondin, S., & McAuley, J. D. (2009). Duration discrimination in crossmodal sequences. *Perception, 38,* 1542–1559.

Grondin, S., & Plourde, M. (2007). Judging multi-minute intervals retrospectively. *Quarterly Journal of Experimental Psychology, 60,* 1303–1312.

Hicks, R. E., Miller, G. W., & Kinsbourne, M. (1976). Prospective and retrospective judgments of time as a function of amount of information processed. *The American Journal of Psychology, 89,* 719–730.

Kearnbach, C. (1991). Simple adaptive testing with the weighted up-down method. *Perception & Psychophysics, 49,* 227–229.

Kuroda, T., & Hasuo, E. (2014). The very first step to start psychophysical experiments. *Acoustical Science & Technology, 35,* 1–9.

Macmillan, N. A., & Creelman, C. D. (1991). *Detection theory: A user's guide.* New York: Cambridge University Press.

Mioni, G., Stablum, F., McClintock, S. M., & Grondin, S. (2014). Different methods for reproducing time, different results. *Attention, Perception, & Psychophysics, 76,* 675–681.

Morgan, M. J., Watamaniuk, S. N. J., & McKee, S. P. (2000). The use of an implicit standard for measuring discrimination thresholds. *Vision Research, 40,* 2341–2349.

Predebon, J. (1996). The effects of active and passive processing of interval events on prospective and retrospective time estimates. *Acta Psychologica, 94,* 41–58.

Tobin, S., Bisson, N., & Grondin, S. (2010). An ecological approach to prospective and retrospective timing of long durations: A study involving gamers. *PLoS One, 5*(2), e9271.

Wallace, M., & Rabin, A. I. (1960). Temporal experience. *Psychological Bulletin, 57,* 213–235.

Zakay, D. (1993). Time estimation methods: Do they influence prospective duration estimates? *Perception, 22,* 91–101.

2 Do Psychophysical Laws Hold for Time Perception?

Psychophysics is a very old discipline and, to some extent, it is even older than psychology itself. The origin of psychophysics dates back to 1860, with the publication of a book by Gustav Fechner entitled *Elemente der Psychophysik*. Interested in the link between the physical reality and the psychological experience we make of it, Fechner proposed in this book different methods for studying this link and the properties of the sensory systems in a scientific way. In fact, during the nineteenth century, the physiology of sensory systems was a very important scientific avenue.

The study of the links between the physical reality—which our sensory systems allow us to capture—and the psychological reality allowed certain laws, or at least major principles, to emerge. These laws sometimes touch on the link between the physical magnitude of stimuli for a given sensory continuum and the magnitude of the sensation, sometimes the link between the capabilities to distinguish two stimuli of the same nature and their physical magnitude. Although there are, strictly speaking, neither stimuli nor receptors dedicated to time, it remains possible to use this framework again for trying to capture the nature of psychological time (Grondin, 2001).

The Psychophysical Law

One question asked in psychophysics concerns the relationship between the perceived intensity of a stimulus and its magnitude on the physical plane. We sometimes refer to the psychophysical law in order to speak about this relationship, or about Stevens's law, who has examined numerous sensory continua for testing the aforementioned relationship (Stevens, 1975).

There are numerous methods for establishing this relationship. For example, we can use magnitude estimation. After having assigned a certain value to a standard stimulus (called modulus), an experimenter asks a participant to assign a numerical value to other stimuli; the magnitude of the value assigned to these stimuli varies according to the initial value assigned to the modulus. We can then establish, based on a participant's responses, a function linking the psychological magnitude and the physical magnitude of stimuli. In the case of time, we can ask a participant, for example, to make a verbal estimation of an interval by means of chronometric units, or we can use the method of production of intervals (see Chapter 1).

The relationships between the perceived intensity of a stimulus and the physical magnitude of the stimulus can take different forms. They will sometimes be linear, sometimes logarithmic, sometimes exponential. In general, it turns out that psychophysical functions linking sensation (S) to physical magnitude (ϕ) can be described using a power function (sometimes referred to as Stevens's power law):

$$S = K\, \phi^b$$

where the exponent b is the signature of a continuum under study. For example, its value will be greater than 1 (exponential) if one studies the impression left by electric shocks, or smaller than 1 (logarithmic) if one studies the length of lines.

Such a relationship can be established for time. In this case, we link the subjective time (S) to the chronometric time (ϕ) and quantify the value of the exponent, b. When the value of b is less than 1, it means that the subjective time increases more and more slowly as chronometric time increases; if this value is greater than 1, the subjective time increases more rapidly as the chronometric time increases. There are hundreds of studies about this psychophysical relationship for time. Most often, the values of b obtained vary between .9 and 1 (Eisler, 1976). However, these estimates of b may vary depending on the magnitude estimation methods used. They also vary according to other factors such as the sex of the participant (Grondin & Laflamme, 2015).

Weber's Law

The psychophysical law described earlier makes it possible to take a general look, over a given range of durations, at the deviation of subjective duration as a function of chronometric duration. This is a concern related to the perceived duration. Weber's law focuses on the other basic concern in the study of psychological time, variability, and, as we will see in Chapter 4, has proved crucial in the development of theoretical propositions for explaining the mechanisms in the processing of temporal information. This important theoretical impact explains why we will study it more thoroughly.

In Chapter 1, some of the methods described made it possible to estimate the value of a differential threshold, i.e., the smallest amount necessary to discriminate two stimuli. In the case that concerns us, the "stimuli" are time intervals. Weber's law was developed in the context of the study of sensory systems, Ernst Weber having specifically studied the kinesthetic system (the ability to discriminate weights). It is, therefore, a law on the capacity to discriminate. More specifically, it aims at describing the link between the differential threshold for given sensory quantities and the magnitude of these quantities.

In its strict form, Weber's law states that for a given sensory continuum, the value of a differential threshold ($\Delta\phi$) increases proportionally as a function of the magnitude (ϕ) of the stimuli under study. In other words, the ratio between the differential threshold and the magnitude remains constant on this continuum:

$$\Delta\phi = K\phi \quad (\text{or } \Delta\phi/\phi = K)$$

where K, Weber's fraction, is a constant.

In reality, we know that Weber's law is inaccurate. When dealing with low magnitude stimuli, the value of Weber's fraction tends to be much higher than it is for slightly higher magnitude stimuli. Algebraically, this increase of the Weber fraction can be easily accounted for with a simple transformation of the equation. It suffices to add a constant, a, interpreted as the result of sensory noise:

$$\Delta\phi = K\phi + a$$

Weber's law, in its generalized form, provides a tool for looking at the mechanisms involved in discrimination tasks, in this case, the discrimination of time intervals (see Killeen & Weiss, 1987).

In the realm of subjective time, we sometimes refer to the scalar property of time, rather than to Weber's fraction. Many studies have been conducted in the field of animal timing for testing the validity of this scalar property (Church & Gibbon, 1982). Later, various methods borrowed from these animal studies were used to test the scalar property in humans. Thus, several empirical demonstrations, often conducted with durations to estimate ranging from a few seconds to about 30 seconds, suggest that the property is respected (see for example Rakitin et al., 1998; Wearden, 1992). In the same vein, Weber's law, or its generalized form, is useful and sometimes seems to hold for the processing of brief intervals (Grondin, 1993; Karampela, Holm, & Madison, 2015; Killeen & Weiss, 1987; Merchant, Zarco, & Prado, 2008).

That said, there are multiple examples in the time perception literature showing that Weber's law, even in its generalized form, does not hold (Bizo, Chu, Sanabria, & Killeen, 2006; Grondin, 2010; see the reviews of Grondin, 2001, 2014). For example, in a study to test different expressions of Weber's law, Getty (1975) reports data for the discrimination of intervals marked by sounds showing that, in durations above two seconds, the Weber fraction increases considerably. Similar results are observed for the discrimination of intervals marked by sequences of brief sounds (tempo: Drake & Botte, 1993) or for time interval production (Madison, 2001); note however that in these cases, this increase of the Weber fraction occurs with intervals much shorter than two seconds. Such a trend (increased Weber fractions) was already observable in a composite figure reported in 1978 by Fraisse who showed that this increase applies to intervals marked by signals delivered from different sensory modalities. Along the same line, Gibbon, Malapani, Dale, and Gallistel (1997) report a figure that depicts Weber fractions from dozens of animal and human studies. These authors conclude that there appears to be an increase of these fractions at around 1.5 s. Crystal (2006) even reported a peak time sensitivity in animals around 1.2 s.

More recently, a systematic study on this issue has been conducted with three different methods (discrimination, production and categorization), with intervals ranging from 1 to 1.9 s, and involving the use of single or sequential intervals (Grondin, 2012). On many occasions, an increase of Weber fraction occurs at around 1.3 s. As we will see in the next chapter, this duration range may well mark a point of critical transition on the psychological timescale.

Law of Vierordt

Another phenomenon known as Vierordt's law can also be traced back to the beginnings of experimental psychology in Germany in the nineteenth century (Eisler, Eisler, & Hellström, 2008; Lejeune & Wearden, 2009). An interesting side of this law is that it stems from investigations dedicated to the study of psychological time. Consequently, the question asked at the beginning of this chapter loses part of its meaning.

In its strict form, this law states that in a set of intervals, shorter ones will be judged to be longer than they really are, while longer ones will be judged to be shorter than they really are. Vierordt had reported this law first on the basis of data obtained with the method of interval reproduction.

With such tendencies, we inevitably end up with a point where this tendency to overestimate or underestimate disappears. This point is called the indifference interval. Since this point changes according to the distribution of the intervals under study, it is not reasonable to conclude that such points have any specific meaning about psychological time. Nevertheless, we know that a simple central tendency effect would not account for the appearance of this indifference interval and that the use of feedback cancels in some cases these over- and under-estimation effects (Lejeune & Wearden, 2009).

Finally, it is reasonable to posit that this effect (Vierordt's law and indifference interval) is related to a more general phenomenon called the *adaptation level* (Helson, 1964, see Eisler et al., 2008), that is, the fact of taking into consideration prior judgments about a given stimulus and the context in which the stimulus is presented (the value of other stimuli to be estimated).

Conclusion

If the question is whether Stevens's law holds for time, it must be answered yes in the sense that this law allows the relationship between a psychological magnitude and a physical magnitude to be logarithmic, linear, or exponential. However, there is a wide variety of estimates in the literature of the value of exponent b for psychological time.

As for the question of whether Weber's law, even in its generalized form, holds for psychological time, the answer seems to be no. But the usefulness of this law remains great since this violation of the law forces us to look at the psychological meaning of the point from which it stops holding. Note, finally, that the violation of Weber's law is not specific to the study of time, this law being faulted in the study of many other sensory continua (Masin, 2009).

References

Bizo, L. A., Chu, J. Y. M., Sanabria, F., & Killeen, P. R. (2006). The failure of Weber's law in time perception and production. *Behavioural Processes, 71*, 201–210.

Church, R. M., & Gibbon, J. (1982). Temporal generalization. *Journal of Experimental Psychology: Animal Behavior Processes, 8*, 165–186.

Crystal, J. D. (2006). Sensitivity to time: Implications for the representation of time. In E. A. Wasserman & T. R. Zentall (Eds.), *Comparative cognition: Experimental explorations of animal intelligence* (pp. 270–284). New York: Oxford University Press.

Drake, C., & Botte, M.-C. (1993). Tempo sensitivity in auditory sequences: Evidence for a multiple-look model. *Perception & Psychophysics, 54*, 277–286.

Eisler, H. (1976). Experiments on subjective duration 1868–1975: A collection of power function exponents. *Psychological Bulletin, 83*, 185–200.

Eisler, H., Eisler, A., & Hellström, A. (2008). Psychophysical issues in the study of time perception. In S. Grondin (Ed.), *Psychology of time* (pp. 75–110). Bingley, UK: Emerald Group Publishing.

Fechner, G. (1860). *Elements of psychophysics*. Trad. par H. E. Adler, D. H. Howes, & E. G. Boring (1966). New York: Holt, Rinehart & Winston.

Fraisse, P. (1978). Time and rhythm perception. In E. Carterette & M. Friedman (Eds.), *Handbook of perception VIII* (pp. 203–254). New York: Academic Press.

Getty, D. (1975). Discrimination of short temporal intervals: A comparison of two models. *Perception & Psychophysics, 18*, 1–8.

Gibbon, J., Malapani, C., Dale, C. L., & Gallistel, C. (1997). Toward a neurobiology of temporal cognition: Advances and challenges. *Current Opinion in Neurobiology, 7*, 170–184.

Grondin, S. (1993). Duration discrimination of empty and filled intervals marked by auditory and visual signals. *Perception & Psychophysics, 54*, 383–394.

Grondin, S. (2001). From physical time to the first and second moments of psychological time. *Psychological Bulletin, 127*, 22–44.

Grondin, S. (2010). Unequal Weber fraction for the categorization of brief temporal intervals. *Attention, Perception & Psychophysics, 72*, 1422–1430.

Grondin, S. (2012). Violation of the scalar property for time perception between 1 and 2 seconds: Evidence from interval discrimination, reproduction, & categorization. *Journal of Experimental Psychology: Human Perception and Performance, 38*, 880–890.

Grondin, S. (2014). About the (non)scalar property for time perception. In H. Merchant & V. de Lafuente (Eds.), *Neurobiology of interval timing* (pp. 17–32). New York: Springer. (Advances in Experimental Medicine and Biology, Vol. 829).

Grondin, S., & Laflamme, V. (2015). Stevens's law for time: A direct comparison of prospective and retrospective judgments. *Attention, Perception, & Psychophysics, 77*, 1044–1051.

Helson, H. (1964). *Adaptation-level theory*. New York, NY: Harper & Row.

Karampela, O., Holm, L., & Madison, G. (2015). Shared timing variability in eye and finger movements increases with interval duration: Support for a distributed timing system below and above one second. *Quarterly Journal of Experimental Psychology, 68,* 1965–1980.

Killeen, P. R., & Weiss, N. A. (1987). Optimal timing and the Weber function. *Psychological Review, 94,* 455–468.

Lejeune, H., & Wearden, J. (2009). Vierordt's *The experimental study of the time sense* (1868) and its legacy. *European Journal of Cognitive Psychology, 21,* 941–960.

Madison, G. (2001). Variability in isochronous tapping: Higher order dependencies as a function of intertap interval. *Journal of Experimental Psychology: Human Perception and Performance, 27,* 411–421.

Masin, S. (2009). The (Weber's) law that never was. In M. Elliott & S. Antonijevic (Eds.), *Fechner Day 2009: Proceedings of the 25th annual meeting of the international society for psychophysics* (pp. 441–446). Galway, UK: The ISP.

Merchant, H., Zarco, W., & Prado, L. (2008). Do we have a common mechanism for measuring time in the hundreds of millisecond range? Evidence from multiple-interval timing tasks. *Journal of Neurophysiology, 99,* 939–949.

Rakitin, B. C., Gibbon, J., Penney, T. B., Malapani, C., Hinton, S. C., & Meck, W. H. (1998). Scalar expectancy theory and peak-interval timing in humans. *Journal of Experimental Psychology: Animal Behavior Processes, 24,* 15–33.

Stevens, S. S. (1975). *Psychophysics: Introduction to its perceptual, neural and social prospects.* New York: Wiley.

Wearden, J. H. (1992). Temporal generalization in humans. *Journal of Experimental Psychology: Animal Behavior Processes, 18,* 134–144.

3 Is Psychological Time Punctuated With Critical Durations?

We could imagine that physical time is continuous, without interruption, an infinitely divisible stream. Most of the time, without knowing exactly what the physical time is (Buccheri, Saniga, & Stuckey, 2003), we extract from it chronometric time, that we also consider continuous, every second following one another and having the same value.

As far as psychology is concerned, it is not sure that time is continuous. We saw in the previous chapter that the correspondence between psychological time and physical time, or between the variability of temporal estimations and the magnitude of time, is not necessarily linear. Actually, researchers in the field of psychological time make every effort to identify temporal windows or moments, ranges of particular durations that would mark the transition from a state to another, from a temporal experience to another.

Nature of Temporal Experiences

The adaptation to everyday life requires temporal regulations, which extend from some hundreds of microseconds to several hours or even several days. All of these regulations do not require an explicit judgment of duration. They rather cover different phenomena (Buonomano, 2007; Wackermann, 2007).

Among experiences connected to time, we note the necessity of knowing the order of arrival of auditory stimuli for identifying their origin. Sound localization is particularly based on the capacity to say if a sound first arrived at the left ear or at the right ear: If the sound seems to have arrived at the left ear first, it is because the source is located to the left. Less than one millisecond is necessary for a sound to arrive at the second ear after reaching the first one. The fact that human beings manage to determine this order of arrival shows how precise the temporal processing system turns out to be in hearing. This process is based on the capacity of certain neurons to reveal the intersection point between the action potentials launched in the left ear and the right ear.

At the other end of the spectrum, we find long periodicities like the circadian rhythm or the menstrual cycle (of about 28 days). The circadian rhythm is necessary because of the earth's rotation every 24 hours. The adaptation relies on a kind of clock whose description, which comes from specific proteins synthesis within cells, is beyond the scope of this book. This clock notably requires one to be capable of following the cycles of day and night despite the change of their duration during the year. Those who have experienced jet-lag caused by trips (for instance, by going from America to Europe) probably know how rigid this rhythm is.

Between these two ends of the spectrum, other facts lead us to believe that psychological time is not a single process and that the human body hides different mechanisms to overcome the temporal requirements essential to adaptation.

Around Time 0

There is a gap between physical reality and conscious perception. The neuronal processes that allow the transmission of stimulation from a sensory receptor up to the cerebral cortex are not instantaneous. For instance, at least 100 ms are needed for a conscious perception of a visual stimulus after its arrival on retina (Hubbard, 2014). Thus, the processing of visual information requires a mechanism to compensate for this gap.

To illustrate the fact that the processing of all stimuli requires a certain delay, we can take as an example a visual effect called flash-lag, which can be observed in multiple situations. Essentially, this phenomenon occurs when a flashing object and a moving stimulus (target) should be aligned: the flashing object will seem to appear behind the target, will accuse a certain delay (Hubbard, 2014). In the auditory modality, there are conditions where, depending on the composition of sounds presented successively, the perceived order of these sounds will not follow the real, physical, order; this is an example of what is called temporal displacement (Vicario, 2003).

The situation is even more complicated if we consider the temporal sequence connected to the will to act. This would be preceded, according to Libet, by a cerebral activity. This activity, collected with the electroencephalographic recording, would arise 550 ms before this intention to act, even if the people realize this intention only approximately 200 ms before acting (see Libet, 2002). It thus means that the brain unconsciously triggers in a person the voluntary process at least 350 ms before the person knows of this will to act.

Psychological Moment

When talking about information processing, certain authors evoke the existence of a "window", of a *psychological moment* inside which sensory events would be processed as if they were together. Beyond the limit of this moment, which would be below 50 ms, the events would be perceived as successive rather than being "co-temporal" (Elliott & Giersch, 2016; Poppël, 2004; see also Chapter 12).

If it is necessary to judge whether or not one auditory stimulus and one visual stimulus were delivered simultaneously, the temporal integration window would be rather about 200 ms (van Wassenhove, Grant, & Poeppel, 2007). This window would indeed be asymmetric, in the sense that we perceive more easily that a sound arrives before a flash than the opposite.

So, psychologically, the connection of an individual with the environment would not be made on the basis of a temporal continuity. This connection would rather occur within pieces of time. If some authors refer to psychological moment, others evoke the existence of a *phenomenal present* (Vicario, 2003, 2005), which makes possible a phenomenon like temporal displacement.

Automatic Processing

In the domain closer to the present concern, that of the explicit judgments about time, the temporal intervals most often investigated extend from about 100 ms to several seconds. Even for such a restricted duration range, there are reasons to believe that psychological time might not be continuous. First, we often evoke the possibility that short intervals benefit from an automatic mode of processing, while longer intervals would require the contribution of control processes like attention (Rammsayer, 2008). If such was the case, this would mean that there is in some place on the time continuum some transition from an automatic to a controlled mode of processing. An empirical demonstration of this transition remains necessary, especially considering that there are reasons for believing that the processing of the intervals of less than 500 ms, for example, is sensitive to a manipulation of the level of attention assigned to time (Grondin & Macar, 1992; Macar, Grondin, & Casini, 1994).

The idea of automatic processing could hide in fact another reality, i.e., another way of approaching the question of time in a phenomenon. It is reasonable to believe that phenomena such as speech processing, motor coordination, and musical perception require the integration of a temporal dimension. In fact, without requiring an explicit judgment about time, these phenomena require an implicit integration of short intervals, for example, between words or between notes, or an implicit integration that would allow exerting, during a precise period, an adequate strength for the motor coordination or for producing a note. This might not tell whether there is or not a continuity of the temporal experience; nevertheless, it may reveal a different type of temporal requirement. This requirement would touch very brief intervals and would require the contribution of a different mechanism.

Maximum Sensitivity

If we strictly stick to explicit judgments on duration, we rapidly meet on the road, i.e. for short time intervals, indications of some discontinuity of the temporal experience. In other words, all temporal intervals would not have the same status, would not offer the same processing possibility, the same efficiency. One example of this special status is the highly debatable, but commonly reported notion of indifference interval, which is defined as an interval in which no bias occurs when intervals are compared; there would be no tendency to overestimate or underestimate durations (see the previous chapter; or Eisler, Eisler, & Hellström, 2008). This indifference interval would be located circa 700 ms.

For tempo sensitivity, the performances are apparently better between 300 and 800 ms (Drake & Botte, 1993), and maybe specifically better around 500 ms (Friberg & Sundberg, 1995) or 600 ms (Fraisse, 1957). This idea of an optimal tempo is compatible with that of the existence of a spontaneous preferred tempo. We determine this spontaneous preferred tempo simply by asking people to make a series of finger taps at a rhythm that comes to them spontaneously, and that feels convenient to them. By the way, the intervals between the taps would be about 600 ms for young adults, 700 ms for elderly, but would be much shorter (350 ms) for children (McAuley, Jones, Holub, Johnston, & Miller, 2006).

This idea of spontaneous tempo, or maximal sensitivity, whether it be located at 500, 600, or 700 ms, is not however compatible with Weber's law (see the previous chapter). In fact, for this restricted range of durations, there are reasons for believing that the Weber fraction remains constant (Getty, 1975; Grondin, Ouellet, & Roussel, 2001; Mioni, Labonté, Cellini, & Grondin, 2016). Would the Weber fraction remain constant for a given duration range, no point within this range would lead to a particularly good performance. The idea of constant Weber fraction and that of optimal sensitivity are paradoxical.

One Second as a Transition Point

In spite of the frequent use of the distinction between the intervals of more or less than one second (*supra* by opposition to the *sub-second intervals*) for presenting the mechanisms involved in timing and time perception, as well as the results of studies (see for example Penney & Vaitilingam, 2008; Rammsayer, 2008), this distinction seems to hold more on linguistic convenience, based on the general and assumed knowledge of one second, than on a scientific reality. Sometimes, differences are reported, for example for the cerebral structures involved in the processing of 600-ms intervals as opposed to those involved in the processing of one-second intervals (Lewis & Miall, 2003), or between the processes involved in the discrimination of 50-ms temporal intervals and that of intervals lasting one second (Rammsayer & Lima, 1991). If this supra- vs. sub-second distinction remains useful, it does not however rely on any critical difference occurring at one second. Such a difference would be revealed if intervals lasting 700, 900, 1100, and 1300 ms, for example, were compared and if the data would indicate a point of transition or disruption.

A method for approaching the question consists in returning to what Weber's law teaches when a close look is taken at what is going on around one second. As seen in the previous chapter, it seems that there is a transition taking place, that there is, at some place, an increase of the Weber fraction when intervals become longer. This transition arrives in the neighborhood of 1.2 to 1.3 s. This fact seems even more interesting if we consider that humans actually possess a system to supply, to maintain their efficiency, even beyond this value, when they have to keep track of time. So, when the intervals to be estimated last more than 1.2 or 1.3 s, there is an advantage to adopting an explicit counting strategy (Grondin, Meilleur-Wells, & Lachance, 1999). In other words, when intervals become too long, it is better to segment them to minimize variability. The literature, in fact, abounds with demonstrations showing how advantageous it is to adopt a strategy allowing the segmentation of long temporal intervals into smaller pieces (Grondin, Ouellet, & Roussel, 2004; Hinton & Rao, 2004).

The increase of the Weber fraction with intervals longer than 1.2 s could be interpreted as the reflection of a fundamental value of the system responsible of the processing of temporal information, a value that would indicate a capacity limitation in memory, a kind of temporal span or limited temporal space. Indeed, in a task where it is simply necessary to count at a given pace rhythm until a certain target is reached, for a certain number of trials, precision (target reached) will be greater, and variability in the course of the trials smaller, if there 0.8 rather than 1.6 s between counts, that is, if the interval used to count remains within this temporal limitation (Grondin, Laflamme, & Mioni, 2015).

Psychological Present

Various researchers in the field of time perception emphasize another distinction. Fraisse (1978) used the term *psychological present*, or *perceived present*, to speak about "the temporal extent of stimulations that can be perceived at a given time, without the intervention of rehearsal during or after the stimulation" (p. 205). For his part, James (1890) rather referred to the notion of *specious present*. For Fraisse, who also distinguishes time perception from time estimation (Fraisse, 1984), this present would extend over a range lasting two to five seconds. Besides, Poppël (2004) supports that the neurocognitive mechanics would be based on a temporal integration occurring within a window lasting two to three seconds and which would provide an impression of *nowness* (phenomenological present). This idea of a three-second temporal window remains however very debatable. According to White (2017), temporal integration should not be defined in terms of duration, but rather in terms of density of the information.

Conclusion

We find numerous concepts in the literature supposed to be closely linked to a specific duration, or range of durations, as if there was a discontinuity of temporal experience. We sometimes search for some unity within a "moment", which would extend over dozens of milliseconds, or within a "present", which would extend over a few seconds, without knowing the exact value. Rather than a unified duration range, maybe there is a point corresponding to maximal sensitivity, between 500 and 700 ms, which would reveal a non-continuity of the temporal experience. However, such a maximal sensitivity would entail a violation of Weber's law. We certainly find such violation when the temporal judgments involve slightly longer intervals, the Weber fraction beginning to increase in the neighborhood of 1.2 to 1.3 seconds.

References

Buccheri, R., Saniga, M., & Stuckey, M. (Eds.). (2003). *The nature of time: Geometry, physics and perception*. Dordrecht, The Netherlands: Kluwer Academic Publishers.

Buonomano, D. V. (2007). The biology of time across different scales. *Nature Chemical Biology, 3*, 594–597.

Drake, C., & Botte, M.-C. (1993). Tempo sensitivity in auditory sequences: Evidence for a multiple-look model. *Perception & Psychophysics, 54*, 277–286.

Eisler, H., Eisler, A., & Hellström, A. (2008). Psychophysical issues in the study of time perception. In S. Grondin (Ed.), *Psychology of time* (pp. 75–110). Bingley, UK: Emerald Group Publishing.

Elliott, M. A., & Giersch, A. (2016). What happens in a moment. *Frontiers in Psychology, 6*, 1905. doi:10.3389/fpsyg.2015.01905.

Fraisse, P. (1957). *Psychologie du temps* (Psychology of time). Paris: Presses universitaires de France.

Fraisse, P. (1978). Time and rhythm perception. In E. Carterette & M. Friedman (Eds.), *Handbook of Perception* (Vol. 8, pp. 203–254). New York: Academic Press.

Fraisse, P. (1984). Perception and estimation of time. *Annual Review of Psychology, 35*, 1–36.

Friberg, A., & Sundberg, J. (1995). Time discrimination in a monotonic, isochronic sequence. *Journal of Acoustical Society of America, 98*, 2524–2531.

Getty, D. (1975). Discrimination of short temporal intervals: A comparison of two models. *Perception & Psychophysics, 18*, 1–8.

Grondin, S., Laflamme, V., & Mioni, G. (2015). Do not count too slowly: Evidence for a temporal limitation in short-term memory. *Psychonomic Bulletin & Review, 22*, 863–868.

Grondin, S., & Macar, F. (1992). Dividing attention between temporal and nontemporal tasks: A performance operating characteristic (POC) analysis. In F. Macar, V. Pouthas, & W. Friedman (Eds.), *Time, action, cognition: Towards bridging the gap* (pp. 119–128). Dordrecht, The Netherlands: Kluwer Academic Publishers.

Grondin, S., Meilleur-Wells, G., & Lachance, R. (1999). When to start explicit counting in a time-intervals discrimination task: A critical point in the timing process of humans. *Journal of Experimental Psychology: Human Perception and Performance, 25*, 993–1004.

Grondin, S., Ouellet, B., & Roussel, M.-E. (2001). About optimal timing and stability of Weber fraction for duration discrimination. *Acoustical Science & Technology, 22*, 370–372.

Grondin, S., Ouellet, B., & Roussel, M.-E. (2004). Benefits and limits of explicit counting for discriminating temporal intervals. *Canadian Journal of Experimental Psychology, 58*, 1–12.

Hinton, S. C., & Rao, S. M. (2004). "One-thousand one . . . one-thousand two . . .": Chronometric counting violates the scalar property in interval timing. *Psychonomic Bulletin & Review*, *11*(1), 24–30.

Hubbard, T. L. (2014). The flash-lag effect and related mislocalizations: Findings, properties and theories. *Psychological Bulletin*, *140*, 308–338.

James, W. (1890). *The Principles of Psychology*. New York: Henry Holt and Company.

Lewis, P. A., & Miall, R. C. (2003). Brain activation patterns during measurement of sub- and supra-second intervals. *Neuropsychologia*, *41*, 1583–1592.

Libet, B. (2002). The timing of mental events: Libet's experimental findings and their implications. *Consciousness and Cognition*, *11*, 291–299.

Macar, F., Grondin, S., & Casini, L. (1994). Controlled attention sharing influences time estimation. *Memory & Cognition*, *22*, 673–686.

McAuley, J. D., Jones, M. R., Holub, S., Johnston, H. M., & Miller, N. S. (2006). The time of our lives: Life span development of timing and event tracking. *Journal of Experimental Psychology: General*, *135*, 348–367.

Mioni, G., Labonté, K., Cellini, N., & Grondin, S. (2016). Relationship between daily fluctuations of body temperature and the processing of sub-second intervals. *Physiology & Behavior*, *164*, 220–226.

Penney, T., & Vaitilingam, L. (2008). Imaging time. In S. Grondin (Ed.), *Psychology of time* (pp. 261–294). Bingley, UK: Emerald Group Publishing.

Poppël, E. (2004). Lost in time: A historical frame, elementary processing units and the 3-second window. *Acta Neurobiologiae Experimentalis*, *64*, 295–301.

Rammsayer, T. H. (2008). Neuropharmacological approaches to human timing. In S. Grondin (Ed.), *Psychology of time* (pp. 295–320). Bingley, UK: Emerald Group Publishing.

Rammsayer, T. H., & Lima, S. D. (1991). Duration discrimination of filled and empty auditory intervals: Cognitive and perceptual factors. *Perception & Psychophysics*, *50*, 565–574.

van Wassenhove, V., Grant, K. W., & Poeppel, D. (2007). Temporal window of integration in auditory-visual speech perception. *Neuropsychologia*, *45*, 598–607.

Vicario, G. B. (2003). Temporal displacement. In R. Buccheri, M. Saniga, & M. Stuckey (Eds.), *The nature of time: Geometry, physics and perception* (pp. 53–66). Dordrecht, The Netherlands: Kluwer Academic Publishers.

Vicario, G. B. (2005). *Il tempo*. Bologna: Il Mulino.

Wackermann, J. (2007). Inner and outer horizons of time experience. *The Spanish Journal of Psychology*, *10*, 20–32.

White, P. (2017). The three-second "subjective present": A critical review and a new proposal. *Psychological Bulletin*, *143*, 735–756.

4 Do We Have an Internal Clock?

We could always believe that there is no internal clock inside us. However, it would be audacious to respond no to the question that is opening this chapter, considering that one may even argue that there are several internal clocks. That said, we know that we are able, for instance, to synchronize actions and make accurate judgments about time. As well, if a traffic light delays turning from red to green, it will not have been necessary to begin an explicit timing activity to have, at some moment, the intuition that there is a delay. This intuition, this impression of delay, necessarily has to be the fruit of a mechanism allowing some measurement of time.

Types of Mechanisms

The description of the mechanism which helps to report time depends in fact on what type of time experience we want to describe or to understand. If we want to consider retrospectively how long an activity has lasted, it will be necessary to refer to memory mechanisms, without relying on an internal clock. Other researchers, rather interested in prospective timing and by the perception of very long intervals (several seconds), will rely on an explanation based on cognitive processes, without evoking the potential contribution of an internal biological clock (Block, 2003; Ornstein, 1969).

Indeed, as we will see in this chapter and in the next chapters, the time perception literature is full of models. Because of its popularity during the last decades, a particular type of internal clock model will hold attention in this chapter. Essentially, this model is based on the idea that a pacemaker is providing pulses and it is the accumulation of these pulses that becomes the basis for making judgments about the passage of time.

There are various models where it is argued that there is a type of clock, or chronometer, without postulating the presence of a pacemaker or of a counter of pulses. Among these, we note that of Staddon and Higa (1996, 1999), which is assuming the presence of a cascade of chronometers where specific periods depend on the strength of traces left in memory, or that of Wackermann and Ehm (2006) based on an accumulator system (klepsydra), but which is not a counter of pulses.

Pacemaker-Counter Device

To understand well the interest of a model based on a pacemaker, let's start with a simple example. Almost everybody can make the difference between a sound of 200 ms and a sound of 400 ms, and distinguishing sounds of 200 ms and 250 ms remains relatively easy for most people. However, to distinguish sounds of 200 ms and 205 ms might not be that easy. In fact, for every person, there is a zone where the difference between sounds is generally sufficient to determine which one is longer, but where this difference is sometimes insufficient; this zone depends on personal capabilities (difference threshold). The question becomes: why do we sometimes make errors, given that most of the time, we do not commit them?

There are counter models based on the assumption that there is a pacemaker providing pulses (Rammsayer & Ulrich, 2001). With such a pacemaker-counter device, the accumulation of the pulses, in the counter mechanism, determines the perceived duration of a given interval. The errors that occur when time is estimated could very well come from the properties of the pacemaker (the pace of emission of pulses). Temporal estimation errors are committed if the exact timing between the discrete pulses is random, as is the case with a Poisson process, for instance (Creelman, 1962). In brief, if the emission of pulses is a random process, the pacemaker will be a source of errors. Therefore, if we encode that a physical time interval corresponds to the mean accumulation of 20 pulses, and that during a following trial, for the same interval, we would accumulate 18, 19, 21, or 22 such pulses because of the pacemaker's variability, time would not be perceived as being the same; duration would seem a little shorter or a little longer.

Other models rather posit the hypothesis that the emission frequency of pulses is deterministic: the inter-pulse intervals are fixed. With such a property, duration discrimination errors would not be caused by the variability of pulses emitted by the pacemaker. They would rather be attributable to the process responsible for signaling the beginning and end of the timekeeping activity. For example, if we estimate the duration of a sound, this activity begins with the detection of the arrival of this sound and ends at some moment after its disappearance. Because this internal beginning and end of the sound may both occur at various moments between two pulses supplied by the pacemaker, there is in this process a source of errors for estimating time (Allan, Kristofferson, & Wiens, 1971). The errors linked to the marking of intervals would explain, at least partially, various sensory effects or effects due to the structure of an interval, in duration discrimination tasks (Bendixen, Grimm, & Schröger, 2006; Grondin, 2003; Tse & Penney, 2006).

Treisman (1963) rather posits the hypothesis of a pacemaker having a deterministic property, but susceptible over a long period to vary according to the changes of the state of physiological activation of an individual. This hypothesis is reasonable if we consider that the internal temperature of the body will exert influence on perceived duration (François, 1927). For example, a feverish person could, at the end of a 35-second period, indicate that one minute has passed by (Hoagland, 1935), whereas a person in immersion in cold water would indicate the passage of one minute only after 66 second have elapsed (Baddeley, 1966). We shall see in Chapter 23 that the idea of physiological activation is useful for explaining some temporal distortions linked to emotion.

Besides, it is not totally excluded that the counter be a source of errors in the timekeeping activities, especially when long intervals have to be estimated (Killeen & Fetterman, 1988; Killeen & Weiss, 1987). In particular, Killeen and Taylor (2000) proposed the presence of a cascade of counter systems. If the counting activity is made in a hierarchical way, as it is the case when binary and decimal systems are used, then the magnitude of potential timing errors should grow in a disproportionate way every time a new step in the counting system is reached. These steps are for example tens or hundreds when a decimal system is used.[1]

An Information Processing Version

Most of the hypotheses about the pacemaker-counter devices described in the previous paragraphs arose from works with human participants. However, it is from research involving nonhuman animals that was developed the timing theory that was, over the past 40 years, the most cited one in the field of timing and time perception: the scalar expectancy theory (SET). This theory is based on the hypothesis that there is a pacemaker-counter device (Gibbon, 1977) and contains two fundamental characteristics. The mean representation of a given interval during a series of trials in a task where it is necessary to estimate the time should equal the chronometric (real) value of this interval. In other words, the relationship between psychological time and chronometric time is linear. The other characteristic touches the variability of judgments. This variability should increase proportionally as a function of the mean representation. This is the scalar property: the ratio between the variability and mean should be constant, which is to say that Weber's law, in its strict form, should hold.[2]

In the version of SET integrated into an information processing perspective, the sources of errors at the moment of making judgments about time is not restricted to the components of the pacemaker-counter mechanism. The domain of information processing is a branch of cognitive psychology developed by the researchers in experimental psychology in the second half of the twentieth century. In this perspective, the sources of errors are located only at the level of the internal clock (pacemaker-counter device, but also at the levels of memory processes and decision-making).

Within the clock process, there is a cognitive component: the accumulation of the pulses is under the control of attention. Because of the importance of attention, in general, in the study of time perception, a complete chapter (see Chapter 9) is dedicated to its role. For the main part, it is necessary to remember that the more attention is given to time, the more time will be perceived as being long. Moreover, there is a part of the errors committed in temporal estimation tasks that are located at two other levels. So, the errors would be partly explained by the imperfect memory mechanisms involved in these estimations and by a certain variance within the decision-making process at the moment of making the comparison between the interval to be estimated and what is retained in memory (Grondin, 2005; Ogden, Wearden, & Jones, 2008; Rattat & Droit-Volet, 2010).

During a trial series in bisection tasks for instance, there is some variability when the content of the accumulator is transferred into memory. This variability would be normally distributed (Jones & Wearden, 2003). According to some researchers, the short and long intervals presented at the beginning of a bisection task would be combined in memory to form a unique representation (Allan & Gerhardt, 2001; Ng, Tobin, & Penney, 2011). When the duration of the interval presented during a given trial exceeds the one held in memory, the presented interval is judged as being closer to the long interval. If the temporal task contains a direct comparison of a standard and a comparison interval, some systematic errors linked to the temporal order of presentation of the intervals may occur (Eisler, Eisler, & Hellström, 2008; Hellström, 1985; Hellström & Rammsayer, 2015). Also, the internal representation of the standard, for a given trial, is not independent from preceding trials, this representation being built over the course of trials during the experiment (Dyjas, Bausenhart, & Ulrich, 2014).

There are several other studies on the implication of the memory processes in temporal generalization and bisection tasks. In particular, we know that the intervals marked by stimuli of various sensory modalities likely use a common memory representation (see Grondin, 2005, for intervals < 1 s; and Penney, Gibbon, & Meck, 2000, for intervals from 3 to 6 s) and the influence of an interval type on another would last at least a few minutes (Gamache & Grondin, 2010). We also know that when we use, within blocks of trials, intervals belonging to clearly different duration distributions (for example, a distribution from 200 ms to 300 ms; and a distribution from 600 ms to 900 ms), the participants use distinct representations for each distribution; however, if these distributions are too close to each other, there will be interference between these representations (Grondin, 2005; Jones & Wearden, 2004; Ogden et al., 2008).

Conclusion

The last pages do not contain material which proves that there is an internal clock. However, for the researchers in the field of time perception, the hypothesis of the existence of such a clock has proved extremely useful. This pacemaker-counter clock allows to account for a very large number of phenomena observed in laboratory, especially when this clock is presented within an information processing perspective. In this last case, the sources of errors are not limited to the properties of pulse distribution by the pacemaker or to the fallibility of the counter, but are also located in the more general cognitive processes contributing at the moment to complete the temporal tasks. These sources are the attentional processes, which act within the internal clock functioning, as well as the memory processes and those associated with decision-making. We shall see in the next chapters that there exist many more interpretations developed for explaining our capacity to estimate the passage of time. It might well be possible that there is such an internal clock, but it might not be the sole mechanism at the disposal of the brain for making judgments about time.

Notes

1. There are other models in the family of pacemaker-accumulator models. A recent one connects with the drift-diffusion model of perceptual decision-making (Simen, Rivest, Ludvig, Balci, & Killeen, 2013).
2. We have seen in Chapter 2 that there are reasons to dispute the idea that the Weber fraction (the scalar property) is constant for time perception.

References

Allan, L. G., & Gerhardt, K. (2001). Temporal bisection with trial referents. *Perception & Psychophysics, 63*, 524–540.

Allan, L. G., Kristofferson, A. B., & Wiens, E. W. (1971). Duration discrimination of brief light flashes. *Perception & Psychophysics, 9*, 327–334.

Baddeley, A. (1966). Time-estimation at reduced body-temperature. *American Journal of Psychology, 79*, 475–479.

Bendixen, A., Grimm, S., & Schröger, E. (2006). The relation between onset, offset, & duration perception as examined by psychophysical data and event-related brain potentials. *Journal of Psychophysiology, 20*, 40–51.

Block, R. A. (2003). Psychological timing without a timer: The roles of attention and memory. In H. Helfrich (Ed.), *Time and mind II: Information processing perspectives* (pp. 41–59). Göttingen, Germany: Hogrefe & Huber Publishers.

Creelman, C. D. (1962). Human discrimination of auditory duration. *Journal of the Acoustical Society of America, 34*, 582–593.

Dyjas, O., Bausenhart, K., & Ulrich, R. (2014). Effects of stimulus order on duration discrimination sensitivity are under attentional control. *Journal of Experimental Psychology: Human Perception and Performance, 40*, 292–307.

Eisler, H., Eisler, A., & Hellström, A. (2008). Psychophysical issues in the study of time perception. In S. Grondin (Ed.), *Psychology of time* (pp. 75–110). Bingley, UK: Emerald Group Publishing.

François, M. (1927). Contributions à l'étude du sens du temps: la température interne comme facteur de variation de l'appréciation subjective des durées. *L'Année psychologique, 27*, 186–204.

Gamache, P.-L., & Grondin, S. (2010). The life span of time intervals in reference memory. *Perception, 39*, 1431–1451.

Gibbon, J. (1977). Scalar expectancy theory and Weber's law in animal timing. *Psychological Review, 84*, 279–325.

Grondin, S. (2003). Sensory modalities and temporal processing. In H. Helfrich (Ed.), *Time and mind II* (pp. 61–77). Göttingen, Germany: Hogrefe & Huber Publishers.

Grondin, S. (2005). Overloading temporal memory. *Journal of Experimental Psychology: Human Perception and Performance, 31*(5), 869–879.

Hellström, Å. (1985). The time-order error and its relatives: Mirrors of cognitive processes in comparing. *Psychological Bulletin, 97*, 35–61.

Hellström, Å., & Rammsayer, T. H. (2015). Time-order errors and standard-position effects in duration discrimination: An experimental study and an analysis by the sensation-weighting model. *Attention, Perception & Psychophysics, 77*, 2409–2423.

Hoagland, H. (1935). *Pacemakers in relation to aspects of behavior*. New York: MacMillan.

Jones, L. A., & Wearden, J. H. (2003). More is not necessarily better: Examining the nature of the temporal reference memory component in timing. *Quarterly Journal of Experimental Psychology, 56*, 321–343.

Jones, L. A., & Wearden, J. H. (2004). Double standards: Memory loading in temporal reference memory. *The Quarterly Journal of Experimental Psychology B: Comparative and Physiological Psychology, 57B*, 55–77.

Killeen, P. R., & Fetterman, J. G. (1988). A behavioral theory of timing. *Psychological Review, 95*, 274–295.

Killeen, P. R., & Taylor, T. (2000). How the propagation of error through stochastic counters affects time discrimination and other psychophysical judgments. *Psychological Review, 107*, 430–459.

Killeen, P. R., & Weiss, N. A. (1987). Optimal timing and the Weber function. *Psychological Review, 94*, 455–468.

Ng, K. K., Tobin, S., & Penney, T. B. (2011). Temporal accumulation and decision processes in the duration bisection task revealed by contingent negative variation. *Frontiers in Integrative Neuroscience, 5*, 77. doi:10.3389/fnint.2011.00077.

Ogden, R. S., Wearden, J. H., & Jones, L. A. (2008). The remembrance of times Past: Interference in temporal reference memory. *Journal of Experimental Psychology: Human Perception and Performance, 34*, 1524–1544.

Ornstein, R. E. (1969). *On the experience of time*. Harmondsworth, England: Penguin.

Penney, T. B., Gibbon, J., & Meck, W. H. (2000). Differential effects of auditory and visual signals on clock speed and temporal memory. *Journal of Experimental Psychology: Human Perception and Performance, 26*, 1770–1787.

Rammsayer, T., & Ulrich, R. (2001). Counting models of temporal discrimination. *Psychonomic Bulletin & Review, 8*, 270–277.

Rattat, A. C., & Droit-Volet, S. (2010). The effects of interference and retention delay on temporal generalization performance. *Attention, Perception & Psychophysics, 72*(7), 1903–1912.

Simen, P., Rivest, F., Ludwig, E. A., Balci, F., & Killeen, P. R. (2013). Timescale invariance in the pacemaker-accumulator family of timing models. *Timing & Time Perception, 1*, 159–188.

Staddon, J. E. R., & Higa, J. J. (1996). Multiple time scales in simple habituation. *Psychological Review, 103*, 720–733.

Staddon, J. E. R., & Higa, J. J. (1999). Time and memory: Towards a pacemaker-free theory of interval timing. *Journal of the Experimental Analysis of Behavior, 71*, 215–251.

Treisman, M. (1963). Temporal discrimination and the indifference interval: Implications for a model of the "internal clock". *Psychological Monographs*, *77* (Whole n° 576).

Tse, C.-Y., & Penney, T. B. (2006). Preattentive timing of empty intervals is from marker offset to onset. *Psychophysiology*, *43*, 172–179.

Wackermann, J., & Ehm, W. (2006). The dual klepsydra model of internal time representation and time reproduction. *Journal of Theoretical Biology*, *239*, 482–493.

5 Which Parts of the Brain Are Involved in the Processing of Temporal Information?

It is quite difficult to provide a simple answer to this question because of the immense technological progress realized in the past 20 years and which generally serves science, particularly the field of neurosciences, so well. Already in the nineteenth century, it was possible to link certain functions and the localization of brain damages for spotting the cerebral structures involved in these functions.

For about the last 50 years, electroencephalography (EEG) has served well the experts in psychophysiology interested in the cerebral bases of timing. If the EEG allows one to offer a precise temporal resolution of the events occurring during timing activities, it is now possible to detect in a more precise way the cortical areas allocated in some way to the processing of temporal information. This spatial resolution relies notably on the magnetoencephalography (MEG), which allows measuring this magnetic activity, and on the contribution of imaging techniques like the tomography by emission of positrons (TEP) or the functional magnetic resonance imaging (fMRI) which allows observing metabolic changes inside the brain (Harrington & Haaland, 1999). In addition to these techniques, researchers can also count on those that are based on neurostimulation (Mioni, Grondin, Bardi, & Stablum, in press). It is now possible to create, with transcranial magnetic stimulation (TMS; or TMSr, r for repetitions), that is by means of small magnetic impulses, a change of the cerebral activity for a very brief period. Finally, with a technique called transcranial direct-current stimulation (tDCS), it is possible to increase or to inhibit the synaptic transmission in a precise brain location.

It is in fact the convergence of the results stemming from all these techniques that will lead one day to the specification of the neuronal networks involved in the timing activities and the processing of temporal information. At this point, the challenge is to pinpoint the brain structures involved in each type of task requiring the processing of temporal information. Indeed, the challenge comes from the fact that there does not seem to be a cerebral area specific to the processing of temporal information, or to time perception, just like there is one, for example, for audition or for vision.

Positioning of the Problem

Merchant, Harrington, and Meck (2013) propose three approaches to the question of the biological bases of timing and time perception. In the first place, they evoke, following the works of Buonomano (2007), a perspective where the possibility of timing is omnipresent. According to such a perspective, there would be, strictly speaking, no internal clock and the timing would rather rely on a mechanism that is not central.

Secondly, Merchant and his collaborators (2013) propose the hypothesis of a general or central timing mechanism. In this perspective, there would be a structure of the brain responsible for the processing of temporal intervals, intervals extending over a wide range. The internal clock described in the previous chapter belongs to such a perspective. However, given the contribution of numerous cerebral structures which reveal the studies based in particular on the fMRI, it is probably better to adopt a third avenue which consists in supposing a mechanism which includes a division of the responsibilities at two levels: There would be, on the one hand, an inevitable contribution of some cerebral structures (a basic network), and a contribution of necessary structures in certain specific contexts, for example an implication of a local activity specific to a sensory modality.

Several other taxonomies were proposed to define what would correspond to categories of different temporal experiences and, as a result, to the implication of different cerebral mechanisms. Authors invite the researchers to glimpse the various works, for example through the scope of a dichotomy between cognitively-controlled timing by opposition to automatic timing (Ciullo, Spalletta, Caltagirone, Jorge, & Piras, 2016). To some extent, this means distinguishing short intervals from longer ones, with a somewhat artificial cut at one second (see Chapter 3). Besides, we can also distinguish explicit from implicit timing. The latter case would include activities containing a motor component.

Noncentral Timing

Among the diverse models which would fit what Merchant and collaborators (2013) describe as a system of omnipresent timing, there are those who are based on multiple oscillators (Buonomano & Laje, 2010; Gu, van Rijn, & Meck, 2015). For example, a class of models suggests that timing depends on the state of neural networks at a given moment (*time-dependent networks*: Karmarkar & Buonomano, 2007). The shift between the short-term changes in the synaptic strength and the balance between the inhibition and the excitement would serve to tell a neuron the moment to point out specific intervals. It is thus with a directory of changes in time of synaptic and cellular properties that cortical networks could allow to judge the length of intervals. So, with this mechanism, which would apply to the processing of short temporal intervals (< 500 ms), timing would not be centralized, would not rely on a neuronal circuitry allowing the temporal integration.

Furthermore, we could classify in the category of noncentral timing mechanisms, but nevertheless non-omnipresent, all the proposals where the processing would be made within the sensory modality used for marking a given interval (see Chapter 7).

Cortical Areas

The various methods of investigation of the link between brain anatomy and the functions that have to be assumed allowed to highlight, besides the contributions of the subcortical structures and of the cerebellum, the participation of numerous areas of the cerebral cortex in the processing of temporal information (see Grondin, 2010; Meck, Doyere, & Gruart, 2012; Merchant & de Lafuente, 2014; Merchant et al., 2013).

Among the cerebral areas most frequently evoked for explaining the processing of temporal information, there is the frontal cortex, and more particularly the dorsolateral prefrontal cortex (DLPFC). In fact, this part of the brain is often requested in the processing of cognitive tasks in general, and in particular during tasks requiring memory. Electrophysiological investigations have shown the importance of the activity in the frontal lobe during the encoding of temporal information (see Macar & Vidal, 2009). In particular, the negative contingent variation (CNV) allowed to show that expecting a memorized duration, as is the case with a generalization task, comes along with a gradual increase, in the frontal area, of electrical activity, an activity which returns more quickly to normal when the comparison duration is shorter than the standard duration. This holds true whether the standard duration lasts 700 ms (Pfeuty, Ragot, & Pouthas, 2008) or 2.5 s (Macar, Vidal, & Casini, 1999). Such data are easily interpretable within the scope of the pacemaker-accumulator model, the CNV amplitude reflecting the accumulation of pulses. Since then, brain imaging studies have provided support to the idea of the involvement of the DLPFC in the processing of short intervals (Pouthas et al., 2005; Tregellas, Davalos, & Rojas, 2006) or of the right part of the prefrontal cortex in the processing of short and long durations (see Penney & Vaitilingam, 2008).

Furthermore, the importance of the supplementary motor area (SMA) has been established (see Wiener, Turkeltaub, & Coslett, 2010). Its role was highlighted as well in the tasks involving short durations (Tregellas et al., 2006) as in those involving the intervals longer than one second (Rao, Mayer, & Harrington, 2001). Furthermore, even when a participant is required to use explicit counting during a temporal task, at the rate of one per second, the SMA would contribute to the processing (Hinton, Harrington, Binder, Durgerian, & Rao, 2004).

During the last fifteen years, especially because of the introduction of TMS in the study temporal information processing, the hypothesis of an active role of the parietal cortex in timing and time perception has been tested. In particular, rTMS-based studies show how important the right posterior parietal cortex is in the treatment of short time intervals, whether these intervals are delimited by auditory or visual stimuli (Bueti, Bahrami, & Walsh, 2008). Studies based on the fMRI also showed the importance of the parietal cortex in timing. This area would serve as an interface between the sensory and motor processes for making possible the transformation of the temporal information into action (Bueti, Walsh, Frith, & Rees, 2008). N'Diaye, Ragot, Garnero, and Pouthas (2004) reported as well, on the basis of EEG and MEG investigations, the contribution of the parietal cortex in the processing of short time intervals, once again whether these intervals are delimited by a sound or by a flash. Finally, the role of the parietal cortex in temporal processing was also highlighted in a study on hemineglect patients who had to estimate long intervals (Danckert et al., 2007).

Subcortical Structures

As numerous studies based on the fMRI reveal, the processing of temporal information requires the contribution of several subcortical structures. So, from the first stages of processing, the contribution of the basal ganglia is observable (Bueti et al., 2008). In particular, the caudate nucleus and the putamen will be activated during the encoding of temporal intervals (Rao et al., 2001; to see Harrington & Haaland, 1999) and they would also be involved in the temporal tasks based on the use of rhythm (Teki, Grube, Kumar, & Griffiths, 2011; see the next chapter).

When temporal processing is concerned with intervals of less than one second, some authors report a contribution of the right portion of the caudate nucleus (Pouthas et al., 2005) or of caudate nucleus and putamen (Tragellas et al., 2006). For intervals of more than one second, we also note an activation of the caudate nucleus and of the putamen (Harrington et al., 2004; Hinton & Meck, 2004).

In fact, the subcortical structures have a crucial role in the explanation of the temporal information processing proposed by Meck and his collaborators (Matell & Meck, 2004; Meck & Benson, 2002). These authors propose a contribution of a fronto-striatal circuitry, the striatum consisting of the caudate nucleus and the putamen. The striatum, which receives millions of impulses of cortical cells, would be called to play a computational role. The signal of the beginning of a timing activity is sent when the striatum cells receive signals from the cortical neurons. These cells have a rhythm of activity of about 10 to 40 cycles per second. Their activity is not usually synchronized, but will be, during a short moment, in such a way that their neural activity will form a specific pattern of activity. At the end of the interval, when timing should end, the substantia nigra sends a message to the striatum. Thanks to a dopaminergic activity, there is at this moment a recording of this pattern. This pattern will serve to determine the specific length of an interval. The contribution of dopamine is most plausible, its importance in the temporal treatment being documented (Rammsayer, 2008).

Cerebellum

For the past thirty years, there has been an accumulation of demonstrations that leads one to believe that another subcortical structure, the cerebellum, has a key role in the processing of temporal information. In particular, we know that lateral cerebellar lesions in humans entail an increase of variability during the production of temporal intervals (Keele & Ivry, 1991). The impaired performance is not only observed in a motor task, the cerebellum being recognized for its role in motor control, but also when the discrimination of short temporal intervals delineated by sounds has to be performed (Ivry & Keele, 1989). In this latter case, if the cerebellar patients and the participants of a control group showed differences for temporal processing, they showed no such differences for the discrimination of the intensity of these sounds. So, the observed temporal deficit could not be attributed to a general problem related to the processing of auditory information.

The cerebellum would also have a role in a variety of tasks where the timing of short temporal intervals is crucial. Among these tasks, we note palpebral conditioning (close the eyelid upon the arrival of a single sound, after this sound had been associated to the arrival of an air puff in the eye), as well as speech perception and production. In fact, the contribution of the cerebellum in the temporal component of a task associated with the production of movement would depend on the exact nature of this task. The task should require an explicit representation of duration, as is the case during the production of discontinuous movements, as opposed to movements containing a continued, rhythmic activity (Teki et al., 2011; Zelaznik, Spencer, & Ivry, 2008; see next chapter). Other data, based on the use of rTMS, also show how important the cerebellum is in the processing of short intervals, be it a bisection task (Lee et al., 2007) or an interval reproduction task (Koch et al., 2007).

The data of some other studies, however, rather indicate that the cerebellum could be involved in the processing of long intervals (Harrington, Lee, Boyd, Rapcsak, & Knight, 2004). A brain imaging study allowed to emphasize the contribution of the cerebellum in a production task involving intervals lasting 12 or 24 seconds (Tracy, Faro, Mohamed, Pinsk, & Pinus, 2000). Furthermore, a study with patients having cerebellar degeneration reveals that these patients have difficulty completing a temporal bisection task when it involves intervals of a few seconds, but not when it involves intervals in the range of a quarter second (Nichelli, Always, & Grafman, 1996).

Conclusion

Or course, the present chapter offers only a partial view on the overall work related to the cerebral structures involved, at one time or another, in the processing of temporal information. For a reader interested in other tasks, or in other species, other cerebral areas may reveal themselves relevant in processing duration. For example, when a monkey produces short intervals after having been synchronized with a metronome, the medial premotor cortex turns out to be essential (Merchant, Zarco, Pérez, Prado, & Bartolo, 2011). Besides, a meta-analysis[1] involving about forty neuro-imaging studies shows that, no matter the range of durations in the study and the task used, the processing of duration generates an activation of the SMA and of the inferior frontal gyrus (Wiener et al., 2010); it seems therefore that there is some stability. In their evaluation of what appears to be the basis of temporal information processing, Merchant and his collaborators (2013) identify the SMA and the basal ganglia. For their part, Koch, Oliveri, and Caltagirone (2009) arrive at the conclusion that the cerebellum contributes to the processing of short intervals whereas the striatum and the substantia nigra would contribute to the processing of longer durations, the prefrontal cortex being necessary for the processing of long intervals when they must be kept in memory.

In brief, beyond the heterogeneousness of the temporal tasks used, the ranges of durations studied and the neuroscientific investigation methods employed, it seems reasonable to conclude the following line. The main cortical areas involved in timing and time perception are the SMA and the frontal and parietal cortices, and the main subcortical structures are the basal ganglia. Finally, the cerebellum has a computational role in various tasks requiring the processing of temporal information.

Note

1. A quantitative review of scientific data about a given question.

References

Bueti, D., Bahrami, B., & Walsh, V. (2008). Sensory and associative cortex in time perception. *Journal of Cognitive Neuroscience, 20*, 1054–1062.

Bueti, D., Walsh, V., Frith, C., & Rees, G. (2008). Different brain circuits underlie motor and perceptual representations of temporal intervals. *Journal of Cognitive Neuroscience, 20*, 204–214.

Buonomano, D. V. (2007). The biology of time across different scales. *Nature Chemical Biology, 3*, 594–597.

Buonomano, D. V., & Laje, R. (2010). Population clocks: Motor timing with neural dynamics. *Trends Cognitive Sciences, 14*, 520–527.

Ciullo, V., Spalletta, G., Caltagirone, C., Jorge, R. E., & Piras, F. (2016). Explicit time deficit in schizophrenia: Systematic review and meta-analysis indicate it is primary and not domain specific. *Schizophrenia Bulletin, 42*, 505–518.

Danckert, J., Ferber, S., Pun, C., Broderick, C., Striemer, C., Rock, S., & Stewart, D. (2007). Neglected time: Impaired temporal perception of multisecond intervals in unilateral neglect. *Journal of Cognitive Neuroscience, 19*, 1706–1720.

Grondin, S. (2010). Timing and time perception: A review of recent behavioral and neuroscience findings and theoretical directions. *Attention, Perception & Psychophysics, 72*, 561–582.

Gu, B.-M., van Rijn, H., & Meck, W. H. (2015). Oscillatory multiplexing of neural population codes for interval timing and working memory. *Neuroscience & Biobehavioral Reviews, 48*, 160–185.

Harrington, D. L., & Haaland, K. Y. (1999). Neural underpinnings of temporal processing: A review of focal lesion, pharmacological, & functional imaging research. *Reviews in the Neurosciences, 10*, 91–116.

Harrington, D. L., Lee, R. R., Boyd, L. A., Rapcsak, S. Z., & Knight, R. T. (2004). Does the representation of time depend on the cerebellum? *Brain, 127*, 1–14.

Hinton, S. C., Harrington, D. L., Binder, J. R., Durgerian, S., & Rao, S. M. (2004). Neural systems supporting timing and chronometric counting: An FMRI study. *Cognitive Brain Research, 21*, 183–192.

Hinton, S. C., & Meck, W. H. (2004). Frontal-striatal circuitry activated by human peak-interval timing in the supra-seconds range. *Cognitive Brain Research, 21*, 171–182.

Ivry, R. B., & Keele, S. W. (1989). Timing functions of the cerebellum. *Journal of Cognitive Neuroscience, 1*, 136–152.

Karmarkar, U. R., & Buonomano, D. V. (2007). Timing in the absence of clocks: Encoding time in neural network states. *Neuron, 53*, 427–438.

Keele, S. W., & Ivry, R. B. (1991). Does the cerebellum provide a common computation for diverse tasks? In A. Diamond (Ed.), *The developmental and neural bases of higher cognitive functions: Annals of the New York academy sciences* (Vol. 608, pp. 179–211). New York: New York Academy of Sciences.

Koch, G., Oliveri, M., & Caltagirone, C. (2009). Neural networks engaged in milliseconds and seconds time processing: Evidence from transcranial magnetic stimulation and patients with cortical or subcortical dysfunction. *Philosophical Transactions of the Royal Society, 364*, 1907–1918.

Koch, G., Oliveri, M., Torriero, S., Salerno, S., Lo Gerfo, E., & Caltogirone, C. (2007). Repetitive TMS of cerebellum interferes with millisecond time processing. *Experimental Brain Research, 179*, 291–299.

Lee, K. H., Eagleston, P. N., Brown, W. H., Gregory, A. N., Barker, A. T., & Woodruff, P. W. R. (2007). The role of the cerebellum in subsecond time perception: Evidence from repetitive transcranial magnetic stimulation. *Journal of Cognitive Neuroscience, 19*, 147–157.

Macar, F., & Vidal, F. (2009). Timing processes: An outline of behavioural and neural indices not systematically considered in timing models. *Canadian Journal of Experimental Psychology, 63*, 227–239.

Macar, F., Vidal, F., & Casini, L. (1999). The supplementary motor area in motor and sensory timing: Evidence from slow brain potential changes. *Experimental Brain Research, 135*, 271–280.

Matell, M. S., & Meck, W. H. (2004). Cortico-striatal circuits and interval timing: Coincidence detection of oscillatory processes. *Cognitive Brain Research, 21*, 139–170.

Meck, W. H., & Benson, A. M. (2002). Dissecting the brain's internal clock: How frontal-striatal circuitry keeps time and shifts attention. *Brain and Cognition, 48*, 195–211.

Meck, W. H., Doyere, V., & Gruart, A. (Eds.). (2012). *Interval timing and time-based decision making*. Lausanne: Frontiers e-book. doi:10.3389/978-2-88919-034-8.

Merchant, H., & de Lafuente, V. (Eds.). (2014). *Neurobiology of interval timing*. New York: Springer. (Advances in Experimental Medicine and Biology, Vol. 829).

Merchant, H., Harrington, D. L., & Meck, W. M. (2013). Neural basis of the perception and estimation of time. *Annual Review of Neuroscience, 36*, 313–336.

Merchant, H., Zarco, W., Pérez, O., Prado, L., & Bartolo, R. (2011). Measuring time with different neural chronometers during a synchronization-continuation task. *PNAS, 108*, 19784–19789.

Mioni, G., Grondin, S., Bardi, L., & Stablum, F. (in press). Understanding time perception through non-invasive brain stimulation techniques: A review of studies. *Behavioural Brain Research*.

N'Diaye, K., Ragot, R., Garnero, L., & Pouthas, V. (2004). What is common to brain activity evoked by the perception of visual and auditory filled durations? A study with MEG and EEG co-recordings. *Cognitive Brain Research, 21*, 250–268.

Nichelli, P., Always, D., & Grafman, J. (1996). Perceptual timing in cerebellar degeneration. *Neuropsychologia, 34*, 863–871.

Penney, T., & Vaitilingam, L. (2008). Imaging time. In S. Grondin (Ed.), *Psychology of time* (pp. 261–294). Bingley, UK: Emerald Group Publishing.

Pfeuty, M., Ragot, R., & Pouthas, V. (2008). Brain activity during interval timing depends on sensory structure. *Brain Research, 1024*, 112–117.

Pouthas, V., George, N., Poline, J.-B., Pfeuty, M., VandeMoorteele, P.-F., Hugueville, L., . . . Renault, B. (2005). Neural network involved in time perception: An fMRI study comparing long and short interval estimation. *Human Brain Mapping, 25*, 433–441.

Rammsayer, T. H. (2008). Neuropharmacological approaches to human timing. In S. Grondin (Ed.), *Psychology of time* (pp. 295–320). Bingley, UK: Emerald Group Publishing.

Rao, S. M., Mayer, A. R., & Harrington, D. L. (2001). The evolution of brain activation during temporal processing. *Nature Neuroscience, 4*(3), 317–323.

Teki, S., Grube, M., Kumar, S., & Griffiths, T. D. (2011). Distinct neural substrates of duration-based and beat-based auditory timing. *Journal of Neuroscience, 31*, 3805–3812.

Tracy, J. I., Faro, S. H., Mohamed, F. B., Pinsk, M., & Pinus, A. (2000). Functional localization of a "time keeper" function separate from attentional resources and task strategy. *NeuroImage, 11*, 228–242.

Tregellas, J. R., Davalos, D. B., & Rojas, D. C. (2006). Effect of task difficulty on the functional anatomy of temporal processing. *NeuroImage, 32*, 307–315.

Wiener, M., Turkeltaub, P., & Coslett, H. B. (2010). The image of time: A voxel-wise meta-analysis. *NeuroImage, 49*, 1728–1740.

Zelaznik, H. N., Spencer, R. M. C., & Ivry, R. B. (2008). Behavioral analysis of human movement timing. In S. Grondin (Ed.), *Psychology of time* (pp. 233–260). Bingley, UK: Emerald Group Publishing.

6 Is Temporal Information Processing Based on Rhythm?

Most of the time, the works on the sensory systems in psychophysics concern simple conditions and it is possible to describe exactly the effects of experimental manipulations. Consequently, numerous works on the discrimination or the categorization of intervals consist in the presentation of simple intervals, as opposed to the presentation of sequences of intervals. Nevertheless, there is literature on the discrimination of sequences of temporal intervals, and it happens that this literature reveals something very important: generally, increasing the number of presentations of intervals increases the capacity to discriminate them.

Number of Intervals and Their Role

Increasing the number of intervals presented in a task from one to three improves discrimination, but increasing the number of intervals from three to five results in only a little change (Grondin, 2012). In fact, in the auditory modality, we know that beyond four presentations, there is no more improvement to be expected (ten Hoopen, van den Berg, Memelink, Bocanegra, & Boon, 2011). In the visual modality, we can also take advantage of the increase of the number of intervals, but, probably because of the requirements imposed by the resolution of the signals themselves, increasing the number of intervals decreases the efficiency when these intervals are very short (300 ms or less) and when there is no inter-stimulus interval between one or several standards and the interval of comparison (Grondin, 2001).

Several years ago, Drake and Botte (1993) reported that increasing the number of interval presentations increases performance (decreases the variability), and attributed this effect to the possibility of stabilizing the representation of the repeated intervals (see also Ivry & Hazeltine, 1995). These authors thus opted for an explanation based on memory. By positing that a part of the variability in the temporal judgments relies on memory processes, the so-called *multiple-look hypothesis* turned out to be compatible with the information processing version of the internal clock described in Chapter 4 and where every interval is estimated on the basis of the accumulation of pulses emitted during this interval.

An alternative hypothesis would be that the multiplication of intervals would allow to make available a different way of handling temporal information: Instead of estimating the duration of each interval, per se, it would become possible to base judgments on the basis of the rhythm dictated by the sequence and on the expectation of the moment of arrival of the next stimulus. We speak here about processing based on the beat, by opposition to processing based on the interval.

In the study of Drake and Botte (Experiment 1), the number of standard intervals, presented first, and the number of intervals of comparison, presented second, co-varied (1, 2, 4, or 6 on each side). If the explanation of Drake and Botte holds water, it would mean that it is the rehearsal of the standard intervals kept in memory that would determine the effect of the number of interval presentations. It has proved that it is not the first sequence, the one that contains standard intervals, that is critical; it is rather the number of intervals presented in the second sequence that is crucial (McAuley & Miller, 2007; Miller & McAuley, 2005). More particularly, no matter whether they are presented in first or second, it is the number of comparison intervals which will have the most influence on the capacity to discriminate correctly (Grondin & McAuley, 2009). In other words, it is reasonable to reject multiple-look hypothesis, i.e., the idea that a part of the variability in the discrimination process, when repeated intervals are at play, is due to the quality of the representation in memory of the standard interval.

It is finally important to mention that the influence of a rhythmic sequence on the discrimination of intervals is not limited to a local effect, that is, to what is presented during a given trial, in the immediate context. This sequence will also exert a global effect, that is, an influence that takes place during an entire block of trials (Jones & McAuley, 2005). Finally, the duration of the delay between the standard and the comparison intervals, whether or not the comparison intervals are a multiple of the standard interval, will influence the discrimination level (Barnes & Jones, 2000).

Unique Intervals vs. Rhythm

This difference in the levels of temporal discrimination, according to the fact that single intervals or sequences of intervals are presented, invariably leads to the hypothesis that there is at least two different ways, two distinct mechanisms, for processing temporal information (Grube, Cooper, Chinnery, & Griffiths, 2010; Grube, Lee, Griffiths, Barker, & Woodruff, 2010). Apparently, according to a study based on the use of fMRI, the brain would actually have in its arsenal more than a single system for reporting time (two indeed), and the use of one of these systems or the other would depend on the temporal structure of the events arising in the environment.

In the study of Teki, Grube, Kumar, and Griffiths (2011), two experimental contexts were created for the same task which consisted in discriminating between the duration of two successive intervals. In a case, auditory stimuli (clicks) were presented in an irregular way, which forces the participants to encode the absolute duration of the penultimate interval so that it may be distinguished from the final interval. In the other context, this penultimate interval was in the continuity of a regular sequence of sounds, which delineated several times this duration. It generated an expectation about the moment of arrival of the next sound, had the last interval been of the same duration. The arrival of the next sound before or after this moment could thus serve for discriminating the last two intervals. In other words, they were comparing a processing based on a representation of the penultimate interval, per se, and a processing based on expectation generated by the beat, by the rhythm.

These researchers distinguished two cerebral mechanisms for responding to the requirements imposed by these types of temporal processing. In the first case, the processing of absolute duration is based on a representation of the interval, the mechanism is an olivo-cerebellar network including the inferior olivary nucleus, the vermis, and the dentate nucleus. In the second case, where the processing is based on rhythm, the mechanism is a striato-thalamo-cortical network which involves numerous parts of the brain: putamen, caudate nucleus, premotor cortex, SMA, dorsolateral prefrontal cortex and, naturally, the thalamus. The use of one or the other of these systems depends on the regularity that the events of the environment have to offer.

Attending, Attention, and Entrainment

There are numerous cases in nature where we can perceive that there is physical regularity in the stream of events. This regularity can be observed in different spheres of normal life through music, speech, or the coordination between body members during locomotion. The repetition of events arising with regularity allows one to anticipate the arrival of the next event (Jones, 1976). The beginnings and ends of the temporal extents could therefore be clearly determined. According to the *dynamic attending theory*, this regularity even allows the regulation of the internal mechanisms of attention (Jones, 2018; Jones & Boltz, 1989). In the context of these regularities, the forthcoming events become predictable and an observer can enter into a future-oriented mode of attending. So, the efficiency of judgments on the duration will rest heavily on the temporal coherence of these events. It will also depend on the capacity to synchronize the internal rhythmicity specific to the cyclic nature of attention with the appropriate rhythmic level that the environment has to offer. It will thus be here a matter of *attunement* between internal and external activities.

A more recent version of the dynamic attending model posits the existence of a two-component oscillator: a nonlinear oscillator and a rhythm of impulse of attentional energy (Large & Jones, 1999). It is the summation of these two components that supplies an attentional rhythm, this one having an adaptive property. In other words, the period and the phase of this internal oscillator can change and adapt themselves (Barnes & Jones, 2000; Jones, 2018; Large, 2008).

In summary, the dynamic attention theory does not posit that all the efficiency for discriminating time intervals comes from the simple repetition of the intervals. It attributes specifically this efficiency to the consequence of this repetition on an internal oscillator. This one adapts itself to the context so as to synchronize the attentional pulses and the beginning of stimuli. There is thus an entrainment effect; we sometimes speak about an entrainment model. Ultimately, this entrainment effect aims for maximum efficiency by tending towards the possibility of aligning the attentional peak with the beginning of the expected stimulus.

Regularity, Cognitive Efficiency, and Brain

The repercussions of the internalization of a rhythm led by the regularity of external events in the environment are not limited solely to temporal performances. This is what reveals, for example, a study of Brochard, Tassin, and Zagar (2013) based on the dynamic attending theory of Jones and Boltz. In this study, participants had to determine as rapidly as possible if the five letters presented on the screen of a computer form a word or not. These words, all bi-syllabic, had the peculiarity of being segmented into two parts, presented successively, which respected the syllabic division of the word (for example "pan" in "pan/da") or not (for example "pa" in "panda"). Series of five sounds were generated, so that they generated an expectation for the moment of arrival of the sixth sound. Instead of the sound, it is the first syllable that was presented, either at the exact moment when the sound was supposed to arrive, or with a slight delay.

The authors expected faster and more correct responses when the appearance of the first syllable of the words was going to be synchronized with the moment of arrival of the following sound. This prediction was based on the idea that this moment was going to correspond to a maximal deployment of the attention. The results indicate that the arrival of the first syllable at the expected moment facilitates the visual recognition of the word, when compared to a condition where the word does not arrive in synchrony with the expected moment of arrival. In return however, in the conditions where the syllabic division of the word was not respected, the difficulty in recognizing the word was even larger.

In fact, even when there is neither a temporal task nor a perceptive or cognitive task of some sort, the brain will detect the regularities of the environment. This is what the study of Mento, Tarantino, Sarlo, and Bisiacchi (2013) demonstrates. In this study, participants heard a sound of 500 ms at the same time as an image was presented. Sounds and images which delineated the beginning of the interval were always the same, and they were different from the sounds and images, also always the same, which delineated the end of an interval. These intervals lasted 1500 ms, 2500 ms, or 3000 ms, and occurred respectively 70%, 15%, and 15% of times. The participants in Mento and collaborators' study received no instruction and had no response or motor activity to make. The fact that they were exposed much more often to the 1500-ms interval has resulted in creating expectancy. This expectancy was in fact revealed by the recording of the electroencephalographic activity, and more specifically by the negative contingent variations. The latter reached their maximum at the moment when the second stimulus was supposed to occur.

Conclusion

Apparently, the brain makes every effort to detect regularities in the environment; if any are present, they will be captured. So, in a task where it is necessary to estimate time, if regular sequences of events arise, they will serve as the basis for making these estimations. If such regularities are not available, it will always be possible to rely on a more analytical system, apparently less effective, which is the processing of single intervals, probably based on a kind of internal clock, maybe a pacemaker-accumulator process.

References

Barnes, R., & Jones, M. R. (2000). Expectancy, attention, & time. *Cognitive Psychology, 41*, 254–311.

Brochard, R., Tassin, M., & Zagar, D. (2013). Got rhythm [. . .] for better and for worse: Cross-modal effects of auditory rhythm on visual word recognition. *Cognition, 127*, 214–219.

Drake, C., & Botte, M.-C. (1993). Tempo sensitivity in auditory sequences: Evidence for a multiple-look model. *Perception & Psychophysics, 54*, 277–286.

Grondin, S. (2001). Discriminating time intervals presented in sequences marked by visual signals. *Perception & Psychophysics, 63*, 1214–1228.

Grondin, S. (2012). Violation of the scalar property for time perception between 1 and 2 seconds: Evidence from interval discrimination, reproduction, & categorization. *Journal of Experimental Psychology: Human Perception and Performance, 38*, 880–890.

Grondin, S., & McAuley, J. D. (2009). Duration discrimination in crossmodal sequences. *Perception, 38*, 1542–1559.

Grube, M., Cooper, F. E., Chinnery, P. F., & Griffiths, T. D. (2010). Dissociation of duration-based and beat-based auditory timing in cerebellar degeneration. *Proceedings of the National Academy of Sciences, 107*, 11597–11601.

Grube, M., Lee, K. H., Griffiths, T. D., Barker, A. T., & Woodruff, P. W. (2010). Transcranial magnetic theta-burst stimulation of the human cerebellum distinguishes absolute, duration-based from relative, beat-based perception of subsecond time intervals. *Frontiers in Psychology, 1*, 171.

Ivry, R. B., & Hazeltine, R. E. (1995). The perception and production of temporal intervals across a range of durations: Evidence for a common timing mechanism. *Journal of Experimental Psychology: Human Perception and Performance, 21*, 3–18.

Jones, M. R. (1976). Time, our lost dimension: Toward a new theory of perception, attention, & memory. *Psychological Review, 83*, 323–355.

Jones, M. R. (2018). *Time will tell: A theory of dynamic attending.* Oxford: Oxford University Press.

Jones, M. R., & Boltz, M. (1989). Dynamic attending and responses to time. *Psychological Review, 96,* 459–491.

Jones, M. R., & McAuley, J. D. (2005). Time judgments in global temporal contexts. *Perception & Psychophysics, 67,* 398–417.

Large, E. W. (2008). Resonating to musical rhythm: Theory and experiment. In S. Grondin (Ed.), *Psychology of time* (pp. 189–232). Bingley, UK: Emerald Group Publishing.

Large, E. W., & Jones, M. R. (1999). The dynamics of attending: How people track time-varying events. *Psychological Review, 106,* 119–159.

McAuley, J. D., & Miller, N. S. (2007). Picking up the pace: Effects of global temporal context on sensitivity to the tempo of auditory sequences. *Perception & Psychophysics, 69,* 709–718.

Mento, G., Tarantino, V., Sarlo, M., & Bisiacchi, P. S. (2013). Automatic temporal expectancy: A high-density event-related potential study. *PLoS One, 8,* e62896. doi:10.1371/journal.pone.0062896.

Miller, N., & McAuley, J. D. (2005). Tempo sensitivity in isochronous tone sequences: The multiple-look model revisited. *Perception & Psychophysics, 67,* 1150–1160.

Teki, S., Grube, M., Kumar, S., & Griffiths, T. D. (2011). Distinct neural substrates of duration-based and beat-based auditory timing. *Journal of Neuroscience, 31,* 3805–3812.

ten Hoopen, G., van den Berg, S., Memelink, J., Bocanegra, B., & Boon, R. (2011). Multiple-look effects on temporal discrimination within sound sequences. *Attention, Perception, & Psychophysics, 73,* 2249–2269.

7   Does the Perception of Time Emerge From Our Senses?

Put so, the question gives the impression that the perception of time or, in a more general way, psychological time, is not a "sixth sense". In fact, contrary to what is possible with other senses, we could hardly indicate specifically the nature of a temporal stimulus, describe a receptor for such a stimulus, or highlight a cerebral area dedicated to time (see Chapter 5).

In the present chapter, the question of the relation between time and the senses will be approached in two ways. First, the processing of temporal information will be posited as being amodal and we will try to see how the temporal performances differ according to whether the sensory stimuli used to interrogate the mechanisms necessary for this processing come from one modality or from another. In the second approach, we shall try to see if it is reasonable to think that the processing might emerge from senses. The accent in the chapter will be put mainly on the auditory and visual modalities, which are the most commonly used in the study of duration.

Senses for Addressing the Internal Clock Issue

A classical result in the field the time perception concerns the comparison of the perceived duration of intervals marked by a sound vs. by a light. Even if there are no decisive reports on this matter (see Grondin, 2003), the studies show that most of the time, intervals lasting from 0.1 to 1.2 seconds are judged as being longer when marked by auditory stimuli than when marked by visual stimuli (Wearden, Edwards, Fakhri, & Percival, 1998). The same conclusion seems to apply to longer intervals (Penney, Gibbon, & Meck, 2000). In fact, this result turns out to be more robust when filled intervals rather than empty intervals are used to mark time (Lhamon & Goldstone, 1974). Furthermore, perceived duration is partially a matter, in the auditory modality, of the intensity of the signal marking time (Eisler & Eisler, 1992) and a matter, in the visual modality of whether there is movement (Goldstone & Lhamon, 1974). In particular, the influence of the intensity of sound on the duration would depend on the relative intensity between the sound marking the interval and the one used in the background (Matthews, Stewart, & Wearden, 2011). Finally, in sensory conditions where the auditory interval is perceived as longer than the same visual interval, if the same auditory and visual signals mark simultaneously the interval, the perceived duration will be closer to the one obtained solely with the auditory presentation, an effect that Walker and Scott (1981) call auditory dominance.

Various hypotheses aim at explaining why an interval seems longer in the auditory modality. One of these, elaborated in a perspective that there is an internal clock (see Chapter 4), consists in supposing that auditory stimuli, more than visual stimuli, contribute to an acceleration of the rhythm of emission of pulses (Wearden et al., 1998). Most of the studies reporting this distortion are developed with a within-subjects design, which suggests that a direct comparison of the stimuli of both modalities would be necessary to obtain this effect. Another hypothesis relies on the possibility that the timing activity begins more quickly (efficiency to close the switch; see Chapter 9) when the intervals are marked by auditory rather than by visual stimuli.

As for the comparison of the levels of discrimination of intervals marked by signals delivered in various sensory modalities, the pinnacle of efficiency unarguably goes to audition. The discrimination is much finer, much better, with sounds than with visual or tactile signals (see Grondin, 2003). Furthermore, whether it is about the presentation of single intervals or about sequences of intervals, the discrimination is better with successions of short sounds than with successions of flashes (Grondin & McAuley, 2009). Also, whether the intervals are empty or filled, the superiority of audition over vision is manifest for intervals from 0.125 to four seconds (Grondin, 1993). Given the use of sounds in speech and music, and the necessity of adjusting efficiently the succession of events in these activities, it is tempting to believe that auditory superiority depends on the resolution for processing the signal itself. However, if we mark a brief interval, for example, with a short auditory signal and a short visual signal (intermodal condition) rather than with two short visual signals (intramodal condition) the discrimination will be much better with both visual signals (Gontier, Hasuo, Mitsudo, & Grondin, 2013; Grondin, Roussel, Gamache, Roy, & Ouellet, 2005; Rousseau, Poirier, & Lemyre, 1983). This effect of intermodality turns out to be very strong when the intervals are very short and also occurs when tactile signals serve to mark intervals (Azari, Mioni, Rousseau, & Grondin, in press; Grondin & Rousseau, 1991; Kuroda, Hasuo, & Grondin, 2013; Mayer, Di Luca, & Ernst, 2014).

Intramodal Processing of Duration

This effect of intermodality during the discrimination of intervals, added to the hearing dominance reported for perceived duration, gives the impression that every sensory modality could be responsible for its own processing of temporal information (Bueti, 2011; Bueti, Bahrami, & Walsh, 2008). Within such a perspective, the intermodal intervals, not being able to be processed within one modality, would be taken in charge by a mechanism—maybe the internal clock (to see Chapter 4)—less effective than what is offered within the modalities.

Before describing how it could take place within a modality, let us note that other models of functioning were proposed. For example, Kanai, Lloyd, Bueti, and Walsh (2011) observed, with transcranial magnetic stimulations (TMS), that a stimulation of the auditory cortex impaired the processing of temporal intervals marked either by sound or by visual stimuli, but that a stimulation of the visual cortex impaired only the processing of intervals marked by visual stimuli. This observation led the authors to suppose that any temporal processing involves the auditory cortex. So, the weaker temporal performances in vision than in hearing would be understandable if one considers the necessity of transferring the visual sensory signals into an auditory code. Other data, based on an investigation by means of the transcranial direct-current stimulation, support the idea of the crucial role of the auditory cortex in temporal processing (Mioni et al., 2016).

The explanation based on the necessity of transforming markers of non-auditory intervals into an auditory code is interesting. However, we may wonder why an intermodal interval that includes at least an auditory marker would be more poorly discriminated than a non-auditory intramodal interval, which requires the transfer of two signals into an auditory code (Grondin, 2014).

If information processing occurs within modalities, then the differences between the efficiency levels of processing would simply depend on the differences of efficiency between the specific mechanisms. In the visual modality, some theoretical proposals were moved forward to determine how temporal processing within the visual cortex could become possible. So, when a flickering visual stimulus is presented in a specific location of the visual space until one can have a local adaptation there, there is a decrease of the perceived duration of subsequent stimuli if these are presented exactly in the same place, but not if they are presented somewhere else in the visual field (Johnston, Arnold, & Nishida, 2006). Besides, we know that the brief and fast eye movements, ocular saccade, exert an influence on the perceived duration of visual events, but not of auditory events (Morrone, Ross, & Burr, 2005). We also know that the timing of visual events is characterized by a spatial selectivity (Burr, Tozzi, & Morrone, 2007) and, more specifically, for a same region, the effect that an adaptation to an upward movement has on temporal compression only holds true for upward movements (Curran & Benton, 2012). In brief, there are many reasons that support, at least partially, the idea that processing of the duration of visual events would directly depend on the neuronal mechanisms belonging to vision.

In the auditory modality, the problem is different. If the question of spatial resolution turns out to be crucial in vision, the resolution of the rapid succession of events proves to be imperative in audition (see the previous chapter). So, instead of depending on the properties of an internal clock, the quality of the processing of temporal information would depend on the quality of the organization of successive events. Just like there is a perceptual organization of visual stimuli displayed in space, during the perception of a visual scene (Grondin, 2016), there would be a perceptual organization of the auditory events in time. This organization would depend in particular on the similarity of the features such as the frequency of the auditory signals. The use of successive sounds of different frequencies, rather than of the same frequency, gives rise to more difficulty when it is necessary to discriminate the duration between these sounds (van Noorden, 1975). Also, the level of discrimination of short temporal intervals varies considerably according to the length of sounds, too long sounds hindering the discrimination (Grondin et al., 2005; Kuroda et al., 2013). According to Rammsayer and Leutner (1996), who worked with standard intervals of 30 ms or 300 ms, if one or the other of the markers of an empty interval lasts more than 200 ms, the capacity to discriminate decreases. Let us note as well that using longer markers also has an influence on perceived duration (Kuroda, Hasuo, Labonté, Laflamme, & Grondin, 2014).

Conclusion

It would be exaggerated to claim that temporal judgments are based on the functioning within the senses. However, the perspective stipulating that judgments on the duration of short intervals can depend on the processing of information within the cortical areas specific to these senses is attractive. In order to do so, the temporal markers used during an experiment have to belong to the same sensory modality. If the markers come from different sensory modalities, the temporal information will be much more difficult to process. This decrease of processing capacities is attributed by certain researchers to the necessity of transferring any marker that is not auditory into a hearing code.

So, we find ourselves in front of a proposal where the nature of the mechanism dedicated to the processing of temporal information would depend on the length of the intervals. With short intervals, we can rely on the processing within the modalities, whereas with longer intervals, it is necessary to rely on an amodal, central, mode of processing, like the pacemaker-accumulator mechanism described earlier (see Chapter 4). Not to mention that we also find somewhere else, in the study of the various sensory systems, proposals where more than one mechanism would serve to satisfy the requirements demanded by the environment. It is the case, for example, of the auditory system which offers a processing based on the location (place theory and traveling wave) for processing high frequencies and a processing based on a temporal coding (with the volley principle) for the processing of low frequencies.

Finally, when we question the processing capacity of temporal information with sensory stimuli to mark time intervals, we generally observe that the duration seems longer when markers are auditory rather than visual; therefore, the capacity to discriminate time intervals is much better when time is marked by sounds than when marked by visual or tactile stimuli.

References

Azari, L., Mioni, G., Rousseau, R., & Grondin, S. (in press). An analysis of the processing of intra- and intermodal time intervals. *Attention, Perception, & Psychophysics*.

48 Basic Temporal Processes

Bueti, D. (2011). The sensory representation of time. *Frontiers of Integrative Neuroscience*, 5, doi:10.3389/fnint.2011.00034.

Bueti, D., Bahrami, B., & Walsh, V. (2008). Sensory and associative cortex in time perception. *Journal of Cognitive Neuroscience*, 20, 1054–1062.

Burr, D., Tozzi, A., & Morrone, M. C. (2007). Neural mechanisms for timing visual events are spatially selective in real-world coordinates. *Nature Neuroscience*, 10, 423–425.

Curran, W., & Benton, C. P. (2012). The many directions of time. *Cognition*, 122, 252–257.

Eisler, H., & Eisler, A. (1992). Time perception: Effects of sex and sound intensity on scales of subjective duration. *Scandinavian Journal of Psychology*, 33, 339–358.

Goldstone, S., & Lhamon, W. T. (1974). Studies on auditory-visual differences in human time judgment: Sounds are judged longer than lights. *Perceptual and Motor Skills*, 39, 63–82.

Gontier, E., Hasuo, E., Mitsudo, T., & Grondin, S. (2013). EEG investigations of duration discrimination: The intermodal effect is induced by an attentional bias. *PLoS One*, 8(8), e74073. doi:10.1371/journal.pone.0074073.

Grondin, S. (1993). Duration discrimination of empty and filled intervals marked by auditory and visual signals. *Perception & Psychophysics*, 54, 383–394.

Grondin, S. (2003). Sensory modalities and temporal processing. In H. Helfrich (Ed.), *Time and mind 02* (pp. 75–92). Göttingen, Germany: Hogrefe & Huber Publishers.

Grondin, S. (2014). Why studying intermodal duration discrimination matters. *Frontiers in Psychology: Perception Science*, 5, 628.

Grondin, S. (2016). *Psychology of perception*. Cham, Switzerland: Springer.

Grondin, S., & McAuley, J. D. (2009). Duration discrimination in crossmodal sequences. *Perception*, 38, 1542–1559.

Grondin, S., & Rousseau, R. (1991). Judging the relative duration of multimodal short empty time intervals. *Perception & Psychophysics*, 49, 245–256.

Grondin, S., Roussel, M.-E., Gamache, P.-L., Roy, M., & Ouellet, B. (2005). The structure of sensory events and the accuracy of judgments about time. *Perception*, 34, 45–58.

Johnston, A., Arnold, D. H., & Nishida, S. (2006). Spatially localized distortions of event time. *Current Biology*, 16, 472–479.

Kanai, R., Lloyd, H., Bueti, D., & Walsh, V. (2011). Modality-independent role of the primary auditory cortex in time estimation. *Experimental Brain Research*, 209, 465–471.

Kuroda, T., Hasuo, E., & Grondin, S. (2013). Discrimination of brief gaps marked by two stimuli: Effects of sound length, repetition and rhythmic grouping. *Perception*, 42, 82–94.

Kuroda, T., Hasuo, E., Labonté, K., Laflamme, V., & Grondin, S. (2014). Discrimination of two neighboring intra- and intermodal empty time intervals marked by three successive stimuli. *Acta Psychologica*, 149, 134–141.

Lhamon, W. T., & Goldstone, S. (1974). Studies on auditory-visual differences in human time judgment: More transmitted information with sounds than lights. *Perceptual and Motor Skills*, 39, 295–307.

Matthews, W. J., Stewart, N., & Wearden, J. H. (2011). Stimulus intensity and the perception of duration. *Journal of Experimental Psychology: Human Perception and Performance*, 37, 303–313.

Mayer, K., Di Luca, M., & Ernst, M. O. (2014). Duration perception in crossmodally-defined intervals. *Acta Psychologica, 147*, 2–9.

Mioni, G., Grondin, S., Forgione, M., Fracasso, V., Mapelli, D., & Stablum, F. (2016). The role of primary auditory and visual cortices in temporal processing: A tDCS approach. *Behavioural Brain Research, 313*, 151–157.

Morrone, M. C., Ross, J., & Burr, D. (2005). Saccadic eye movements cause compression of time as well as space. *Nature Neuroscience, 8*, 950–954.

Penney, T. B., Gibbon, J., & Meck, W. H. (2000). Differential effects of auditory and visual signals on clock speed and temporal memory. *Journal of Experimental Psychology: Human Perception and Performance, 26*, 1770–1787.

Rammsayer, T. H., & Leutner, D. (1996). Temporal discrimination as a function of marker duration. *Perception & Psychophysics, 58*, 1213–1223.

Rousseau, R., Poirier, J., & Lemyre, L. (1983). Duration discrimination of empty time intervals marked by intermodal pulses. *Perception & Psychophysics, 34*, 541–548.

van Noorden, L. P. A. S. (1975). *Temporal coherence in the perception of tone sequences.* Unpublished doctoral dissertation, Eindhoven University of Technology, Eindhoven, the Netherlands.

Walker, J. T., & Scott, K. J. (1981). Auditory-visual conflicts in the perceived duration of lights, tones and gaps. *Journal of Experimental Psychology: Human Perception and Performance, 7*, 1327–1339.

Wearden, J. H., Edwards, H., Fakhri, M., & Percival, A. (1998). Why "sounds are judged longer than lights": Application of a model of the internal clock in humans. *Quarterly Journal of Experimental Psychology, 51B*, 97–120.

8 Can We Improve the Processing of Temporal Information?

The question asked here does not concern long trainings extending over years, as is the case in music (see Chapter 21). It is neither concerned with training aiming at being able to guess what time it is correctly or to wake up at a precise moment without an alarm. We rather wonder to what extent we can improve capabilities to solve the temporal requirements in simple tasks, and to what extent this learning, if any, could be transferred to another temporal task. The following lines will illustrate temporal tasks, classical and quite simple, used in experimental psychology and which have been the object of training.

Training and Intramodal Transfer

The opportunity to benefit from training seems to depend on the type of task being studied. The production of continuous intervals improves with training, but this does not seem to be the case for time interval discrimination.

Madison, Karampela, Ullen, and Holm (2013) have tackled directly the question of the effect of training on an interval production task. In a first experiment, they compared four ways of producing: with a finger tap on a sensor, passing a finger through a light beam when the hand is at rest, with a tap with a drumstick, or with the same stick, but not leaving the wrist free to move. The participants could not see their hand. After 70 taps synchronized with a sound delivered by headphones (500, 536, or 574 ms between the sounds), participants had to continue to tap at the same rhythm so as to produce 70 other intervals. The study included six 30-minute sessions distributed over different days. The results reveal that the coefficients of variation are lower (performances are better) with the stick conditions than in the other two conditions, and the prolonged training does not make it possible to reduce the difference between these conditions. Also, there is a training effect. As a second experiment by Madison et al., which focused on producing 500 to 1624 ms intervals, also reveals, this effect occurs very quickly. The learning in the timing of this motor task occurs after 60 to 90 minutes of training. This improvement probably affects more the motor component than the properly temporal component of the task.

Improving Temporal Information Processing? 51

With respect to short interval discrimination, some studies indicate that there is little improvement to be expected from even very long training. In their attempt to replicate the data of Kristofferson (1980), who hoped to demonstrate the quantum nature of psychological time, Matthews and Grondin (2012) used the same method consisting of spending 20 sessions for each of the 13 durations under study (from 100 to 1480 ms). Kristofferson thought that a long training would make it able to remove the nontemporal noise which masks the real value of the differential thresholds for interval discrimination. In addition to not being able to replicate the step function that Kristofferson reported when only the last sessions of each duration were taken into consideration, the two participants in the Matthews and Grondin study showed only weak improvements over sessions and, when there were signs of improvement, they occurred for the longest intervals of the study. Rammsayer (1994) had also shown, for 50-ms intervals, whether empty or filled, that training does not improve temporal discrimination.

Thus, the improvement of the ability to discriminate time intervals that can be expected from training sometimes seems rather slim. However, some authors report that it is possible to transfer a certain learning of the processing of short time intervals, of the order of a few hundred milliseconds, from one situation to another within a modality (Karmarkar & Buonomano, 2003). For example, the gains obtained after training with 100-ms intervals delimited by 1-kHz sounds could be transferred to a situation where the intervals of the order of 100 ms were delimited by 4-kHz sounds. However, they were not transferred to the discrimination of intervals of 50, 200 or 400 ms, although 1-kHz sounds delimited these intervals (Wright, Buonomano, Mahncke, & Merzenich, 1997).

Just as it seems that we can transfer a temporal learning of a given duration between frequencies in the auditory modality, it seems possible to transfer within the visual modality as well as within the tactile modality (Wright et al., 1997). In the case of vision, the improvement due to training in a task of discrimination of intervals marked by signals processed by one cerebral hemisphere can be transferred to the other hemisphere (Westheimer, 1999). Similarly, gains in an interval discrimination task obtained as a result of learning with tactile stimuli at a given location can be transferred elsewhere to the skin (Nagarajan, Blake, Wright, Byl, & Merzenich, 1998).

Training and Intermodal Transfer

In addition to offering some demonstrations of an intramodal transfer of the learning of temporal information processing, the literature on the subject contains some studies indicating that intermodal transfer of this learning also seems possible. Nagarajan et al. (1998), who had demonstrated an intramodal tactile transfer, even report that this learning of duration with tactile stimuli can be transferred to the auditory modality. Moreover, it seems that the learning made during time discrimination in the auditory modality can be transferred to the production of time intervals, provided that the intervals involved in the production and discrimination tasks are of the same order of magnitude (Meegan, Aslin, & Jacobs, 2000).

In the area of interval discrimination, the results are much better in the auditory modality than in the other modalities (see previous chapter). Thus, one can expect to observe more improvement if a training is done in audition and that the effect of this training is then examined in the visual or tactile modalities, than in the opposite conditions (training in visual condition or tactile, and transfer in auditory condition). However, despite what Nagarajan and his collaborators report (1998), studies show that there is no real gain to be expected from an intermodal transfer of the processing of temporal information. Lapid, Ulrich, and Rammsayer (2009) asked participants to discriminate short auditory intervals marked by two brief sounds in order to examine the transfer of some temporal learning to another auditory condition or to the visual modality. They showed that there seems to be an intramodal transfer (from an empty auditory interval to a filled auditory interval), but no transfer to the visual modality. For their part, Grondin, Bisson, Gagnon, Gamache, and Matteau (2009) first showed that after five sessions of 300 tests of discrimination of intervals delimited by visual stimuli the result had hardly improved from the first to the fifth session. In subsequent sessions, simultaneous presentations of auditory and visual signals were used to delineate the empty intervals to be discriminated. The discrimination was better with signals presented simultaneously in both modalities with respect to a condition comprising only visual cues. In other words, as soon as the auditory signals are available to mark intervals, the discrimination is improved. Once the auditory signals were removed, there was only a slight improvement in the discrimination of intervals delimited only by visual stimuli. Targeted learning, by association between auditory and visual markers, ultimately resulted in only a slight improvement in performance; this improvement was in fact dependent on the participants' initial level of ability and the small gains quickly disappeared after the withdrawal of auditory stimuli.

Another study investigated whether one can improve the discrimination of time intervals delimited by visual stimuli by playing on the context in which the intervals are presented (Grondin, Gamache, Tobin, Bisson, & Hawke, 2008). The experimental sessions included only the presentation of auditory intervals, only the presentation of visual intervals, or included some tests with visual intervals in a context where it was mainly necessary to discriminate intervals delimited by sounds (auditory presentations). The Weber fraction for auditory interval discrimination remained about 6%, with or without the addition of visual tests. For visual interval discrimination, the Weber fraction was approximately 10% without the addition of auditory testing but increased to almost 15% in the context where auditory signals were also presented. In short, instead of assisting with discrimination, presenting visual intervals in a context where there is mainly auditory temporal processing rather seems to diminish the ability to discriminate intervals delimited only by visual stimuli.

In addition, another experiment aimed to improve the discrimination of intervals of 220 ms vs. 280 ms presented in the visual modality. This time, the experiment allowed the testing of the influence of a massive, regrouped, condensed training, as opposed to a training lasting a few days (Grondin & Ulrich, 2011). Thus, between the two portions of the experiment (pretraining and post-training) where the stimuli were visual, there were five portions of 360 trials (1800 training trials in total) where 240- vs. 260-ms intervals delimited by two brief sounds were to be discriminated. Although there was a slight improvement in the second testing session with visual intervals, it was about the same for a control group as for the group of participants who received massive training. In short, again, what could have been gained from an auditory training seems difficult to transfer to visual conditions.

Transfer Towards Other Types of Activity

Is it reasonable to believe that the training involving the processing of temporal information can contribute to improving performance in a different sphere of activity than time? Chen and Zhou (2014) report that a short training (15 minutes) on the discrimination of the duration of short time intervals improves another perceptual ability. Specifically, it is an improvement in the ability to categorize the apparent movement (which involves visual stimuli) and this improvement occurs whether the training has been completed with intervals delimited by auditory stimuli or by tactile stimuli; with a training involving visual stimuli the improvement was less pronounced. Also, when the task rather involved a discrimination of the frequency for example, there was no improvement.

Beyond a perceptual improvement, we know that there are links between the level of processing of temporal information and certain cognitive abilities. We do not know if this is a transfer of skills, but the phenomena are related. For example, the level of performance in temporal reproduction tasks is related to mnemonic capabilities (Baudouin, Vanneste, Isingrini, & Pouthas, 2006). Similarly, levels of performance in temporal production or discrimination tasks are related to intelligence level (Madison, Forsman, Blom, Karabanov, & Ullén, 2009, Rammsayer & Brandler, 2002, 2007).

Moreover, we know the crucial role of attention in the processing of temporal information (see the next chapter). One might think that training in the processing of temporal information, by the attention it would require, could be beneficial for some aspect of attention. Karampela, Madison, and Holm (2017) have demonstrated this. These researchers trained participants in a motor synchronization task with a sound presented every 1024 ms. After five training sessions spread over five consecutive days, each session comprising five trials during which 200 synchronizations were required, they observed an improvement in the performance of the Connors test (*Continuous Performance Test II*) which measures sustained attention.

Conclusion

The possibility of improving a temporal performance seems to depend on the task at hand. The discrimination of very short intervals delimited by sounds does not always seem to be able to benefit from a training effect. On the other hand, 60 to 90 minutes of training in the continuous production of short time intervals can reduce the inter-tap variability, probably due to the reduced variability of the motor component in the task.

The transfer of the processing capabilities of a time interval seems possible within a sensory modality if it is an interval of the same duration. However, the ability to transfer temporal information processing capabilities from one sensory modality to another remains questionable. Nevertheless, there appears to be some gains associated with the training of temporal information processing that can be exported to other spheres of activity than just temporal processing. The question remains, however, what the real magnitude of these gains is, and, more importantly, how long they can last.

References

Baudouin, A., Vanneste, S., Isingrini, M., & Pouthas, V. (2006). Differential involvement of internal clock and working memory in the production and reproduction of duration: A study on older adults. *Acta Psychologica, 121,* 285–296.

Chen, L., & Zhou, X. (2014). Fast transfer of crossmodal time interval training. *Experimental Brain Research, 232,* 1855–1864.

Grondin, S., Bisson, N., Gagnon, C., Gamache, P.-L., & Matteau, A.-A. (2009). Little to be expected from auditory training for improving visual temporal discrimination. *NeuroQuantology, 7,* 95–102.

Grondin, S., Gamache, P.-L., Tobin, S., Bisson, N., & Hawke, L. (2008). Categorization of brief temporal intervals: An auditory processing context may impair visual performances. *Acoustical Science & Technology, 29,* 338–340.

Grondin, S., & Ulrich, R. (2011). Duration discrimination performance: No crossmodal transfer from audition to vision even after massive perceptual learning. In A. Vatakis, A. Esposito, M. Giagkou, F. Cummins, & G. Papadelis (Eds.), *Time and time perception 2010, LNAI 6789* (pp. 92–100). Berlin: Springer-Verlag.

Karampela, O., Madison, G., & Holm, L. (2017). Motor timing training improves sustained attention performance. In O. Karampela, *Exploring models of time processing: Effects of training and modality, and the relationship with cognition in rhythmic motor tasks.* Doctoral Dissertation, Umea University, Sweden.

Karmarkar, U. R., & Buonomano, D. V. (2003). Temporal specificity of perceptual learning in an auditory discrimination task. *Learning and Memory, 10,* 141–147.

Kristofferson, A. B. (1980). A quantal step function in duration discrimination. *Perception & Psychophysics, 27,* 300–306.

Lapid, E., Ulrich, R., & Rammsayer, T. (2009). Perceptual learning in auditory temporal discrimination: No evidence for a cross-modal transfer to the visual modality. *Psychonomic Bulletin & Review, 16,* 382–389.

Madison, G., Forsman, L., Blom, Ö., Karabanov, A., & Ullén, F. (2009). Correlations between general intelligence and components of serial timing variability. *Intelligence, 37,* 68–75.

Madison, G., Karampela, O., Ullen, F., & Holm, L. (2013). Effects of practice on variability in an isochronous serial interval production task: Asymptotical levels of tapping variability after training are similar to those of musicians. *Acta Psychologica, 143*, 119–128.

Matthews, W. J., & Grondin, S. (2012). On the replication of Kristofferson's (1980) quantal timing for duration discrimination: Some learning but no quanta and not much of a Weber constant. *Attention, Perception, & Psychophysics, 74*, 1056–1072.

Meegan, D. V., Aslin, R. N., & Jacobs, R. A. (2000). Motor timing learned without motor training. *Nature Neuroscience, 3*, 860–862.

Nagarajan, S. S., Blake, D. T., Wright, B. A., Byl, N., & Merzenich, M. M. (1998). Practice-related improvements in somatosensory interval discrimination are temporally specific but generalize across skin location, hemisphere, and modality. *Journal of Neuroscience, 18*, 1559–1570.

Rammsayer, T. H. (1994). Effects of practice and signal energy on duration discrimination of brief auditory intervals. *Perception & Psychophysics, 55*, 454–464.

Rammsayer, T. H., & Brandler, S. (2002). On the relationship between general fluid intelligence and psychophysical indicators of temporal resolution in the brain. *Journal of Research in Personality, 36*, 507–530.

Rammsayer, T. H., & Brandler, S. (2007). Performance on temporal information processing as an index of general intelligence. *Intelligence, 35*, 123–139.

Westheimer, G. (1999). Discrimination of short time intervals by human observers. *Experimental Brain Research, 129*, 121–126.

Wright, B. A., Buonomano, D. V., Mahncke, H. W., & Merzenich, M. M. (1997). Learning and generalization of auditory temporal-interval discrimination in humans. *Journal of Neuroscience, 17*, 3956–3963.

9 What Is the Influence of Attention on Time Perception?

One day, a seven-year-old child asked me: "How is that possible? It looks like the more we look forward to something, the longer it takes". The comment is not trivial when we consider that the question was asked in December, waiting for Christmas. A child asked the question, but the mechanics would be the same for an adult. We have all experienced the slowness or the speed of the passage of time. Waiting, impatience, or boredom transforms the duration into a semblance of eternity! When we want time to pass quickly, we pay attention to it. Actually, paying attention to time largely determines the experience of duration (Brown, 2008).

Retrospective Judgments

In Chapter 1, we distinguished two categories of judgments on duration, prospective vs. retrospective. In the latter case, it is often reported that memory processes are at the heart of perceived duration (Block, Grondin, & Zakay, 2018; Block, Hancock, & Zakay, 2010). However, it turns out that attention also exerts a certain influence on the remembered duration. More specifically, there is a recognized phenomenon in the field which consists of a waiting effect as revealed by this old adage: "A watched pot never boils". Cahoon and Edmonds (1980) wanted to know if, indeed, time seems longer when we wait until the water comes to a boil. They asked participants to settle in front of a kettle full of water placed on a hot plate. The experimenter told the participants that they would come back when the experiment was ready, but some participants were further instructed to warn the experimenter, who was in a room next door, if the water was boiling. No instructions about time measurement were given. After four minutes, the experimenter returned and asked the participants to make a verbal assessment of the time that had elapsed since the beginning of his absence until his return. It turns out that the participants who had received additional instructions, to monitor the possible boiling, found the time longer; that is to say, they overestimated the duration compared to the participants of the control group.

In addition, Boltz (1993) asked participants to detect tonal errors in popular songs as quickly as possible. After 36 trials and three minutes of rest, participants who did not know the true purpose of the study were told that they were at one-third, one-half, or two-thirds of the experience. After a second block of 36 trials, therefore of the same duration as the first block, they had to indicate which of the two blocks had been the longest. It turns out that expectations had an influence on perceived duration. Participants who expected a longer duration in the second block of trials felt that the duration of this second block was longer than that of the first block; in contrast, those expecting a shorter duration in the second block felt that the duration of this second block was shorter than that of the first block. In short, retrospective judgments are influenced by expectations as events or activities unfold.

Prospective Judgments

Attention plays a key role in determining perceived duration and in making more or less errors in time estimation during prospective time judgments. In particular, the attention paid to time during an interval to be judged is crucial and this is what we will discuss shortly. It should be noted, however, that the attention preparation before the interval to be judged, whether it is the duration of the intervals between the trials (Grondin & Rammsayer, 2003; Laflamme, Zakay, Gamache, & Grondin, 2015) or the rhythmicity of events (see Chapter 6), will influence perceived duration. Also, the attentional properties of stimuli that may even occur after the interval may have an influence on perceived duration (see Grondin, 2017).

The most convincing evidence of the role of attention on duration in experimental psychology are most often based on a strategy called the double task (Rousseau, Fortin, & Kirouac, 1993). In general, this amounts to checking to what extent the fact of doing two tasks at the same time affects the quality of the performance in each of them. The demonstration is based on a comparison with the performance when each task is executed alone.

Brown (1997) used this strategy. Participants in his study were expected to produce series of continuous finger taps to produce two- or five-second intervals. During the execution of the temporal task, the participants had to simultaneously complete one of three tasks: a rotor pursuit tracking, a visual search (for distractors), or mental arithmetic (more or less complicated calculations). The results show that, regardless of the nature of the secondary task to be completed, the variability of the intervals produced is much greater in a dual-task situation, and whether the intervals to be produced last for two or five seconds.

Other studies have exploited the use of a dual-task strategy to show the role of attention on psychological time. These studies not only had a dual task, but before each trial, participants had to assign a certain percentage of their attentional resources to each of them (Casini, Macar, & Grondin, 1992; Grondin & Macar, 1992). This strategy has shown, especially for interval discrimination tasks, whether they are delimited by sounds or by flashes, that a greater percentage of attention given to time leads to a higher level of discrimination and to a duration perceived as being longer (Macar, Grondin, & Casini, 1994; see also Coull, Vidal, Nazarian, & Macar, 2004).

Brown, Collier, and Night (2013) later looked at the effect of manipulating resources assigned to cognitive functions on timing efficiency. They used the same dual-task strategy with the allocation of a percentage of attention to each of the temporal and nontemporal tasks. In addition to the temporal task, the secondary tasks used by Brown and his collaborators were related executive functions, namely mental flexibility (shifting), updating ability, and inhibiting ability. They report that there is a bidirectional interference of the timing activity (continuous production of five-second intervals) with each of these three types of tasks which can be summed up as follows. The more attention is paid to time, the better the temporal performance and the lower the performance of the task measuring the executive functions; in contrast, when more attention is paid to tasks measuring executive functions, the inverse results are observed. Timing and these three features of executive functions would therefore share the same resources needed to process information.

With or Without an Internal Clock

There are different models to account for the role of attention in temporal judgments. Some of these models do not use the concept of an internal clock (Block, 2003). In a way, we could talk about a "cognitive clock". For example, with an explanation based solely on the distribution of attentional resources, it will be understood that the attention that is not assigned to a cognitive task can be devoted to the measurement of time. That is how we can explain why the number of stimuli processed during a given time interval is inversely proportional to the subjective duration (Hicks, Miller, Gaes, & Bierman, 1977; Hicks, Miller, & Kinsbourne, 1976). Some researchers interested in short intervals have also provided theoretical descriptions based on attention mechanisms without resorting to the presence of an internal biological clock (Thomas & Cantor, 1978; Thomas & Weaver, 1975). In Thomas's model, there are two independent processors, one responsible for encoding temporal information, the other nontemporal information. A part of attention is allocated automatically to each one of them, which operate in parallel. The perceived time is the weighted average of what these two processors provide.

In recent decades though, the role of attention has been integrated into an "internal clock" perspective. We saw in Chapter 4 that this internal clock is a "pacemaker-accumulator" mechanism. In an information-processing perspective, this clock has a place for attention. In fact, we evoke the contribution of attention to explain a part of what happens in the internal clock. There would be a switch that determines how many pulses provided by the pacemaker access the accumulator. When the switch is closed, there is an accumulation of pulses. The said switch is under the control of attention and would determine a certain efficiency regarding the moments when the timing activity must begin and end.

Other researchers posit the hypothesis of a gate, in addition to the switch, to account for the role of attention within the internal clock process (Zakay & Block, 1997). In the so-called *attentional gate model*, if attention is diverted from time, for example by the need to perform a cognitive task of some kind at the same time, the accumulation of pulses is found diminished and a given interval will appear shorter.

Conclusion

In conditions of prospective time judgments, the way we distribute our attentional resources has a great impact on our experience of time. If we divert our attention from time because of a distraction or because we share it between different tasks or activities, it will result in more variability in time judgments and the duration will seem shorter. On the other hand, paying attention to time, having expectations about it, may have the effect of perceiving it as being longer; this holds true even for retrospective judgments.

With the prospective judgments, we can interpret the results concerning the role of attention within a cognitive framework (mental load, attentional sharing, distraction, expectation generated by the succession of events), but also by resorting to the hypothesis of an internal clock. In this case, the attention will have a role of switch and gate. A switch will determine the moments during which the timing activity (i.e., the count of pulses emitted by a pacemaker) takes place. The gate will determine the magnitude of the flow of arrival of the pulses during timing, with more attention paid to time increasing this flow and, as a result, the perceived duration.

References

Block, R. A. (2003). Psychological timing without a timer: The roles of attention and memory. In H. Helfrich (Ed.), *Time and mind II: Information processing perspectives* (pp. 41–59). Gottingen, Germany: Hogrefe & Huber Publishers.

Block, R. A., Grondin, S., & Zakay, D. (2018). Prospective and retrospective timing processes: Theories, methods, and findings. In A. Vatakis, F. Balci, M. Di Luca, & A. Correa (Eds.), *Timing and time perception: Procedures, measures, and applications* (pp. 32–51). Leiden, The Netherlands: Brill.

Block, R. A., Hancock, P. A., & Zakay, D. (2010). How cognitive load affect duration judgments: A meta-analytic review. *Acta Psychologica, 134*, 330–343.

Boltz, M. G. (1993). Time estimation and expectancies. *Memory and Cognition, 21*, 853–863.

Brown, S. W. (1997). Attentional resources in timing: Interference effects in concurrent temporal and nontemporal working memory tasks. *Perception and Psychophysics, 59*, 1118–1140.

Brown, S. W. (2008). Time and attention: Review of the literature. In S. Grondin (Ed.), *Psychology of time* (pp. 111–138). Bingley, UK: Emerald Group Publishing.

Brown, S. W., Collier, S. A., & Night, J. C. (2013). Timing and executive resources: Dual-task interference patterns between temporal production and shifting, updating, and inhibition tasks. *Journal of Experimental Psychology: Human Perception and Performance, 39,* 947–963.

Cahoon, D., & Edmonds, E. M. (1980). The watched pot still won't boil: Expectancy as a variable in estimating the passage of time. *Bulletin of the Psychonomic Society, 16,* 115–116.

Casini, L., Macar, F., & Grondin, S. (1992). Time estimation and attentional sharing. In F. Macar, V. Pouthas, & W. J. Friedman (Eds.), *Time, action, and cognition: Towards bridging the gap* (pp. 177–180). Dordrecht, The Netherlands: Kluwer Academic Publishers.

Coull, J. T., Vidal, F., Nazarian, B., & Macar, F. (2004). Functional anatomy of the attentional modulation of time estimation. *Science, 303,* 1506–1508.

Grondin, S. (2017). Chronométrage & perception temporelle (Timing and time perception). *Revue canadienne de psychologie expérimentale/Canadian Journal of Experimental Psychology, 71,* 313–327.

Grondin, S., & Macar, F. (1992). Dividing attention between temporal and nontemporal tasks: A performance operating characteristic (POC) analysis. In F. Macar, V. Pouthas, & W. J. Friedman (Eds.), *Time, action, and cognition: Towards bridging the gap* (pp. 119–128). Dordrecht, The Netherlands: Kluwer Academic Publishers.

Grondin, S., & Rammsayer, T. (2003). Variable foreperiods and temporal discrimination. *Quarterly Journal of Experimental Psychology, 56A,* 731–765.

Hicks, R. E., Miller, G. W., Gaes, G., & Bierman, K. (1977). Concurrent processing demands and the experience of time-in-passing. *American Journal of Psychology, 90,* 431–446.

Hicks, R. E., Miller, G. W., & Kinsbourne, M. (1976). Prospective and retrospective judgments of time as a function of amount of information processed. *American Journal of Psychology, 89,* 719–730.

Laflamme, V., Zakay, D., Gamache, P.-L., & Grondin, S. (2015). Foreperiod and range effects on time interval categorization. *Attention, Perception, & Psychophysics, 77,* 1507–1514.

Macar, F., Grondin, S., & Casini, L. (1994). Controlled attention sharing influences time estimation. *Memory and Cognition, 22,* 673–686.

Rousseau, R., Fortin, C., & Kirouac, É. (1993). Sensibilité & diagnosticité de la mesure de la charge mentale par la tâche secondaire de frappe cadencée. *Revue canadienne de psychologie expérimentale, 47,* 493–506.

Thomas, E. A. C., & Cantor, N. E. (1978). Interdependence between the processing of temporal and non-temporal information. In J. Requin (Ed.), *Attention and performance VII* (pp. 43–62). Hillsdale, NJ: Lawrence Erlbaum.

Thomas, E. A. C., & Weaver, W. B. (1975). Cognitive processing and time perception. *Perception and Psychophysics, 17,* 363–367.

Zakay, D., & Block, R. A. (1997). Temporal cognition. *Current Directions in Psychological Science, 6,* 12–16.

10 How Does Space Affect Time Judgments?

The avenues on which the interactions between space and time could bring us are so numerous that it is better first to designate some of them that will not be explored. Thus, we will cover neither the study of the estimation of the arrival time of a moving object at a given point in space, the estimate of when two moving objects should collide (Hecht & Savelsbergh, 2004), nor the spatial/horizontal organization of the representation of time intervals (Frassinetti, Magnani, & Oliveri, 2009). Similarly, the whole Piagetian perspective on the relations between time, space, and speed is not covered in this part (but see Chapter 24).

We will confine ourselves here to the question of explicit judgments on duration by taking two very different paths: when the stimuli delimiting a time interval come from sources arranged in different locations in space and when the interval to be judged is filled with moving stimuli.

Kappa Effect

There is a classical field of research, revealed almost a century ago, in which the influence of space on temporal judgments, the *kappa* effect, and that of time on spatial judgments, the *tau* effect, are paralleled (Jones & Huang, 1982). Most often, these effects are reported for conditions involving visual stimuli.

Consider the following situation. Three visual sources—A, B, and C—are aligned so that B is at the midpoint between A and C. If the three sources are briefly lit one after the other, the segments A-B and B-C will be perceived as equidistant if the duration between the flashes A and B and that between B and C are the same. On the other hand, if the time interval between the presentations of A and B is shorter than that between B and C, the spatial distance between A and B will be perceived as being shorter than that between B and C. Similarly, if the duration between the appearances of A and B is longer than that between B and C, the spatial interval between A and B will appear longer than that between B and C. This influence of time on the perceived distance constitutes an illustration of the tau effect (Sarrazin, Giraudo, & Pittenger, 2007).

On the other hand, if somebody must judge the duration between the appearance of A and B and that between B and C and that these durations are the same, these will appear identical if B is located midpoint between A and C (that is, if the segments A-B and B-C are of the same length). If the A-B segment were to be shorter (less distance) than the B-C segment, even if the duration between the appearances of A and B is the same as that between the appearances of B and C, the time interval between the appearances of A and B will be perceived as being shorter than that between the apparitions of B and C. Conversely, a greater distance between A and B than between B and C would make the duration of the interval between the appearances of A and B overestimated with respect to the duration of the interval between the appearances of B and C. This influence of space on perceived duration is called the kappa effect (Abe, 1935, Cohen, Hansel, & Sylvester, 1953).

One hypothesis explaining the kappa effect consists in supposing that there is an impression of movement created by the succession of flashes and that the speed of movement is constant (*imputed-velocity model*: Jones & Huang, 1982, ten Hoopen, Miyauchi, & Nakajima, 2008). In other words, according to this hypothesis, the set of stimuli is perceived as a single object appearing three times rather than three distinct objects appearing successively. With segments A-B and B-C equal and B appearing in the middle of the time interval, the observer perceives a constant speed. If the segments are not of the same length and B appears in the middle of the time interval, this situation will generate speed inconstancy that will force the perceptual system to readjust. If the distance between A and B is shorter than that between B and C, the first time interval is perceived to be shorter than the second; if the distance between A and B is larger than that between B and C, the first time interval is perceived to be longer than the second. Thus, with this readjustment, the observer will believe that the object moves between space locations at constant speed.

The kappa effect is not limited to the use of visual stimuli. We observe this influence of space on the perceived duration in the tactile modality (Goldreich, 2007) and in the auditory modality when there is a difference between the intensity (Alards-Tomalin, Leboe-McGowan, & Mondor, 2013) or between the frequency (Henry & McAuley, 2009; Shigeno, 1986, 1987) of the sounds. There is also a kappa effect under special conditions, namely when there is a distance between sound sources (Grondin & Plourde, 2007; see Grondin, Hasuo, Kuroda, & Nakajima, 2018 for a detailed description of the results in the auditory modality).

In addition, some demonstrations aimed at showing the influence of space (distance between sources of stimulation) on the perceived duration when only two stimulations (one interval) are involved at the same time, but in a context where more than one spatial condition can be used from one trial to another. Increasing the distance between two flashes increases the reproduced duration (Price-Williams, 1954). On the other hand, for the discrimination of short time intervals, increasing the distance between two visual sources delimiting these intervals causes an impression that the duration seems shorter (Guay & Grondin, 2001). Such a result is rather interpreted according to the need to shift attention from one point to another, which affects the attention to time (see previous chapter). Moreover, the effect of space on duration when time intervals are delimited by two visual stimuli depends on the location of stimuli in the visual field (Kuroda, Grondin, Miyazaki, Ogata, & Tobimatsu, 2016) and on the point fixation (Roussel, Grondin, & Killeen, 2009). Also, the interval delimited by a sequence of two brief flashes will seem longer if it goes from left to right rather than from right to left (Grondin, 1998).

Increasing the distance between two sound sources delimiting an interval also leads to an impression that the duration is shorter (Roy, Kuroda, & Grondin, 2011). In the tactile modality, an interval delimited by electro-tactile stimuli will seem longer if the two signals are delivered on different hands rather than at the same place on the same hand (Grondin, Kuroda, & Mitsudo, 2011; Kuroda & Miyazaki, 2016) or delivered on the index then on the middle finger, rather than on the index twice (Kuroda & Grondin, 2013).

Influence of Movement

There are several experiments showing that observing movements in space has a great influence on perceived duration. We will limit ourselves here to report mainly the results of two relatively recent studies on this subject.

In a series of experiments, Brown (1995) investigated the effect of observing spatial displacements on temporal perception. Using the productions or the reproductions of 6 to 18-second intervals, Brown compared conditions where there were on the screen in front of a participant motionless vs. moving stimuli. It emerges from this investigation that the presence of movements has the effect of increasing perceived duration and that the effect is stronger if the speed of movement of the stimuli is fast rather than slow. The number of stimuli on the screen, however, seems to exert only a small influence on the perceived duration. The fact that the presence of displacements leads to an impression that the duration is longer is consistent with the hypothesis that the amount of change occurring during an interval is a crucial variable to explain perceived duration (Poynter & Homa, 1983).

In another series of experiments on the effect of observing spatial displacements on the processing of time intervals lasting three seconds or less, the displacement of geometric shapes presented to participants was constant or was accelerated or decelerated (Matthews, 2011). With a time-estimation task, duration in the deceleration condition was perceived to be longer than duration in the acceleration condition, but in both cases, relative to the condition where the velocity remains constant, the duration was perceived as being shorter. The interval reproduction task made it possible to replicate the difference between the constant condition and the conditions with acceleration or deceleration, but not the difference between the latter two conditions. These results pose a challenge for the interpretation of the perceived duration in terms of the number or the complexity of changes occurring during an interval, in terms of space occupied in memory by stimuli or in terms of attentional sharing. If one wants to explain the differences in perceived duration between the constant vs. acceleration/deceleration conditions based on a pacemaker-accumulator mechanism, then we must posit bold assumptions like a nonlinear relationship between speed and the rate of accumulation of pulses, and a decrease in the weight given to what the accumulator provides when stimuli are presented. We may rather posit a rate of accumulation inversely related to the speed of the stimuli, which would also include a weighting process emphasizing the most recent portions of the accumulation process.

Note finally that the conclusions could be quite different if the intervals to estimate were to be very long (more than a minute), so closer to what we can be exposed to in everyday life. In a series of experiments with constant, accelerating, or decelerating visual stimuli, or with constant, accelerating, or decelerating auditory tempos (music excerpts), Darlow, Dylman, Gheorghiu, and Matthews (2013) report no difference in perceived duration, whether the participants are placed in prospective or retrospective judgment conditions.

Conclusion

There is a mutual influence of spatial and temporal dimensions. In particular, time can be perceived as being longer or shorter depending on whether the distance between the stimulation sources used to delimit an interval to be estimated is greater or smaller. The kappa effect occurs most often with the use of a sequence of three successive stimuli and in the visual modality: an interval seems longer if the distance between two sources is greater. With only two sources of stimulation, the opposite may be observed: an interval appears shorter if the distance between two sources is greater. A kappa effect can also occur in the auditory or tactile modes. In addition, another avenue of research on space-time interactions reveals that the perception of time is influenced by the observation of moving rather than stationary objects, and the perceived time depends on the speed of movement of objects and on the fact that they are accelerating or decelerating.

References

Abe, S. (1935). Experimental study on the co-relation between time and space. *Tohoku Psychologica Folia*, 3, 53–68.

Alards-Tomalin, D., Leboe-McGowan, L. C., & Mondor, T. A. (2013). Examining auditory kappa effects through manipulating intensity differences between sequential tones. *Psychological Research*, 77, 480–491.

Brown, S. W. (1995). Time, change, and motion: The effects of stimulus movement on temporal perception. *Perception & Psychophysics*, 57, 105–116.

Cohen, J., Hansel, C. E. M., & Sylvester, J. D. (1953). A new phenomenon in time judgment. *Nature*, 172, 901.

Darlow, H. M., Dylman, A. S., Gheorghiu, A. I., & Matthews, W. J. (2013). Do changes in the pace of events affect one-off judgments of duration? *PLoS One, 8*, e59847.

Frassinetti, F., Magnani, B., & Oliveri, M. (2009). Prismatic lenses shift time perception. *Psychological Science, 20*, 949–954.

Goldreich, D. (2007). A Bayesian perceptual model replicates the cutaneous rabbit and other tactile spatiotemporal illusions. *PLoS One, 2*, e333. doi:10.1371/journal.pone.0000333.

Grondin, S. (1998). Judgments of the duration of visually marked empty time intervals: Linking perceived duration and sensitivity. *Perception & Psychophysics, 60*, 319–330.

Grondin, S., Hasuo, E., Kuroda, T., & Nakajima, Y. (2018). Auditory time perception. In R. Bader (Ed.), *Springer handbook of systematic musicology* (pp. 423–440). Berlin: Springer.

Grondin, S., Kuroda, T., & Mitsudo, T. (2011). Spatial effects on tactile duration categorization. *Canadian Journal of Experimental Psychology, 65*, 163–167.

Grondin, S., & Plourde, M. (2007). Discrimination of time intervals presented in sequences: Spatial effects with multiple auditory sources. *Human Movement Science, 26*, 702–716.

Guay, I., & Grondin, S. (2001). Influence on time interval categorization of distance between markers located on a vertical plane. *Proceedings of the 17th Annual Meeting of the International Society for Psychophysics*, Berlin, Germany, 391–396.

Hecht, H., & Savelsbergh, G. (Eds.). (2004). *Time-to-contact* (Advances in Psychology, 135). Amsterdam, The Netherlands: North-Holland & Elsevier Science.

Henry, M. J., & McAuley, J. D. (2009). Evaluation of an imputed pitch velocity model of the auditory kappa effect. *Journal of Experimental Psychology: Human Perception and Performance, 35*, 551–564.

Jones, B., & Huang, Y. L. (1982). Space-time dependencies in psychophysical judgment of extent and duration: Algebraic models of the tau and kappa effect. *Psychological Bulletin, 91*, 128–142.

Kuroda, T., & Grondin, S. (2013). Discrimination is not impaired when more cortical space between two electro-tactile markers increases perceived duration. *Experimental Brain Research, 224*, 303–312.

Kuroda, T., Grondin, S., Miyazaki, M., Ogata, K., & Tobimatsu, S. (2016). The kappa effect with only two visual markers. *Multisensory Research, 29*, 703–725.

Kuroda, T., & Miyazaki, M. (2016). Perceptual versus motor spatiotemporal interactions in duration reproduction across two hands. *Scientific Reports, 6*, 23365. doi:10.1038/srep23365.

Matthews, W. J. (2011). How do changes in speed affect the perception of duration? *Journal of Experimental Psychology: Human Perception and Performance, 37*, 1617–1627.

Poynter, W. D., & Homa, D. (1983). Duration judgment and the experience of change. *Perception & Psychophysics, 33*, 548–560.

Price-Williams, D. R. (1954). The kappa effect. *Nature, 173*, 363–364.

Roussel, M.-E., Grondin, S., & Killeen, P. (2009). Spatial effects on temporal categorization. *Perception, 38*, 748–762.

Roy, M., Kuroda, T., & Grondin, S. (2011). Effect of space on auditory temporal processing with a single-stimulus method. In P. Strumillo (Ed.), *Advances in sound localization* (pp. 95–104). Rijeka, Croatia: InTech. doi:10.5772/14436.

Sarrazin, J.-C., Giraudo, M.-D., & Pittenger, J. B. (2007). Tau and kappa effects in physical space: The case of audition. *Psychological Research, 71*, 201–218.

Shigeno, S. (1986). The auditory tau and kappa effects for speech and nonspeech stimuli. *Perception & Psychophysics, 40,* 9–19.

Shigeno, S. (1987). The auditory tau and kappa effects for voiced stop consonants. *Japanese Psychological Research, 29,* 71–80.

ten Hoopen, G., Miyauchi, R., & Nakajima, Y. (2008). Time-based illusions in the auditory mode. In S. Grondin (Ed.), *Psychology of time* (pp. 139–187). Bingley, UK: Emerald Group Publishing.

11 What Factors Cause Temporal Distortions?

We have seen in the last two chapters that attention to time and the spatial arrangement of sources of stimulation for marking time influence the perceived duration of a time interval. Moreover, as we will see in Chapter 23, emotion also has such an influence. Because the influences on perceived duration of attention, emotion, and space manifest themselves under different forms and are per se large research fields, a chapter is dedicated to each of these three issues. However, many other sources can cause temporal distortions, and some of these are briefly described next.

Perceptual Effects

On the perceptual level, there are many reasons why the perceived duration of an interval may fluctuate. In particular, we have long known that the magnitude of the stimuli presented to mark a short interval influences the perceived duration, the increase in magnitude resulting in an increase in the perceived duration (see Allan, 1979, for a more recent example, see Xuan, Zhang, He, & Chen, 2007).

A perceptual phenomenon likely to exert a strong influence on perceived duration is called chronostasis. This phenomenon sometimes occurs when you look at the second hand on a clock. At the moment of looking, one can have the impression that this second hand is stopped; the moment will appear to be longer than the next few seconds, if we continue to look (Yarrow, Haggard, Heal, Brown, & Rothwell, 2001). There are also some forms of this phenomenon in the tactile modality (Yarrow & Rothwell, 2003) and in the auditory modality; in the latter case, the effect occurs when attention has to be shifted from one ear to another (Hodinott-Hill, Thilo, Cowey, & Walsh, 2002).

The effects of temporal distortions can also occur when a series of brief auditory stimuli delimit successive empty intervals. Suppose that three stimuli delimit two intervals. Under certain conditions, the second interval will appear to be much shorter than the first, an effect known as the *time-shrinking illusion*. Typically, the illusion occurs when the first interval is short (< 250 ms, the illusion being at its maximum at 200 ms), and when the difference between the durations of the first and second intervals is more than 0 ms and less than 100 ms (Nakajima, ten Hoopen, & van der Wilk, 1991; see ten Hoopen, Miyauchi, & Nakajima, 2008). We find such a temporal shortening effect for a succession of empty intervals in the visual (Arao, Suetomi, & Nakajima, 2000) and tactile (Hasuo, Kuroda, & Grondin, 2014) modalities.

Temporal distortions are also observed when series of solid intervals follow each other. Thus, the first of a series of visual stimuli of the same length seems longer (Rose & Summers, 1995). Likewise, in a series of consecutive stimuli, the one differing from the others will appear longer; this effect is called oddball (Tse, Intriligator, Rivest, & Cavanagh, 2004). Rather than talking about an expansion of oddball duration, Pariyadath and Eagleman (2007) take a position that the observed effect would depend on a contraction of the duration of the other stimuli presented. In fact, this position is based on the assumption that subjective duration reflects the magnitude of the neuronal response to stimulation. In other words, the amount of neuronal energy needed to represent a stimulus would serve as a basis for determining the duration. Well, there is a phenomenon in the nervous system called repetition suppression. This phenomenon consists of a decrease in the neural firing rate at a specific brain location, for a given stimulus, when this stimulus is presented several times. This suppression can be interpreted as an increase in efficiency to form a representation of the stimulus. This explanation, founded on the idea that the subjective duration reflects the level of neural activity, is however undermined by recent studies. These studies show an increase in this subjective duration when the rate of repetition is increased (Matthews, 2015) or when the expectations about the arrival of a stimulus, by the increased processing they allow, are confirmed (Birngruber, Schröter, Schütt, & Ulrich, 2017).

Other perceptual phenomena can leave an imprint on temporal judgments. For example, researchers used prismatic glasses to distort visual perception and see how this distortion would influence temporal judgments (Frassinetti, Magnani, & Oliveri, 2009). The effect of wearing these glasses consisted in deviations to the left or to the right relative to the real location of an object. Participants were tested before and after using the glasses on temporal bisection and temporal reproduction tasks. When the glasses caused a consecutive compensation effect to the left, the participants underestimated the duration; conversely, when the glasses caused a consecutive compensation effect to the right, the participants overestimated the duration. These results show not only the general effect of spatial perception on the estimate of duration, but also that there appears to be a horizontal arrangement of the magnitude of duration just like there is an arrangement of numbers from left to right, the small quantities being on the left and the largest on the right (Vicario et al., 2008).

Cognitive Effects

The effect reported in the preceding paragraph was the manipulation of a perceptual effect (following the use of prismatic glasses); it also leads to a more general avenue about the spatial arrangement of magnitudes. If the magnitudes are ordered from left to right, to the point of influencing temporal judgments, perhaps the mere magnitude of a digit presented visually in order to mark a time interval will influence its duration.

Some studies show that this is the case. For example, in a study by Oliveri et al. (2008), participants were asked to determine whether a number, in this case 1 or 9, was presented for more or less time than a reference digit, 5. Their results indicate that the presentation time of 1 is underestimated and that the presentation time of 9 is overestimated. Although no numerical processing was required during the task, the study shows that the representation of the magnitude of numbers influences temporal judgments. In other words, knowing the numbers tints the estimated duration (see also Vicario, 2011; Xuan et al., 2007). In addition, placing units next to numbers, such as grams or kilograms, may modulate the effect of numbers (Lu, Hodges, Zhang, & Zhang, 2009). In fact, the effect of the units depends on the context of the experiment. If the addition of "kilogram" has a greater influence than the addition of "gram" in a context where weight is to be lifted, this will not be the case if the context is that of toxicology and the use of poison (Lu, Mo, & Hodges, 2011).

The influence exerted by the symbolic value extends beyond numbers. In a study based on the temporal bisection of intervals ranging from 400 ms to 1600 ms, these intervals were delimited either by the image of a motorcycle or that of a bicycle, the former representing a higher speed than the second one (Mioni, Zakay, & Grondin, 2015). In the motorcycle presentation conditions, participants were more likely to consider the interval to be short than when a bicycle defined the duration to be estimated. Such a result, as well as those of Lu et al. (2011), is consistent with the ecological perspective of Gibson at the heart of which we find the concept of affordance. This notion refers to the potential utility of an object for someone, a utility that the object itself suggests. By activating what the bicycle or motorcycle is made for, a participant in the Mioni and collaborators study becomes more likely to overestimate or underestimate the duration.

Beyond the symbolic aspect, knowledge can bias the time estimation of an activity. As we will see in Chapter 27, we make bad estimates of the time needed to complete a task; in fact, we often tend to underestimate the time it takes. On a large scale, this can lead to interesting time distortions. For example, if we underestimate the time needed to go somewhere, we may find that the duration will have been longer than expected and we may also be able to adjust upward the prediction for the duration of the return trip. Thus one can end up with an impression that the trip was shorter on the return, a distortion effect referred to as the return-trip effect (Van de Ven, van Rilswijk, & Roy, 2011).

Body Effects

The internal state of the body determines the experience of duration. For example, different aspects of the heart rhythm shape the perception of time

(Cellini et al., 2015; Meissner & Wittmann, 2011). There are different ways to transform this internal state.

One way to influence this state is to meditate. In fact, the twenty-first century has seen the emergence of interest in meditation in order to provide access to a state called mindfulness. In general, this state is characterized by a form of temporal distortion, namely an impression of great slowing down of time and of expansion of the present moment. Some studies provide empirical support for this idea of lengthening of the present moment (of the subjective "now": Sauer et al., 2012). Furthermore, in a study involving 42 participants with extensive experience with mindfulness meditation and 42 participants in a control group, Wittmann et al. (2015) found that, among other things, meditators felt less temporal pressure and have a stronger sense that time is slower than other participants of the study. A week or a month seems to pass less quickly when you meditate. On the other hand, Wittmann and his collaborators did not observe any difference between the groups for the classical psychophysical tasks used in the study, namely temporal estimations ranging from a few hundredths to a few tenths of seconds.

Another way to transform body condition is to use different substances. However, the effect of these substances, especially of different drugs, remains difficult to describe because of individual differences in the distortions they cause. In general, one could distinguish tranquilizers, which should lead to a deceleration of the rhythm of the pacemaker of an internal clock (see Chapter 4), and stimulants, which should rather cause an acceleration of this rhythm. For example, it is known that a stimulant like methamphetamine, by its action on dopamine, will give the impression that more time has elapsed than it actually does, in animals at least (Meck, 1983).

A drug like marijuana, which disrupts the central nervous system, will cause an impression of slowing down of the passage of time, so that a user will overestimate the duration of a given time interval. Thus, the passage of a few minutes may give the impression that an hour has passed. In fact, the temporal distortions caused by marijuana can be even greater, in the sense that they can lead to a form of temporal disintegration, itself associated with an impression of depersonalization (Mathew, Wilson, & Melges, 1992).

In addition, it is important to emphasize that drug abuse can leave a mark on temporal perception well after consumption. Wittmann, Leland, Churand, and Paulus (2007) tested individuals who were addicted to stimulants (methamphetamine or cocaine) but were abstinent for 20 to 40 days. Compared to the participants of the control group, people with addictions had a harder time discriminating intervals of about 1 s, had a faster pace when producing series of 1-s finger taps, and overestimated long intervals. In the latter case, an interval of 53 s appeared to have lasted in average 91 s and 67 s for the addict and control groups, respectively, a result attributable to greater impulsivity among drug users. In fact, such deficits in the processing of temporal information might explain the difficulty of waiting for long-term rewards, since the temptation for immediate use of the drug is too great.

Other substances, however legal, make it possible to disturb the relationship with time and to cause certain distortions. This is the case of alcohol and caffeine. It is very difficult to draw clear conclusions about the effect of alcohol. Compared to a dose of 0 or 0.4 g/kg, the consumption of a dose of 0.6 g/kg of alcohol results in an overestimation of the duration of an interval (prospective judgments) and an impression that time passes quickly, but no difference in the retrospective judgments of duration (Ogden, Wearden, Gallagher, & Montgomery, 2011).

With regard to the effects of caffeine, they seem to depend on the nature of the time estimation task. Curiously though, even though caffeine should increase the pace of the pacemaker of an internal clock, it is its effects on attention that will determine the perceived duration. This is what Gruber and Block (2005) report in a study involving a 200-mg dose of caffeine and timing tasks such as the verbal estimation of 15, 60, or 300-second intervals in experimental settings where more or less attentional resources were required. The results indicate that an active and attention-demanding task will seem much shorter in conditions with, rather than without, caffeine consumption, but this difference is not observed if the task is passive and requires less attention.

Conclusion

Many factors influence the perceived duration of a time interval, sometimes to the point of causing significant distortions. Among these influencing factors, there are perceptual factors, among which are the magnitude of the physical stimuli used to delimit time and their presentation in sequences, whether they are filled or empty intervals. Cognitive effects such as knowing the value of the numbers used to delimit intervals to judge or the symbolic value of the objects presented to bound such intervals will also have a strong influence on perceived duration. Finally, disturbing a person's body condition, by meditating or taking certain substances, might well result in a distortion of perceived duration.

References

Allan, L. G. (1979). The perception of time. *Perception & Psychophysics, 26*, 340–354.

Arao, H., Suetomi, D., & Nakajima, Y. (2000). Does time-shrinking take place in visual temporal patterns? *Perception, 29*, 819–830.

Birngruber, T., Schröter, H., Schütt, E., & Ulrich, R. (2017). Stimulus expectation prolongs rather than shortens perceived duration: Evidence from self-generated expectations. *Journal of Experimental Psychology: Human Perception and Performance.* http://doi.org/10.1037/xhp0000433.

Cellini, N., Mioni, G., Levorato, I., Grondin, S., Stablum, F., & Sarlo, M. (2015). Heart rate variability helps tracking time more accurately. *Brain & Cognition, 101*, 57–63.

Frassinetti, F., Magnani, B., & Oliveri, M. (2009). Prismatic lenses shift time perception. *Psychological Science, 20*, 949–954.

Gruber, R. P., & Block, R. A. (2005). Effects of caffeine on prospective duration judgements of various intervals depend on task difficulty. *Human Psychopharmacology: Clinical and Experimental, 20*, 275–285.

Hasuo, E., Kuroda, T., & Grondin, S. (2014). About the time-shrinking illusion in the tactile modality. *Acta Psychologica, 147*, 122–126.

Hodinott-Hill, I., Thilo, K. V., Cowey, A., & Walsh, V. (2002). Auditory chronostasis: Hanging on the telephone. *Current Biology, 12*, 1779–1781.

Lu, A., Hodges, B., Zhang, J., & Zhang, J. X. (2009). Contextual effects on number-time interaction. *Cognition, 113*, 117–122.

Lu, A., Mo, L., & Hodges, B. H. (2011). The weight of time: Affordances for an integrated magnitude system. *Journal of Experimental Psychology: Human Perception and Performance, 37*, 1855–1866.

Mathew, R. J., Wilson, W. H., & Melges, F. T. (1992). Temporal disintegration and its psychological and physiological correlates changes in the experience of time after marijuana smoking. *Annals of Clinical Psychiatry, 4*, 235–245.

Matthews, W. J. (2015). Time perception: The surprising effects of surprising stimuli. *Journal of Experimental Psychology: General, 144*, 172–197.

Meck, W. H. (1983). Selective adjustment of the speed of internal clock and memory processes. *Journal of Experimental Psychology: Animal Behavior Processes, 9*, 171–201.

Meissner, K., & Wittmann, M. (2011). Body signals, cardiac awareness, and the perception of time. *Biological Psychology, 86*, 289–297.

Mioni, G., Zakay, D., & Grondin, S. (2015). Faster is briefer: The symbolic meaning of speed influences time perception. *Psychonomic Bulletin & Review, 22*, 1285–1291.

Nakajima, Y., ten Hoopen, G., & van der Wilk, R. (1991). A new illusion of time perception. *Music Perception, 8*, 431–448.

Ogden, R. S., Wearden, J. H., Gallagher, D. T., & Montgomery, C. (2011). The effect of alcohol administration on human timing: A comparison of prospective timing, retrospective timing and passage of time judgements. *Acta Psychologica, 138*, 254–262.

Oliveri, M., Vicario, C. M., Salarno, S., Kock, G., Turriziani, P., Mangano, R., . . . Caltagirone, C. (2008). Perceiving numbers alters time perception. *Neurosciences Letters, 27*, 308–311.

Pariyadath, V., & Eagleman, D. M. (2007). The effect of predictability on subjective duration. *PLoS One, 2*, 1264. doi:10.1371/journal.pone.0001264.

Rose, D., & Summers, J. (1995). Duration illusions in a train of visual stimuli. *Perception, 24*, 1177–1187.

Sauer, S., Lemke, J., Wittmann, M., Kohls, N., Mochty, U., & Walach, H. (2012). How long is now for mindfulness meditators? *Personality and Individual Differences, 52*, 750–754.

ten Hoopen, G., Miyauchi, R., & Nakajima, Y. (2008). Time-based illusions in the auditory mode. In S. Grondin (Ed.), *Psychology of time* (pp. 139–188). Bingley, UK: Emerald Group Publishing.

Tse, P. U., Intriligator, J., Rivest, J., & Cavanagh, P. (2004). Attention and the subjective expansion of time. *Perception & Psychophysics, 66*, 1171–1189.

Van de Ven, N., van Rilswijk, L., & Roy, M. M. (2011). The return trip effect: Why the return trip often seems to take less time. *Psychonomic Bulletin & Review, 18*, 827–832.

Vicario, C. M. (2011). Perceiving numbers affects the subjective temporal midpoint. *Perception, 40*, 23–29.

Vicario, C. M., Pecoraro, P., Turriziani, P., Koch, G., Caltagirone, C., & Oliveri, M. (2008). Relativistic compression and expansion of experiential time in the left and right space. *PLoS One, 3*, e1716.

Wittmann, M., Leland, D. S., Churand, J., & Paulus, M. P. (2007). Impaired time perception and motor timing in stimulant-dependent subjects. *Drug and Alcohol Dependence, 90*, 183–192.

Wittmann, M., Otten, S., Schötz, E., Sarikaya, A., Lehnen, H., Jo, H. G., . . . Meissner, K. (2015). Subjective expansion of extended time-spans in experienced meditators. *Frontiers in Psychology, 5*, 1586. doi:10.3389/fpsyg.2014.01586.

Xuan, B., Zhang, D., He, S., & Chen, X. (2007). Larger stimuli are judged to last longer. *Journal of Vision, 7*, 1–5.

Yarrow, K., Haggard, P., Heal, R., Brown, P., & Rothwell, J. C. (2001). Illusory perceptions of space and time preserve cross-saccadic perceptual continuity. *Nature, 414*, 302–305.

Yarrow, K., & Rothwell, J. C. E. (2003). Manual chronostasis: Tactile perception precedes physical contact. *Current Biology, 13*, 1334–1339.

Part 2
Time and Pathologies

12 What Experience of Time Do People With Schizophrenia Have?

Introduced by the Zurich psychiatrist Eugen Bleuler, the term "schizophrenia" in the strict sense means "split mind" and refers to a certain fragmentation of the mind. Nearly 1% of people have schizophrenia, which usually appears in adulthood. It is a kind of psychosis and includes a state of loss of contact with reality (Collard, Pothier, & Roy, 2017).

Schizophrenic patients have clinical disorders of all kinds, including motor or cognitive ones (like attentional or thought disorders). However, it cannot be excluded that the relation to time is at the heart of schizophrenia (Delevoye-Turrell, Wilquin, & Giersch, 2012). However, it is sometimes difficult to separate a psychological-time disorder from a cognitive-related disorder when studying temporal information processing capabilities of people with schizophrenia. Nevertheless, we can list numerous studies highlighting certain deficits related to psychological time in these people.

Continuity and Order of Sensory Events

The difficulties of schizophrenic patients in determining the temporal order of the course of events come in different forms. These patients can be lost in seasons, dates, and sometimes even hours. In fact, the problem of time seems even deeper. They have a loss of the sense of continuity. Rather than integrating events with each other within a certain continuity, as we normally do, time appears as a series of isolated elements; time is fragmented. This fragmentation may be at the root of the feeling of dissociation (feeling of strangeness and loss of coherence of the environment) that characterizes schizophrenia (Lalanne, 2011; Minkowski, 1995).

One way to address the issue of continuity is to refer to the idea of a time window, sometimes referred to as the "perceptual moment" (see Chapter 3). This window would in fact be a short time interval within which all events that occur would be judged to occur simultaneously. This window would have a span of about 30 ms (Lalanne, 2011), but there are various estimations of this span, or of this perceptual moment (Elliott & Giersch, 2016). Thus, events that would occur successively, but separated by only a few milliseconds, would belong to the same present. There would be a neural integration of what happens within this window; the past, the immediate present, and the near future would belong to the same subjective present, which would ensure a sense of continuity.

Schizophrenic patients have much more difficulty than individuals in a control group in determining whether two stimuli are presented simultaneously or in succession (Giersch et al., 2009). However, this loss of sense of continuity may depend on the fusion of events over time (the inability to separate them) or on the difficulty of segregating events, a difficulty that would be caused by an inability to encode a structure linking time and event. The members of the Strasbourg team used the Simon effect to determine which of these two explanations holds water. Their results indicate that the threshold difference, 20% higher in patients than in control group participants, is not explained by a fusion of events in the patient window, but by their inability to anticipate what should happen in the very near future (Lalanne, van Assche, & Giersch, 2012; Lalanne, van Assche, Wang, & Giersch, 2012).

In addition, the difficulty of schizophrenic patients is apparent not only when deciding whether stimuli have arrived simultaneously or in succession, but also when deciding on their order of arrival. In fact, even when 96 ms separate the arrival of a square on a screen from that of another square, people with schizophrenia remain unable to determine their order of arrival (Capa, Duval, Blaison, & Giersch, 2014).

Explicit Judgments on Duration

The distortions of temporal perception, in explicit judgments about duration, could be one of the features of schizophrenia. It is in order to bring a certain objectivity to the reported distortions that laboratory work, with the classical tasks of psychophysics, is conducted.

Recent meta-analyses synthesize the reported results on the question (Ciullo, Spalletta, Caltagirone, Jorge, & Piras, 2016; Thönes & Oberfeld, 2017). Thus, schizophrenic patients tend to overestimate duration in a verbal estimation task, but they underproduce duration in a temporal production task. Also, in a continuous 500-ms interval production task, the pace of taps by schizophrenic people is faster than that of participants in a control group (Carroll, O'Donnell, Shekhar, & Hetrick, 2009a). Moreover, there is little difference between these groups regarding the duration of reproductions, the studies with this task being few and perhaps even less relevant.

The study of the variability of judgments makes it possible to distinguish much more clearly between schizophrenic patients and non-patients (Thönes & Oberfeld, 2017). For instance, Carroll, O'Donnell, Shekhar, and Hetrick (2009b) compared schizophrenic and control group participants in bisection tasks where durations ranged from 0.3 to 0.6 s or from 3 to 6 s. In both cases, the variability of judgments was higher in patients with schizophrenia than in the control group. The same authors also tested the same groups on a continuous 500-ms interval production task (Carroll et al., 2009a). Again, people with schizophrenia showed more variability, not only when time came to synchronize taps with sound, but also when continuing to tap without sounds. Overall, these data indicate that there is a difficulty in schizophrenic individuals to correctly estimate time, whether in production tasks or in perceptual tasks involving different ranges of durations. Many other data show that beyond methodological differences, there is much variability in the temporal judgments of schizophrenic individuals (Davalos, Kisley, & Ross, 2002, 2003; Lee et al., 2009).

It is unclear whether the problems faced by people with schizophrenia stem from cognitive problems. We know that the problems for processing temporal information are often accompanied by attentional or working memory problems (Roy, Grondin, & Roy, 2012). However, there seems to be problems belonging to the processing of temporal information per se, according to the light provided by neuroscience.

Neuroscience Data

Neuroscience results support the idea that there is a basic problem of temporal estimation in schizophrenics. This is notably what we learn from the results obtained with a response called mismatch negativity (MMN). MMN is a particular electroencephalographic (EEG) response occurring strongly when an unexpected stimulus occurs after many identical stimuli have been presented, especially when these stimuli have identical durations (Davalos, Kisley, & Freedman, 2005; Davalos et al., 2003; see Umbricht & Krljes, 2005). However, the EEG response in a MMN task is reduced in people with schizophrenia, compared to that of participants in a control group, in tasks involving the arrival of an unexpected duration. Such a deficit is explained by a problem specific to the processing of temporal information and not by an attentional or mnemic processes deficit.

Data based on functional magnetic resonance imaging (fMRI) also suggest that poorer temporal information processing in schizophrenic patients would be a consequence of a dysfunction of a large network of brain regions. This network includes the supplementary motor area, the dorsolateral prefrontal cortex, the striatum, the thalamus, and the insula/operculum (Davalos, Rojas, & Tregellas, 2011). Also, there is less activation in schizophrenic people of the regions of the right hemisphere involved in timing activities (Alústiza et al., 2016). In fact, when tasks are difficult and require many cognitive resources, a vast network of brain regions, cortical and subcortical, becomes activated, whether tasks involve the processing of temporal information or other cognitive components. It is as if there is a "temporal cognitive" control network (Alústiza et al., 2016). This suggests that the general deficit of temporal information processing could be a marker of the cognitive profile in schizophrenic patients; that is what Alústiza and collaborators claim after conducting a fine meta-analysis of the fMRI studies conducted in schizophrenic patients and comparing the activated regions in temporal tasks and those activated in difficult cognitive tasks.

Conclusion

The temporal problems encountered in people with schizophrenia have several forms. They manifest themselves in the ability to determine the simultaneity or the succession of events and in the classical tasks of temporal estimations. In addition, people with schizophrenia show much more variability in the processing of temporal information. Some neuroscience data suggest that these temporal information processing problems are not just a consequence of attentional or memory disorders.

References

Alústiza, I., Radua, J., Albajes-Eizagirre, A., Domínguez, M., Aubá, E., & Ortuño, F. (2016). Meta-analysis of functional neuroimaging and cognitive control studies in schizophrenia: Preliminary elucidation of a core dysfunctional timing network. *Frontiers in Psychology*, 7, 192. doi:10.3389/fpsyg.2016.00192.

Capa, R. L., Duval, C. Z., Blaison, D., & Giersch, A. (2014). Patients with schizophrenia selectively impaired in temporal order judgments. *Schizophrenia Research*, 156, 51–55.

Carroll, C. A., O'Donnell, B. F., Shekhar, A., & Hetrick, W. P. (2009a). Timing dysfunctions in schizophrenia as measured by a repetitive finger tapping task. *Brain & Cognition*, 71, 345–353.

Carroll, C. A., O'Donnell, B. F., Shekhar, A., & Hetrick, W. P. (2009b). Timing dysfunctions in schizophrenia span from millisecond to several-second durations. *Brain & Cognition*, 70, 181–190.

Ciullo, V., Spalletta, G., Caltagirone, C., Jorge, R. E., & Piras, F. (2016). Explicit time deficit in schizophrenia: Systematic review and meta-analysis indicate it is primary and not domain specific. *Schizophrenia Bulletin*, 42, 505–518.

Collard, C., Pothier, W., & Roy, M.-A. (2017). Les troubles psychotiques. In S. Grondin (Ed.), *La psychologie au quotidien* (Vol. 3, pp. 1–27). Québec: Les Presses de l'Université Laval.

Davalos, D. B., Kisley, M. A., & Freedman, R. (2005). Behavioral and electrophysiological indices of temporal processing dysfunction in schizophrenia. *The Journal of Neuropsychiatry and Clinical Neurosciences*, 17, 517–525.

Davalos, D. B., Kisley, M. A., & Ross, R. G. (2002). Deficits in auditory and visual temporal perception in schizophrenia. *Cognitive Neuropsychiatry*, 7, 273–282. doi:10.1080/13546800143000230.

Davalos, D. B., Kisley, M. A., & Ross, R. G. (2003). Mismatch negativity in detection of interval duration in schizophrenia. *Cognitive Neuroscience and Neuropsychology*, 14, 1283–1286.

Davalos, D. B., Rojas, D. C., & Tregellas, J. R. (2011). Temporal processing in schizophrenia: Effects of task-difficulty on behavioral discrimination and neuronal responses. *Schizophrenia Research*, 127, 123–130.

Delevoye-Turrell, Y., Wilquin, H., & Giersch, A. (2012). A ticking clock for the production of sequential actions: Where does the problem lie in schizophrenia? *Schizophrenia Research*, 135, 51–54.

Elliott, M. A., & Giersch, A. (2016). What happens in a moment. *Frontiers in Psychology*, 6, 1905. doi:10.3389/fpsyg.2015.01905.

Giersch, A., Lalanne, L., Corves, C., Seubert, J., Shi, Z., Foucher, J., & Elliott, M. A. (2009). Extended visual simultaneity thresholds in patients with schizophrenia. *Schizophrenia Bulletin, 35*, 816–825.

Lalanne, L. (2011). *Codage des événements dans le temps: perturbations chez les patients schizophrènes.* Doctoral Dissertation, Strasbourg Université, France.

Lalanne, L., van Assche, M., & Giersch, A. (2012). When predictive mechanisms go wrong: Disordered visual synchrony thresholds in schizophrenia. *Schizophrenia Bulletin, 38*, 506–513.

Lalanne, L., van Assche, M., Wang, W., & Giersch, A. (2012). Looking forward: An impaired ability in patients with schizophrenia? *Neuropsychologia, 50*, 2736–2744.

Lee, K. H., Bhaker, R. S., Mysore, A., Parks, R. W., Birkett, P. B. L., & Woodruff, P. W. R. (2009). Time perception and its neuropsychological correlates in patients with schizophrenia and in healthy volunteers. *Psychiatry Research, 166*, 174–183.

Minkowski, E. (1995). *Le temps vécu.* Paris: Presses universitaires de France.

Roy, M., Grondin, S., & Roy, M.-A. (2012). Time perception disorders are related to working memory impairment in schizophrenia. *Psychiatry Research, 200*, 159–166.

Thönes, S., & Oberfeld, D. (2017). Meta-analysis of time perception and temporal processing in schizophrenia: Differential effects on precision and accuracy. *Clinical Psychology Review, 54*, 44–64.

Umbricht, D., & Krljes, S. (2005). Mismatch negativity in schizophrenia: A meta-analysis. *Schizophrenia Research, 76*, 1–23.

13 What Relation to Time Do Autistic People Have?

Autistic Spectrum Disorder (ASD) impairs a person's ability to communicate and interact with others. The term ASD, adopted in 2013, includes a wide range of symptoms and severity, which includes what was once known as Asperger's syndrome. In addition to the problems of understanding social interactions, ASD is characterized by a limited range of interests and activities, rigidity in behavior, and a great need for stability. People with autism have difficulty recognizing and understanding the expectations and intentions of others. As a result, they misunderstand what others are doing or are about to say.

Temporal Rigidity

It is recognized that people with autism may have some difficulty with executive functions, namely a general difficulty in organization (Hughes, Russell, & Robbins, 1994). Autistic people are also distinguished by their poor time management. They have difficulty planning their activities and distributing them over time (Attwood, 2007). In fact, people with ASD need routine, having trouble coping with unexpected events; they struggle to travel in time in their head.

Diachronic thinking is this ability that people have to deal with the different events that are distributed over time. This means that people are not only in relation to the present moment; they can consider what was before and what will be after. Diachronic thinking also includes the ability to understand that transformations take place over time, and that these transformations do not mean that identities were changed. Diachronic thinking also means that events occurring successively in time can be part of the same whole. Children normally acquire these abilities between 7 and 12 years old. Children with ASD clearly have a deficit of diachronic thinking (Boucher, Pons, Lind, & Williams, 2007). Also, Boucher et al. report that, since it does not seem to correlate significantly with verbal or nonverbal skills, with age, or with mentalizing abilities, diachronic thinking would therefore be a specific skill in itself, independent of any other cognitive skill.

Otherwise, it seems that people with ASD have a reduced episodic memory capacity, that is, a difficulty to remember events from the past that touches on personal experiences. Lind, Williams, Bowler, and Peel (2014) wanted to know if these people also have difficulty to project themselves into the future, to imagine future personal experiences. They asked 27 adults with ASD and 29 adults without ASD to imagine fictitious scenes, with no temporal or self-reference, to imagine self-related episodes that might eventually occur, and finally to remember personal events that have already occurred. In all three cases, the narrative of ASD individuals was less detailed, and this did not depend on poorer general narrative ability. Lind et al. conclude that the problems of episodic memory and projection into the future would be based on the same incapacity of constructing a scene, that is to say of linking together multiple, multisensory elements, coming from an imaginary scene.

The difficulty of ASD people in organizing themselves over time is also evident in prospective memory tasks. The latter is a skill that makes it possible to remember doing an activity that must be done in the more or less near future. This skill is based on two mechanisms, one based on the arrival of an event, the other based on time, that is to say on having to do something at a specific time. After a meta-analysis, Landsiedel, Williams, and Abbot-Smith (2017) report that ASD individuals have clear deficits for time-based prospective memory, but also report that, for the event-based mechanism, studies lead to more uncertain conclusions. The introspection difficulty of ASD individuals and their difficulty in remembering their own intentions would be the cause of the time-based prospective memory deficit.

Performances With Classical Temporal Tasks

The various studies comparing control groups and participants with ASD for standard temporal estimation tasks do not provide a clear picture of the situation. Nevertheless, the studies on the subject most often show that people with ASD are less successful than those in a control group in estimating or reproducing time intervals.

In a study of children aged 8 to 13, 21 with and 21 without ASD, Maister and Plaisted-Grant (2011) used an interval reproduction task. The task was to observe a blue square on the screen and, one second after this presentation, a purple square was presented, and the participant had to interrupt this presentation by pressing a button when the duration of it appeared to be equivalent to the first one. During each of the presentations, participants heard words that they had to repeat. Maister and Plaisted-Grant found differences between the groups for short (0.5 s) and long (45 s) reproductions, but not for reproductions of intermediate durations (4 to 30 s). The deficit observed at 0.5 s is attributed by the authors of the study to attentional factors. The performance obtained at 45 s is correlated with episodic memory capacity in children of the control group, but there is no such correlation for children with ASD. It should be noted that, during the reproduction of 45 s, the participants could not count explicitly. They had to rely on a construction in memory of the duration. Maister and Plaisted-Grant suggest that problems of estimating very short time intervals may interfere in the socio-cognitive development of children with ASD, for example in face-to-face interactions that require some sensitivity to time, while problems in estimating long durations could be the source of episodic memory problems. In the latter case, it is difficult to establish the direction of the link, but one might think that the difficulty in processing temporal information prevents one from correctly learning the duration of events and, consequently, of predicting their duration and maybe even their occurrence.

For their part, Brenner et al. (2015) tested children and adolescents with or without ASD on a reproduction task of intervals lasting 4 to 20 seconds. Study participants tended to show much variability with shorter durations, especially younger participants or those who had a weak outcome in a task related to working memory. Also, the accuracy of the reproductions (remaining more or less close to the target) was lower for younger participants with ASD, which, according to the authors, is related to the abilities in working memory, but not to a measure of inattention or hyperactivity. Szelag, Kowalska, Galkowski, and Pöppel (2004) also reported difficulties in autistic children asked to reproduce intervals, difficulties they also attributed to a limitation of working memory capacities. In adults, in an interval reproduction task, participants with ASD moved further away from the target duration and showed more variability in their responses than participants in the control group (Martin, Poirier, & Bowler, 2010). This effect tended to increase with longer durations.

After an investigation with the temporal generalization method with short intervals (0.6 and 1 s), Falter, Noreika, Wearden, and Bailey (2012) showed that autistic participants have a lower sensitivity to time, whether intervals are delimited by auditory or visual stimuli. They also report that the intervals presented in the auditory modality appear longer than those presented in the visual modality, a result consistent with what is normally reported in the literature on the subject. The results of Brodeur, Gordon Green, Flores, and Burack (2014), with temporal bisection and generalization tasks and intervals of less than one second, also show a weaker sensitivity to time in ADS participants compared to that of neurotypical children. The results of ASD children in a bisection task (1 to 4-s intervals and 2 to 8-s intervals) are also more variable than those of children without ASD, especially when the intervals range from 2 to 8 s (Allman, DeLeon, & Wearden, 2011). In contrast, the study by Gil, Chambers, Hyvert, Fanget, and Droit-Volet (2012) shows no difference between children who have ASD compared to children who do not in a time bisection task involving intervals of 0.5 to 1 seconds, 1.25 to 2.5 seconds, 3.12 to 6.25 seconds, and 7.81 to 16.62 seconds.

Conclusion

People with ASD clearly have difficulty dealing with the temporal demands of everyday life. They have a deficit in diachronic thought, problems of episodic memory, and difficulty in projecting themselves into the future. In the latter two cases, it could depend on the inability to build a scene. They also have problems with the time-based mechanism of prospective memory. Finally, most often, during estimation and time interval replication tasks, their results are worse than those of neurotypical individuals.

References

Allman, M. J., DeLeon, I. G., & Wearden, J. H. (2011). Psychophysical assessment of timing in individuals with autism. *American Journal on Intellectual and Developmental Disabilities, 116*, 165–178.

Attwood, T. (2007). *Le syndrome d'Asperger: Guide complete.* Montréal: Chenelière.

Boucher, J., Pons, F., Lind, S., & Williams, D. (2007). Temporal cognition in children with autistic spectrum disorders: Tests of diachronic thinking. *Journal of Autism and Developmental Disorders, 37*, 1413–1429.

Brenner, L. A., Shih, V. H., Colich, N. L., Sugar, C. A., Bearden, C. E., & Dapretto, M. (2015). Time reproduction performance is associated with age and working memory in high-functioning youth with autism spectrum disorder. *Autism Research, 8*, 29–37.

Brodeur, D. A., Gordon Green, C., Flores, H., & Burack, J. A. (2014). Time estimation among low-functioning individuals with autism spectrum disorders: Evidence of poor sensitivity to variability of short durations. *Autism Research, 7*, 237–244.

Falter, C. M., Noreika, V., Wearden, J. H., & Bailey, A. J. (2012). More consistent, yet less sensitive: Interval timing in autism spectrum disorders. *The Quarterly Journal of Experimental Psychology, 65*, 2093–2107.

Gil, S., Chambres, P., Hyvert, C., Fanget, M., & Droit-Volet, S. (2012). Children with autism spectrum disorders have "the working raw material" for time perception. *PLoS One, 7*(11), e49116. doi:10.1371/journal.pone.0049116.

Hughes, C., Russell, J., & Robbins, T. W. (1994). Evidence for executive dysfunction in autism. *Neuropsychologia, 32*, 477–492.

Landsiedel, J., Williams, D. M., & Abbot-Smith, K. (2017). A meta-analysis and critical review of prospective memory in autism spectrum disorder. *Journal of Autism and Developmental Disorders, 47*, 646–666.

Lind, S. E., Williams, D. M., Bowler, D. M., & Peel, A. (2014). Episodic memory and episodic future thinking impairments in high-functioning autism spectrum disorder: An underlying difficulty with scene construction or self-projection? *Neuropsychology, 28*, 55–67.

Maister, L., & Plaisted-Grant, K. C. (2011). Time perception and its relationship to memory in autism spectrum conditions. *Developmental Science, 14*, 1311–1322.

Martin, J. S., Poirier, M., & Bowler, D. M. (2010). Brief report: Impaired temporal reproduction performance in adults with autism spectrum disorder. *Journal of Autism and Developmental Disorders, 40*, 640–646.

Szelag, E., Kowalska, J., Galkowski, T., & Pöppel, E. (2004). Temporal processing deficits in high-functioning children with autism. *British Journal of Psychology, 95*, 269–282.

14 How Is ADHD Linked to Temporal Problems?

Attention deficit hyperactivity disorder (ADHD) is a persistent problem of inattention that is sometimes accompanied by hyperactivity, which interferes with the normal functioning of the person and may interfere with their development. More concretely, it means that people with ADHD may have trouble getting organized, staying focused on a task; they can easily be distracted and often experience procrastination. This cognitive problem risks compromising the chances of success in school and work and even creating emotional, relational, and financial problems (Laplante, 2017). With hyperactivity, we observe behaviors that reflect an inability to wait or a tendency to interrupt others during a conversation. Behaviors associated with hyperactivity subside during adolescence, but attention disorders do not diminish.

Given the importance of attention in the perception of time (see Chapter 9), it is not surprising to learn that the temporal estimation capabilities of people with ADHD are affected. But the problems related to psychological time go beyond the estimation of short time intervals.

Deficits in the Processing of Temporal Information

The studies on temporal estimation in ADHD are quite numerous. In the detailed review of Toplak, Dockstader, and Tannock (2006), we learn that differences between the control and ADHD groups are reported in five of the six studies involving interval discrimination, in 12 of the 13 studies on interval reproduction, and in seven of the eight studies where tasks involving finger tapping (adoption of a spontaneous tempo, synchronization with an external stimulus, and synchronization followed by continuation).

Since then, many other studies have shown effectiveness differences between the two groups in the processing of temporal information. Suarez, Lopera, Pineda, and Casini (2013) used a time bisection task with stimuli from the auditory (150 to 450 ms) and visual (300 to 900-ms intervals) modalities. They tested 15 adults with ADHD and 16 adults without this diagnosis. The results showed that, compared to participants in the control group, ADHD participants overestimate duration in both auditory and visual conditions. In addition, participants in the ADHD group obtain significantly higher differential thresholds (are less sensitive to time), both in auditory and visual conditions, once again. The authors explain the poorer results of participants with ADHD, on the one hand, by a lower efficiency of attentional mechanisms (the switch—see Chapter 9) and, on the other hand, by a certain failure of the memory processes involved in the bisection task.

As for tasks involving interval production, a relatively recent study has shown that people with ADHD are less effective than those without ADHD (Zelaznik et al., 2012). These authors asked 27 children with ADHD and 51 children in a control group to do a synchronization-continuation task at the rate of one stroke every 500 ms. On the basis of an analysis of the continuation phase allowing to separate the motor-related part of inter-tap variability observed in this task from the part of a variability belonging to the fluctuations in the internal clock, the authors showed that not only does the control group remain closer to the target (500 ms) over the course of trials, but that the time-related variability is much greater in participants with ADHD.

The ability to do this synchronization-continuation task of people with ADHD and of those who do not have ADHD has also been tested with adults. Gilden and Marusich (2009) compared a group of 11 adults with ADHD to a group of 11 adults with no attentional problems. While the performances of the two groups are the same during a production task of 1-second intervals, those of the ADHD group become significantly less good from the moment the intervals last 1.5 seconds (increase of the variability, as quantified with the coefficient of variation, a kind of Weber fraction—see Chapter 2). For the same interval length, participants in the control group are able to continue to produce the 1.5-second interval just as effectively as 1-second interval. For 2-second intervals, participants in both groups show an increase of this coefficient of variation.

In the same vein, that is to say in the perspective of reaching a time limit that can differentiate the two groups, Marusich and Gilden (2014) asked participants with or without ADHD to complete the trajectory of the movement they perceived after seeing a rectangle appearing successively for 100 ms in two places. When the duration between the presentations of the rectangles is 200, 300, 500, or 1100 ms, the trajectories are perceived correctly by the two groups. In other words, the temporal integration is done correctly. When the duration between presentations of the rectangle is 2300 ms, the participants of both groups fail to integrate the information properly in time. Finally, unlike participants with ADHD, when the duration is 1700 ms, participants in the control group show sensory integration capacity. According to the authors, the time scale that dictates the rate of decline in the strength of association between stimuli would be contracted in people with ADHD.

Neurological Bases of Temporal Disorders in ADHD

The idea that there is a deficit in temporal information processing in ADHD is supported by data from functional magnetic resonance imaging (fMRI).

These data reveal in particular a lower activity of the prefrontal cortex, recognized for its contribution to the processing of duration (see Chapter 5). More specifically, according to Rubia, Halari, Christakou, and Taylor (2009), the impulsivity problems sometimes encountered in ADHD are linked to a malfunctioning of the timing mechanisms involved in tasks such as discrimination of short time intervals, temporal productions involving motor skills and temporal discounting which involves the appreciation of very long intervals. With fMRI, it has been possible to locate the source of these temporal information processing disorders in the prefrontal, striatal, and cerebellar regions.

What seems particularly interesting are efforts to develop a time-based biomarker to diagnose ADHD (Hart et al., 2014). Based on the cerebral activation (fMRI) of some regions involved in temporal discrimination (including parietal and dorsolateral prefrontal cortex, basal ganglia, and cerebellum), it was possible to distinguish the 20 adolescents with ADHD from the 20 without ADHD with a 75% success rate.

Aversion to Delays

Part of the literature related in some way to psychological time in people with ADHD is related to the difficulty of postponing reward (Jackson & Mackillop, 2016). According to Sonuga-Baret and collaborators, these people seem to prefer getting a small reward in the immediate future rather than having to wait to get a bigger reward. This preference, or aversion to waiting or delay, would explain why people with ADHD underestimate the duration in an anticipatory task (Sonuga-Barke, Saxton, & Hall, 1998, Sonuga-Barke, Taylor, Sembi, & Smith, 1992; Yu, Sonuga-Barke, & Liu, 2015). People with ADHD would have a clock with a pace that accelerates during the wait. Indeed, the shape of the temporal discounting function in ADHD and that of participants in the control group would be different in situations of real expectation of reinforcement, but not in hypothetical situations where one imagines the waiting time (Yu & Sonuga-Barke, 2016).

In fact, there is a whole field of decision-making research in people with ADHD. These people would tend not to make the right choices, in this case the choice to wait. Making the wrong choices would not be explained by differences in the tendency to take more or less risk, but by a difficulty in handling the information about risk and by an aversion to waiting, this aversion showing by a propensity to choose the options that come first (Coghill, Seth, & Matthews, 2014). With their inability to read the future consequences (a kind of "temporal myopia"), people with ADHD are somehow caught in the present (Toplak et al., 2006, Vloet et al., 2010). The reader will find in Sonuga-Barke, Cortese, Fairchild, and Stringaris (2016) a summary of the brain structures involved in decision-making in people with ADHD.

Conclusion

Overall, for standard temporal estimation tasks, there are in most cases differences between people who have ADHD and people who do not. These differences could be explained by differences in the involvement of the brain structures responsible for the processing of temporal information. Differences between groups extend even into the realm of temporal discounting, as people with ADHD find it more difficult to defer gratification.

Finally, for the sake of further information, note that even the usual knowledge about time (for example the order of days of the week), as well as the conservation of time in Piagetian tests, is not as good among children with ADHD than in children without this deficit (Quartier, Zimmermann, & Nashat, 2010).

References

Coghill, D. R., Seth, S., & Matthews, K. (2014). A comprehensive assessment of memory, delay aversion, timing, inhibition, decision making and variability in attention deficit hyperactivity disorder: Advancing beyond the three-pathway models. *Psychological Medicine*, 44, 1989–2001.

Gilden, D. L., & Marusich, L. R. (2009). Contraction of time in attention-deficit hyperactivity disorder. *Neuropsychology*, 23, 265–269.

Hart, H., Marquand, A. F., Smith, A., Cubillo, A., Simmons, A., Brammer, M., & Rubia, K. (2014). Predictive neurofunctional markers of attention-deficit/hyperactivity disorder based on pattern classification of temporal processing. *Journal of the American Academy of Child and Adolescent Psychiatry*, 53, 569–578.

Jackson, J. N. S., & Mackillop, J. (2016). Attention-deficit/hyperactivity disorder and monetary delay discounting: A meta-analysis of case-control studies. *Biological Psychiatry*, 1, 316–325.

Laplante, L. (2017). Le trouble du déficit de l'attention avec ou sans hyperactivité (TDAH) chez l'adulte. In S. Grondin (Ed.), *La psychologie au quotidien* (Vol. 3, pp. 57–72). Québec: Les Presses de l'Université Laval.

Marusich, L. R., & Gilden, D. L. (2014). Assessing temporal integration spans in ADHD through apparent motion. *Neuropsychology*, 28, 585–593.

Quartier, V., Zimmermann, G., & Nashat, S. (2010). Sense of time in children with attention-deficit/hyperactivity disorder (ADHD): A comparative study. *Swiss Journal of Psychology*, 69, 7–14.

Rubia, K., Halari, R., Christakou, A., & Taylor, E. (2009). Impulsiveness as a timing disturbance: Neurocognitive abnormalities in attention-deficit hyperactivity disorder during temporal processes and normalization with methylphenidate. *Philosophical Transactions of the Royal Society of London B*, 364, 1919–1931.

Sonuga-Barke, E. J. S., Cortese, S., Fairchild, G., & Stringaris, A. (2016). Annual research review: Transdiagnostic neuroscience of child and adolescent mental disorders: Differentiating decision making in attention-deficit/hyperactivity disorder, conduct disorder, depression, and anxiety. *Journal of Child Psychology and Psychiatry*, 57, 321–349.

Sonuga-Barke, E. J. S., Saxton, T., & Hall, M. (1998). The role of interval underestimation in hyperactive children's failure to suppress responses over time. *Behavioural Brain Research*, 94, 45–50.

Sonuga-Barke, E. J. S., Taylor, E., Sembi, S., & Smith, J. (1992). Hyperactivity and delay aversion I: The effect of delay on choice. *Journal of Child Psychology and Psychiatry, 33*, 387–398.

Suarez, I., Lopera, F., Pineda, D., & Casini, L. (2013). The cognitive structure of time estimation impairments in adults with attention deficit hyperactivity disorder. *Cognitive Neuropsychology, 30*, 195–207.

Toplak, M. E., Dockstader, C., & Tannock, R. (2006). Temporal information processing in ADHD: Findings to date and new methods. *Journal of Neuroscience Methods, 151*, 15–29.

Vloet, T. D., Gilsbach, S., Neufang, S., Fink, G. R., Herpertz-Dahlmann, B., & Konrad, K. (2010). Neural mechanisms of interference control and time discrimination in attention-deficit/hyperactivity disorder. *Journal of the American Academy of Child and Adolescent Psychiatry, 49*, 356–367.

Yu, X., & Sonuga-Barke, E. (2016). Childhood ADHD and delayed reinforcement: A direct comparison of performance on hypothetical and real-time delay tasks. *Journal of Attention Disorders, 20*, 63–70.

Yu, X., Sonuga-Barke, E., & Liu, X. (2015). Preference for smaller sooner over larger later rewards in ADHD: Contribution of delay duration and paradigm type. *Journal of Attention Disorders*. doi:10.1177/1087054715570390.

Zelaznik, H. N., Vaughn, A. J., Green, J. T., Smith, A. L., Hoza, B., & Linnea, K. (2012). Motor timing deficits in children with attention-deficit/hyperactivity disorder. *Human Movement Science, 31*, 255–265.

15 Does a Depressive State Affect Time Perception?

A depressive state can manifest in different ways, including lack of sleep or appetite, loss of energy, and even a loss of interest in doing things. It is also manifested by problems of concentration, feelings of guilt, excessive feelings of failure and even, sometimes, by suicidal ideation (Provencher, Soucy Chartier, & Mirabel-Sarron, 2015). If this state contains concentration problems, it may affect the processing of temporal information given the prominent role of attention in temporal tasks (see Chapter 9). Moreover, a typical symptom in people with depression is related to the experience of time that seems to flow much more slowly.

Classical Temporal Tasks

It is common to link the perception of time and the psychological disturbances caused by a depressive state (Blewett, 1992; Lehmann, 1967). However, studies involving the use of traditional temporal tasks, such as those described in Chapter 1, do not always lead to the observation of a deficit in the processing of temporal information in depressive persons or people who manifest depressive traits (Hawkins, French, Crawford, & Enzle, 1988; Oberfeld, Thönes, Palayoor, & Hecht, 2014). Following a meta-analysis focusing on four classical methods (verbal estimation, temporal production and reproduction, and duration discrimination), Thönes and Oberfeld (2015) concluded that differences between depressed patients and control participants are not at all systematic, and this is true with each of these methods. Nevertheless, let's try to list some of these studies.

In Bschor et al. (2004), a battery of tests was administered to participants. Among these tests, there was the production of intervals of 7, 35, and 90 s; the estimation of intervals of 8, 43, and 109 s; and the evaluation of the duration of a film of 12 min 40 s; in addition, participants were free to use an explicit counting strategy to do the tasks. The results indicate that the duration of the film is estimated by depressed patients and patients in a manic phase[1] at approximately 20 min and 28 min on average, respectively, and that the estimate of the 8 and 43 s intervals of the two groups does not differ significantly. For the other condition however (109 s), the patients in a manic phase

(M = 133 s), unlike those in a depressive phase (M = 105 s), overestimate time. In the production task, depressed patients (M = 9.1 and 29.3 s) differed significantly from manic patients (M = 5.7 and 25.3 s), the difference observed with a longer target being not significant (M = 64 and 58 s for depressive and manic patients, respectively).

In addition, some studies indicate that depressed people overestimate duration. This is the case of the study of Wyrick and Wyrick (1977) in which target intervals ranging from 160 to 320 s are reported by depressive patients lasting 265 and 406 s, respectively. Similarly, if 30-second intervals have to be produced and the duration is overestimated, it will take less than 30 seconds for a depressed person to complete the productions; this finding is reported by Kuhs, Hermann, Kammer, and Tölle (1989) who asked participants to count up to 10, three consecutive times, to reach 30 s. Depressive patients needed only 24 seconds to feel they were reaching the target. Also, even if the mood of depressed people sometimes varies a lot during the same day, this result remains the same at different times of evaluation and is valid both in patients showing diurnal fluctuations of mood and in patients who do not show such fluctuations.

Based on an investigation involving short intervals (targets of 500, 100, and 1500 ms) Mioni, Stablum, Prunetti, and Grondin (2016) report that depressed patients produce longer intervals than participants in a control group. In fact, compared to the participants in a control group, depressive patients tend to make too long productions of short intervals and too short productions of long intervals (Thönes & Oberfeld, 2015). In addition, Sévigny, Everett, and Grondin (2003) report that participants in a depressive state (estimated by the Beck Inventory) show more variability, when producing one-second intervals with a series of finger taps, than participants who are not in such a depressive state. Because participants in the depressive group make significantly more errors than participants in the control group in the Continuous Performance Test, the difference between groups is attributed to attentional differences. In the same study, participants in depressive states were also less able to discriminate between intervals of about one second, although there was no difference between the groups for interval discrimination of 100 or 500 ms. Similar results, where the control and depressive groups differ for the discrimination of long intervals, but not for the discrimination of short intervals, are also reported by Msetfi, Murphy, and Kornbrot (2012).

Temporal Orientation and Impression

Depressed people are known to be more inclined towards the past than the future. One way of approaching this question of temporal orientation is to use spatial representation. For example, we can ask people if a given moment in time seems more or less distant using, to quantify the impression, a scale of 1 (very close to the present moment) to 10 (very far from the present moment). Rinaldi, Locati, Parolin, and Girelli (2017) did this by asking participants to rate on this scale how far apart they locate "a month ago" (the past) and "in a month" (the future). In this study, participants with depressive traits were compared to participants in a control group. The results show that the very strong tendency that people have, normally, to find that a given distance is closer in the future than it is in the past (Caruso, van Bove, Chin, & Ward, 2013) is greatly diminished in people with depressive personality traits. This observation is consistent with the idea that people who ruminate tend to find that negative emotions (anger, guilt, sadness), which are the object of their ruminations, seem closer in time (Siedlecka, Capper, & Denson, 2015). The results of Rinaldi et al. (2017) are also consistent with the fact that people with depressive traits tend to often look at the past, to have negative thoughts such as personal loss and failure, and what caused sadness.

For Melges (1989), the fact of being turned towards the past during the depression could be explained by an internal rhythm that is slowing down. This slowing of the flow of thoughts and movements would give the impression that the perspective on the future is shortened. Thus, the depressed person is left with the impression of being short of ideas and plans. On the contrary, for people in manic phase, thoughts and actions are accelerated and, by leaving room for the future, this future seems open to all possibilities, to the point that the relationship with reality becomes defective. In a manic phase, the internal flow is too intense and too little room is left for the analysis of external events that reality imposes. The person in a depressive phase lives the opposite: a lack of internal events and too many external events predominate and exert control over them.

Bschor et al.'s (2004) study, cited in the previous section, provides, in addition to data on explicit time judgments, an investigation of the link between depression (and mania) and the impression of time passing. Thus, participants were presented with a 10 cm line symbolizing their experience of the passage of time during the day of the test, and they had to indicate whether the time seemed to pass quickly or slowly, +5 cm corresponding to the impression of time that passes the fastest and -5 cm to the impression of the time that passes the slowest. Bschor and colleagues (2004) have shown that, for the impression of time, depressive patients judge that time passes significantly slower than do participants in a control group, but that patients in a manic phase judge that time passes significantly faster than do the participants of said control group.

Conclusion

When the investigations concern temporal tasks such as those typically used in experimental psychology, the portrait aimed at describing the effect of depression on temporal perception is not clear. This is partly due to the fact that we do not always know whether, in the different studies, a patient is or is not on medication (Oberfeld et al., 2014). It seems nevertheless that depressed people have a tendency to overestimate the long durations.

Phenomenologically, depressive patients most often report an impression that time is passing slowly and clearly seem to be inclined to turn towards the past, unlike people in a manic phase who see the future as being wide open.

Note

1. Part of the work on depression focuses on the comparison of patients in a depressed phase and those in a manic phase, depression disorders sometimes being part of a manic-depressive cycle (bipolar disorder).

References

Blewett, A. E. (1992). Abnormal subjective time experience in depression. *British Journal of Psychiatry, 161*, 195–200.

Bschor, T., Ising, M., Bauer, M., Lewitzka, U., Skerstupeit, M., Müller-Oerlinghausen, B., & Baethge, C. (2004). Time experience and time judgment in major depression, mania, and healthy subjects: A controlled study of 93 subjects. *Acta Psychiatrica Scandinavica, 109*, 222–229.

Caruso, E. M., van Bove, L., Chin, M., & Ward, A. (2013). The temporal Doppler effect: When the future feels closer than the past. *Psychological Science, 24*, 530–536.

Hawkins, W. L., French, L. C., Crawford, B. D., & Enzle, M. E. (1988). Depressed affect and time perception. *Journal of Abnormal Psychology, 97*, 275–280.

Kuhs, H., Hermann, W., Kammer, K., & Tölle, R. (1989). The daily course of the symptomatology and the impaired time estimation in endogenous depression (melancholia). *Journal of Affective Disorders, 17*, 285–290.

Lehmann, H. (1967). Time and psychopathology. *Annals of New York Academy of Sciences, 138*, 798–821.

Melges, F. T. (1989). Disorders of time and the brain in severe mental illness. In J. T. Fraser (Ed.), *Time and mind* (pp. 99–119). Madison: International University Press.

Mioni, G., Stablum, F., Prunetti, E., & Grondin, S. (2016). Time perception in anxious and depressed patients: A comparison between time reproduction and time production tasks. *Journal of Affective Disorders, 196*, 154–163.

Msetfi, R. M., Murphy, R. A., & Kornbrot, D. E. (2012). The effect of mild depression on time discrimination. *The Quarterly Journal of Experimental Psychology, 65*, 632–645.

Oberfeld, D., Thönes, S., Palayoor, B. J., & Hecht, H. (2014). Depression does not affect time perception and time-to-contact estimation. *Frontiers in Psychology, 5*, 810. http://dx.doi.org/10.3389/fpsyg.2014.00810.

Provencher, M. D., Soucy Chartier, I., & Mirabel-Sarron, C. (2015). La dépression & les troubles de l'humeur: mieux les comprendre pour mieux les traiter. In S. Grondin (Ed.), *La psychologie au quotidien* (Vol. 2, pp. 63–94). Québec: Les Presses de l'Université Laval.

Rinaldi, L., Locati, F., Parolin, L., & Girelli, L. (2017). Distancing the present self from the past and future: Psychological distance in anxiety and depression. *The Quarterly Journal of Experimental Psychology, 70*, 1106–1113.

Sévigny, M.-C., Everett, J., & Grondin, S. (2003). Depression, attention and time estimation. *Brain and Cognition, 53*, 351–353.

Siedlecka, E., Capper, M. M., & Denson, T. F. (2015). Negative emotional events that people ruminate about feel closer in time. *PLoS One, 10*, e0117105. doi.org/10.1371/journal.pone.0117105.

Thönes, S., & Oberfeld, D. (2015). Time perception in depression: A meta-analysis. *Journal of Affective Disorders, 175*, 359–372.

Wyrick, R. A., & Wyrick, L. C. (1977). Time experience during depression. *Archives of General Psychiatry, 34*, 1441–1443.

16 Does Anxiety Affect Time Perception?

Anxiety can be viewed as a kind of worry and apprehension, a general state of alert to meet the normal demands of daily life and to see them arrive. But when it persists, anxiety ends up affecting the quality of life; it reflects a chronic feeling of insecurity and is perceived as an uncomfortable state by the person who lives it (Belleville, 2012).

In psychology, one distinguishes state anxiety from trait anxiety. In the first case, it is a state of physiological excitability provoked by a given situation, by an external stimulus. Trait anxiety is rather a stable characteristic related to the personality of a person. In both cases, anxiety is associated with attentional deficits that can be observed in certain cognitive tasks (Eysenck, 1992), especially if they are very demanding.

Classical Temporal Tasks

The link between attention and anxiety suggests that the processing of temporal information of anxious people may be defective. For example, people with high levels of anxiety and people with low levels of anxiety were compared in a study involving the production of 15-, 30-, or 90-second intervals. The results reveal that, on average, the participants in each group produce intervals shorter than the target, but the difference between the target duration and the produced interval is greater among the participants of the anxiety group (Whyman & Moos, 1967). Such a result is poorly explained by an effect of attention, but on the other hand is compatible with an interpretation stipulating that the rhythm of the pacemaker of an internal clock (see Chapter 4) is accelerated in the anxiety group. Such acceleration allows for greater pulse emission during a given period of time and, as a result, the number of pulses corresponding to the target duration is reached more rapidly. An interpretation based on a lack of attention to time would instead have predicted a longer production to reach the number of pulses corresponding to the target duration.

The study by Mioni, Stablum, Prunetti, and Grondin (2016), reported in the previous chapter, also involves the participation of people who are anxious. This study, which revealed that depressed people have difficulty especially in an interval production task, also reveals that anxious people under-reproduce the target intervals lasting 500, 1000, and 1500 ms. Not only do the reproductions of anxious people tend to be shorter than those of a control group, but they are also much shorter than those of a group of depressed patients. This effect observed with anxious people is attributed to the functioning of attention in this temporal reproduction task. Indeed, in this task, it is necessary to encode and then reproduce an interval. Under-reproduction would depend on the gradual erasure of temporal information, the difficulty in maintaining intact a temporal representation being greater in participants with attention problems, which is the case for anxious individuals (Eysenck, 1992).

Another demonstration of the effect of anxiety on temporal perception comes from a strategy of using the inclination of anxious people to direct their attention to threatening sources of information. As will be seen in Chapter 23, emotions and their expression, especially the one related to fear, influence perceived duration. In a study by Bar-Haim, Kerem, Lamy, and Zakay (2010), participants with a strong anxiety trait, as measured by a high score in Spielberger's inventory, were compared to participants who scored low on the same inventory. Participants had to look at a face expressing fear, or remaining neutral, for two, four, or eight seconds, and had to try to remember it. The participants also knew that they would have to reproduce the duration of presentation of the face. Experience shows that there is a difference between anxious and non-anxious groups for the condition where a frightened face is presented and not in the condition of the calm face; also, this difference only appears with the duration of two seconds, and not with the two other durations under study. When a frightened face is presented, people with an anxiety trait judge that the two-second interval is much longer than when a calm face is presented; non-anxious people tend to judge the duration as being longer with a calm face than with a frightened face. The interpretation of this effect on anxious people cannot be due to the loss of attention to time; the effect would rather be attributed to the attention paid to the frightened image, the latter causing an increase in physiological activation, therefore also increasing the rate of emission of the pulses of the internal clock. Also, if such an effect does not occur at four and eight seconds, it may be because of a habituation effect to frightened faces caused by prolonged exposure. This explanation of why an effect occurs at two seconds, but not at four seconds or eight seconds, is consistent with the fact that the attentional bias observed in anxiety occurs at short exposures (< 500 ms) and not at longer exposures (Bar-Haim, Lamy, Pergamin, Bakermans-Kranenberg, & van Ijzendoorn, 2007).

It should also be noted that earlier work has focused on estimating duration under real fear conditions. Thus, Langer, Wapner, and Werner (1961) report that participants placed on a platform at the edge of a precipice, as opposed to being placed far from the precipice, verbally overestimate a five-second interval. Similarly, participants with a phobia of spiders placed near a spider for 45 seconds significantly overestimate this interval, which is not the case for participants who do not have such a phobia (Watts & Sharrock, 1984).

Otherwise, in a study on the retrospective judgments of four-minute intervals, Sarason and Stoops (1978, Experiment 2) distinguished very, moderately and slightly anxious people. These people were placed in conditions that could cause more or less anxiety, emphasizing more or less the importance of a forthcoming intelligence test to be passed. They observed that the four-minute wait before the test and the four-minute duration of the test are much more overestimated by those who are very anxious than those who are moderately or slightly anxious, and that people placed in the anxiety-provoking condition (the test reported to be very important) also overestimate duration much more than people placed in the less anxiety-provoking condition. In fact, the effect of the personal level of anxiety is especially apparent in the condition where participants are placed in anxiety-provoking conditions. This last result also applies to the retrospective estimation of a task lasting 18 minutes (Sarason & Stoops, 1978, Experiment 3).

Temporal Orientation

It is not uncommon in recent clinical studies that the investigation of the effects of anxiety and depression be conducted together. In both cases, it is often said that thoughts about the future are negative. What sets them apart is that, in the case of depression, there is also a reduction in positive thoughts about the future, which is not the case with anxiety (Miloyan, Pachana, & Suddendorf, 2014). Also, anxious people are less inclined to turn to the past than depressed people.

As we saw in the previous chapter, people generally tend to find that a given distance is closer in the future than it is in the past (Caruso, van Bove, Chin, & Ward, 2013). We have seen that this trend is greatly diminished in people with depressive personality traits (Rinaldi, Locati, Parolin, & Girelli, 2017). The same study also teaches us that, unlike depressed people, persons with anxious personality traits tend to exaggerate the impression that a distance is closer in the future than in the past.

Another study parallels the cases of anxiety and depression for orientation over time. While the studies on the subject are aimed at comparing anxious people and depressed people, Eysenck, Payne, and Santos (2006) look instead at the relationship to the past, present, and future of participants (non-clinical population) who are measured on both anxious and depressive traits. In a first study, participants were asked to describe three moments in the past when they felt particularly anxious and three moments when they felt particularly depressed. Eysenck and colleagues report that anxiety is more closely associated with future events than past events, and that the opposite is true for depression. In a second study, participants were asked to rate their level of anxiety and depression after reading different scenarios containing a negative event and imagining themselves to be living the experience. These scenarios, which covered different categories of events (relational, academic success), were related to a past event, an uncertain future event or a probable future event. It turns out that probable future events are more associated with anxiety and depression than uncertain future events; and past events, compared to future events (probable or uncertain), are closely related to depression but not related to anxiety. The idea that anxiety is triggered by negative future events and that depression is rather triggered by negative past events leads one to believe that once the expected negative events are transformed into past negative events, anxiety gives way to depression.

Conclusion

Due to attentional disorders, anxiety seems to lead to shorter reproductions of short time intervals. However, the propensity of anxious people to observe threatening stimuli would make the duration (two seconds) of frightened faces overestimated because of the physiological arousal generated by this observation. Furthermore, while depressed people tend to look back, anxious people feel that the future is very close and have little concern for the past.

References

Bar-Haim, Y., Kerem, A., Lamy, D., & Zakay, D. (2010). When time slows down: The influence of threat on time perception in anxiety. *Cognition & Emotion*, 24(2), 255–263.

Bar-Haim, Y., Lamy, D., Pergamin, L., Bakermans-Kranenburg, M. J., & van Ijzendoorn, M. H. (2007). Threat-related attentional bias in anxious and non-anxious individuals: A meta-analytic study. *Psychological Bulletin*, 133, 1–24.

Belleville, G. (2012). Stress, anxiété & panique: des histoires de peur! In S. Grondin (Ed.), *La psychologie au quotidien* (pp. 95–119). Québec: Les Presses de l'Université Laval.

Caruso, E. M., van Bove, L., Chin, M., & Ward, A. (2013). The temporal Doppler effect: When the future feels closer than the past. *Psychological Science*, 24, 530–536.

Eysenck, M. W. (1992). *Anxiety: The cognitive perspective*. Hove, UK: Psychology Press.

Eysenck, M. W., Payne, S., & Santos, R. (2006). Anxiety and depression: Past, present, and future events. *Cognition & Emotion*, 20, 274–294.

Langer, J., Wapner, S., & Werner, H. (1961). The effect of danger upon the experience of time. *American Journal of Psychology*, 74, 94–97.

Miloyan, B., Pachana, N. A., & Suddendorf, T. (2014). The future is here: A review of foresight systems in anxiety and depression. *Cognition and Emotion*, 28, 795–810.

Mioni, G., Stablum, F., Prunetti, E., & Grondin, S. (2016). Time perception in anxious and depressed patients: A comparison between time reproduction and time production tasks. *Journal of Affective Disorders*, 196, 154–163.

Rinaldi, L., Locati, F., Parolin, L., & Girelli, L. (2017). Distancing the present self from the past and future: Psychological distance in anxiety and depression. *The Quarterly Journal of Experimental Psychology*, 70, 1106–1113.

Sarason, I. G., & Stoops, R. (1978). Test anxiety and the passage of time. *Journal of Consulting and Clinical Psychology*, 46(1), 102–109.

Watts, F. N., & Sharrock, R. (1984). Fear and time estimation. *Perceptual and Motor Skills*, 59, 597–598.

Whyman, A. D., & Moos, R. H. (1967). Time perception and anxiety. *Perceptual and Motor Skills*, 24, 567–570.

17 How Is Parkinson's Disease Related to the Processing of Temporal Information?

Parkinson's disease consists of a degeneration of the central nervous system. It is characterized by slowness and rarity of movement, as well as rigidity, postural instability, and resting tremor. Movement problems include a reduction in facial expression and gestures when speaking.

This disorder of movement capacity is caused by the degradation of the dopaminergic system. In particular, we note the lack of dopamine in the basal ganglia, these nuclei being involved in the control of movement and in cognition (Pagonabarraga & Kulisevsky, 2012). Given the role of dopamine and basal ganglia in the processing of temporal information (see Chapter 5), it is not surprising to learn that some people with Parkinson's disease may have difficulty performing tasks involving timekeeping (Malapani, Deweer, & Gibbon, 2002).

Temporal Tasks Involving Motor Skills

Curiously, even in temporal tasks involving motor skills, there are no systematic weaker results of Parkinson's patients compared to the results of participants in a control group (see Jones & Jahanshahi, 2014). In a synchronization-continuation task involving 750-ms intervals, Cerasa et al. (2006) report that there is more variability in Parkinson's patients during synchronization, but no difference during continuity. On the basis of functional magnetic resonance imaging (fMRI), the same authors report a particularly greater activation of the cerebellum, the supplementary motor area (SMA), and the thalamus in patients during the synchronization phase, and greater cerebellothalamic activation during continuity. With the same method, but with 600-ms intervals, Elsinger et al. (2003) report greater variability among patients in each phase. Namely, they observe, by means of the fMRI, activation of the SMA and of the thalamus, but this observation occurs during the continuation phase and when the patients are on medication. For their part, whether during synchronization or during continuation, Jahanshahi et al. (2010), with intervals of 1000 ms, observe no difference in variability between Parkinson's patients and the control group.

Other studies based on the synchronization-continuation task, but which do not take place in the context of brain imaging, reveal that there is an increase in variability (intervals of about half a second) in the continuation phase in Parkinson's patients (Joundi, Brittain, Green, Aziz, & Jenkinson, 2012). For the same task, but with intervals ranging from 400 to 2000 ms, Pastor, Jahanshahi, Artieda, and Obeso (1992) observe more variability during the continuation phase in patients. In contrast, Jones et al. (2011), with intervals lasting 250 to 2000 ms, fail to draw such clear conclusions about differences between patients and participants from a control group, both for the synchronization phase and for the continuation phase. Similarly, for the continuation phase, other studies failed to observe differences between the two groups with 550-ms intervals (Ivry & Keele, 1989; Spencer & Ivry, 2005).

In interval production and reproduction tasks, where there is also a motor component, but which does not contribute as much to the total variability observed as in a synchronization-continuation production task, the portrait is not very clear. With the production of long intervals (from 5 to 120 s), one can sometimes observe an overestimation of duration by patients compared to participants in a control group (Jones, Malone, Dirnberger, Edwards, & Jahanshahi, 2008), and sometimes an underestimation or no difference when participants can count explicitly (Perbal et al., 2005).

Perceptual Temporal Tasks

Although they do not include a motor component to explain different levels of performance, many studies that used a temporal perception task showed differences between Parkinson's patients and participants in a control group. Such differences are reported for interval discrimination of 50 ms (Guehl et al., 2008; Rammsayer & Classen, 1997) and for 300- and 600-ms intervals (Harrington, Haaland, & Hermanowicz, 1998; Harrington et al., 2011). However, for the same task, Ivry and Keele (1989) did not observe differences between groups with 400-ms intervals, and Hellström, Lang, Portin, and Rinne (1997) did not observe it for intervals ranging from 400 ms to 1600 ms. Riesen and Schnider (2001) found no differences between the groups for the verbal estimation of 12-, 24-, and 48-sec intervals, but reported differences for discrimination of 200- and 1000-ms intervals.

In other studies where the same groups were compared, the bisection method was adopted. Smith, Harper, Gittings, and Abernethy (2007), who worked with patients on medication, report that there is more variability observed in patients when the intervals vary around one second or five seconds, but not when they vary around 100 milliseconds or 500 milliseconds. These results obtained with very short intervals are corroborated by those of Wearden et al. (2008) who do not observe differences between the groups when the intervals vary around 200 ms or 800 ms, whether patients are on medication or not. However, with the bisection method, and intervals ranging from 350 to 1000 ms, Merchant, Luciana, Hooper, Majestic, and Tuite (2008) observe more variability in patients without medication than in participants of a control group.

The work of Merchant and his collaborators is worthy of attention because they have investigated whether it is possible to categorize patients with Parkinson's disease according to their performance in different types of tasks involving temporal information processing whether these tasks are essentially motor or perceptual. Thus, patients had to reproduce intervals, do a synchronization-continuation task and do a bisection task. The results reveal that some patients show a lot of temporal variability in each of the three tasks, while other patients do not differ on each of the tasks from the participants of a control group. However, the results of the two groups of patients do not differ on nontemporal tasks which rather measure perceptual, mnemonic, decision-making, or execution capacities. Besides, the analysis of the continuous interval production task, which makes it possible to separate the temporal and nontemporal shares of the total variability observed, reveals that the variability observed in the most unstable patients in the temporal tasks actually has a temporal origin. Merchant and colleagues also report that the correlations between tasks related to the variability of performance are large among control group participants, but not among patients, particularly those with poorer outcomes; however, after dopaminergic treatment in patients, the correlations between the tasks become larger. It seems that there are subcategories of Parkinson's disease that temporal tasks can highlight.

Emotions

It is known that people who suffer from Parkinson's disease also have difficulty recognizing emotional facial expressions. This difficulty is particularly great when the emotions in question have a negative valence, as is the case with anger or fear. As we will see in Chapter 23, in perceived duration tasks, when duration is delimited by the presentation of a face, the emotional expression contained in this face affects judgments about time.

In a time bisection task where durations of 400 to 1600 ms are delimited by the presentation of neutral faces or expressing joy or sadness, participants in a control group and Parkinson's patients with mild cognitive deficits were compared. Overall, there is an underestimation of duration in patients compared to participants in the control group. More important is the fact that both groups show similar effects with respect to the effect of emotional expression, namely, an overestimation of duration when joyful faces are presented and underestimation when faces express sadness (Mioni et al. 2018).

In another study on the question of the effect of emotion on temporal judgments in Parkinson's patients, the same task was used, but the emotional conditions tested were anger and shame. In addition, the group of patients was divided into two, depending on whether or not they had mild cognitive deficits. The results reveal that the effect of emotional facial expression is apparent in all participants, but is greater in patients with cognitive impairment (Mioni et al. 2016). Compared to patients without cognitive impairment, those who do have impairment underestimate longer intervals and overestimate shorter intervals. The decrease in temporal capacities in patients with cognitive deficits is attributed by these authors to memory function disorders.

Conclusion

Pathologies provide a gateway into the investigation of timing mechanisms. This is particularly true in the case of Parkinson's disease where motor function is very affected. Although the overall results do not allow one to draw a clear portrait of the relative performances of control participants and Parkinson's patients during temporal tasks, the following findings can be extracted from the literature. The deterioration of performance sometimes observed in Parkinson's disease is not limited to motor timing; it is also manifested in perceptual tasks. The overall results help to highlight the critical role of dopamine in timing and temporal perception, the lack of this neurotransmitter being the basis of Parkinson's disease. Finally, it seems that the temporal tasks would make it possible to distinguish two categories of patients suffering from Parkinson's disease.

References

Cerasa, A., Hagberg, G. E., Peppe, A., Bianciardi, M., Gioia, M., Costa, A., Castriota-Scanderbeg, A., Caltagirone, C., & Sabatini, U. (2006). Functional changes in the activity of cerebellum and frontostriatal regions during externally and internally timed movement in Parkinson's disease. *Brain Research Bulletin, 71*, 259–269.

Elsinger, C. L., Rao, S., Zimbelman, J. L., Reynolds, N. C., Blindauer, K. A., & Hoffmann, R. G. (2003). Neural basis for impaired time reproduction in Parkinson's disease: An fMRI study. *Journal of International Neuropsychological Society, 9*, 1088–1098.

Guehl, D., Burbaud, P., Lorenzi, C., Ramos, C., Bioulac, B., Semal, C., & Demany, L. (2008). Auditory temporal processing in Parkinson's disease. *Neuropsychologia, 46*, 2326–2335.

Harrington, D. L., Castillo, G. N., Greenberg, P. A., Song, D. D., Lessig, S., Lee, R. R., & Rao, S. M. (2011). Neurobehavioural mechanisms of temporal processing deficits in Parkinson's disease. *PLoS One, 6*, e17461. doi:10.1371/journal.pone.0017461.

Harrington, D. L., Haaland, K. Y., & Hermanowicz, N. (1998). Temporal processing in the basal ganglia. *Neuropsychology, 12*, 3–12.

Hellström, A., Lang, H., Portin, R., & Rinne, J. (1997). Tone duration discrimination in Parkinson's disease. *Neuropsychologia, 35*, 737–740.

Ivry, R. B., & Keele, S. W. (1989). Timing functions of the cerebellum. *Journal of Cognitive Neuroscience, 1*, 136–152.

Jahanshahi, M., Jones, C. R. G., Zijlmans, J., Katzenschlager, R., Lee, L., Quinn, N., ... Lees, A. J. (2010). Dopaminergic modulation of striato-frontal connectivity during motor timing in Parkinson's disease. *Brain, 133*, 727–745.

Jones, C. R. G., Claassen, D. O., Minhong, Y., Spies, J. R., Malone, T., Dirnberger, G., Jahanshahi, M., & Kubovy, M. (2011). Modeling accuracy and variability of motor timing in treated and untreated Parkinson's disease and healthy controls. *Frontiers in Integrative Neuroscience, 5.* doi:10.3389/fnint.2011.00081.

Jones, C. R. G., & Jahanshahi, M. (2014). Motor and perceptual timing in Parkinson's disease. In H. Merchant & V. de Lafuente (Eds.), *Neurobiology of interval* timing: Advances in experimental medicine and biology (pp. 265–290). New York: Springer-Verlag.

Jones, C. R. G., Malone, T. J. L., Dirnberger, G., Edwards, M., & Jahanshahi, M. (2008). Basal ganglia, dopamine and temporal processing: Performance on three timing tasks on and off medication in Parkinson's disease. *Brain and Cognition, 68*, 30–41.

Joundi, R. A., Brittain, J. S., Green, A. L., Aziz, T. Z., & Jenkinson, N. (2012). High-frequency stimulation of the subthalamic nucleus selectively decreases central variance of rhythmic finger tapping in Parkinson's disease. *Neuropsychologia, 50*, 2460–2466.

Malapani, C., Deweer, B., & Gibbon, J. (2002). Separating storage from retrieval dysfunction of temporal memory in Parkinson's disease. *Journal of Cognitive Neuroscience, 14*, 1–12.

Merchant, H., Luciana, M., Hooper, C., Majestic, S., & Tuite, P. (2008). Interval timing and Parkinson's disease: Heterogeneity in temporal performance. *Experimental Brain Research, 184*, 233–248.

Mioni, G., Grondin, S., Meligrana, L., Perini, F., Bartolomei, L., & Stablum, F. (2018). Effects of happy and sad facial expressions on the perception of time in Parkinson's disease patients with mild cognitive impairment. *Journal of Clinical and Experimental Neuropsychology, 40*, 123–138.

Mioni, G., Meligrana, L., Grondin, S., Perini, F., Bartolomei, L., & Stablum, F. (2016). Effects of emotional facial expression on time perception in patients with Parkinson's disease. *Journal of the International Neuropsychological Society, 22*, 890–899. doi:10.1017/S1355617715000612.

Pagonabarraga, J., & Kulisevsky, J. (2012). Cognitive impairment and dementia in Parkinson's disease. *Neurobiological Disorder, 46*, 590–596.

Pastor, M. A., Jahanshahi, M., Artieda, J., & Obeso, J. A. (1992). Performance of repetitive wrist movements in Parkinson's disease. *Brain, 115*, 875–891.

Perbal, S., Deweer, B., Pillon, B., Vidailhet, M., Dubois, B., & Pouthas, V. (2005). Effects of internal clock and memory disorders on duration reproductions and duration productions in patients with Parkinson's disease. *Brain & Cognition, 58*, 35–48.

Rammsayer, T., & Classen, W. (1997). Impaired temporal discrimination in Parkinson's disease: Temporal processing of brief durations as an indicator of degeneration of dopaminergic neurons in the basal ganglia. *International Journal of Neuroscience, 91*, 45–55.

Riesen, J. M., & Schnider, A. (2001). Time estimation in Parkinson's disease: Normal long duration estimation despite impaired short duration discrimination. *Journal of Neurology, 248*, 27–35.

Smith, J. G., Harper, D. N., Gittings, D., & Abernethy, D. (2007). The effect of Parkinson's disease on time estimation as a function of stimulus duration range and modality. *Brain and Cognition, 64*, 130–143.

Spencer, R. M., & Ivry, R. B. (2005). Comparison of patients with Parkinson's disease or cerebellar lesions in the production of periodic movements involving event-based or emergent timing. *Brain & Cognition, 58*, 84–93.

Wearden, J. H., Smith-Spark, J. H., Cousins, R., Edelstyn, N. M., Cody, F. W., & O'Boyle, D. J. (2008). Stimulus timing by people with Parkinson's disease. *Brain & Cognition, 67*, 264–279.

18 Do People With Traumatic Brain Injury Have Temporal Dysfunctions?

Traumatic brain injury (TBI) often causes damage to the frontal and temporal lobes and it is not uncommon for this to involve diffuse axonal lesions. TBI is often accompanied by a loss of consciousness and a period of confusion. Neurological sequelae can be more or less serious, but long-term cognitive changes are often observed, including attentional deficits, memory loss, and treatment speed. That being said, TBI remains an injury whose nature and extent is difficult to establish precisely, given the heterogeneity of cases. Also, there are only a very few studies that can be used to determine the temporal estimation capabilities of TBI patients and the main results will be listed here (see Mioni, Grondin, & Stablum, 2014).[1]

Perceived Duration

Schmitter-Edgecombe and Rueda (2008) asked TBI participants and a control group to verbally estimate the duration of 10-, 25-, 45-, and 60-second intervals. These authors observed that the estimations are significantly lower in patients under the conditions of 45 and 60 seconds. For example, at 60 seconds, while the average deviation from the target is less than 20 seconds in control group participants, it is more than 25 seconds in patients. In a study where the same method and durations were repeated, Anderson and Schmitter-Edgecombe (2011) observed this time that the durations of 25, 45, and 60 seconds were significantly underestimated by TBI patients compared to the results of the control group, but this observation is only valid for a first evaluation. Later, while deficits in episodic memory persist, the difference between the groups disappears, leading the authors to conclude that episodic memory does not play a critical role in the recovery of TBI patients for the verbal estimation of duration.

When interval production and reproduction methods are used, the conclusions about differences between groups are not the same as those based on the verbal estimate. In a study involving these two methods and involving 5-, 14-, and 18-second intervals, Perbal, Couillet, Azouvi, and Pouthas (2003) found no significant difference between TBI patients and participants in a control group, whether the temporal task is the only one having to be completed (the use of an explicit counting strategy was allowed) or be completed in the context where a cognitive (reading) task has to be done at the same time. Note, however, that participants in both groups tend to underrepresent the target intervals when a nontemporal secondary task is required in addition to the temporal task.

Mioni, Mattalia, and Stablum (2013) compared these two groups with the same two methods, production and reproduction, but this time with shorter intervals. For the perceived duration, their results, obtained with intervals of 500, 1000, and 1500 ms, reveal that there are no differences between the groups for the production task, but that there are for the task of reproduction.

Variability

The overall picture for the variability of temporal tasks is not the same as that observed for the perceived duration. While differences were observed between the groups by Schmitter-Edgecombe and Rueda (2008) for the perceived duration (verbal estimation) of intervals of 45 and 60 s, these authors report no difference in their index of variability, the coefficient of variation, for all durations under study.

In contrast, Perbal et al. (2003), who reported no difference between groups for perceived duration using interval production and reproduction, obtained significant differences between groups for the coefficient of variation for the same tasks, in both experimental conditions under study (with explicit counting and with a reading task in addition to the temporal task). The fact that the dual-task situation has affected the temporal performance of non-patients as much as that of patients shows once again the importance of attention in the processing of temporal information (see Chapter 9).

In addition, during their investigation, Mioni et al. (2013) also used a duration discrimination task (500 to 1500 ms). Similarly, Mioni, Stablum, and Cantagallo (2013) compared groups on interval discrimination with standards of 500 ms and 1300 ms. Interval discrimination tests the level of sensitivity to time, i.e. whether there is more or less variability in judgments. In each of these two studies, TBI patients have much more difficulty than control group participants in discriminating between intervals. Moreover, in the Mioni, Stablum, and Cantagallo study, the temporal order error (Hellström, 1985) is greater in patients than in non-patients, with patients often responding "short" in trials with a standard of 500 ms.

Links With Other Neuropsychological Tasks

Studies of the temporal information processing of TBI patients are often accompanied by other neuropsychological tests. For example, compared to non-patients, TBIs have slower reaction times and lower scores on tests evaluating working memory or episodic memory (Perbal et al., 2003). In fact, in TBI, neuromotor slowing and cognitive disorders, especially those of attention, are documented (Stuss, 2011; Stuss et al., 1989).

More specifically, Perbal et al. (2003) report that the variability of the reproductive task is closely related to scores for working memory and processing speed, whereas the variability of the production task is closely related only to the scores for processing speed. In fact, they conclude that the weaker temporal performance of TBI patients is not due to a problem of the timing mechanisms per se; it would rather be related to attentional, working memory or processing speed problems. Meyers and Levin (1992) noted that the TBI patients having more success on an attention span test tend to under-reproduce 5- or 10-second intervals, while those with poorer scores tend to over-reproduce such intervals.

For the duration discrimination task, Mioni et al. (2013) report, for 1300-ms intervals, significant correlations between temporal performance and working memory and processing speed tasks, and this finding applies to both TBI patients and non-patients; at 500 ms, these significant links are limited to patients. In addition, Mioni et al. (2013) report significant correlations between performances obtained in 500-, 1000-, and 1500-ms interval reproduction and discrimination tasks, for which the control and TBI groups are different, and tests measuring attention, working memory, and executive functions. However, they do not observe such links with the interval production task for which the two groups do not differ. Finally, note that Schmitter-Edgecombe and Rueda (2008), as well as Anderson and Schmitter-Edgecombe (2011), do not report any significant link between the verbal estimations of their TBI patients and certain clinical characteristics, such as the severity of the trauma or the time elapsed since the incident causing the injury.

Conclusion

It seems that people who suffer from TBI do not stand out much from control group participants when looking at perceived duration as measured by long interval production and reproduction tasks. Nevertheless, with a temporal estimation task, TBI patients seem to underestimate very long intervals more than do non-patients. Where the two groups differ the most is the variability of performance, whether it is the estimation, the production or the reproduction of long intervals, or the discrimination of short intervals. Finally, the problems encountered by the TBI patients would not have temporal roots, strictly speaking, but would arise from other cognitive deficits.

Note

1. The overview of the studies does not include those on time-based prospective memory which consists in remembering that at some point in the future something will have to be done. In such a task, TBI patients tend to monitor time more often and be less specific than non-patients; also the performances of this "temporal task" are strongly related to the executive functions, in particular the updating and inhibition skills (Mioni, Stablum, McClintock, & Cantagallo, 2012).

References

Anderson, J. W., & Schmitter-Edgecombe, M. (2011). Recovery of time estimation following moderate to severe traumatic brain injury. *Neuropsychology, 25,* 36–44.

Hellström, Å. (1985). The time-order error and its relatives: Mirrors of cognitive processes in comparing. *Psychological Bulletin, 97,* 35–61.

Meyers, C., & Levin, H. S. (1992). Temporal perception following closed head injury: Relationship of orientation and attention span. *Neuropsychiatry, Neuropsychology, and Behavioural Neurology, 5,* 28–32.

Mioni, G., Grondin, S., & Stablum, F. (2014). Temporal dysfunction in traumatic brain injury patients: Primary or secondary impairment? *Frontiers in Human Neuroscience, 8,* 269. doi:10.3389/fnhum.2014.00269.

Mioni, G., Mattalia, G., & Stablum, F. (2013). Time perception in severe traumatic brain injury patients: A study comparing different methodologies. *Brain & Cognition, 81,* 305–312.

Mioni, G., Stablum, F., & Cantagallo, A. (2013). Time discrimination in traumatic brain injury patients. *Journal of Clinical and Experimental Neuropsychology, 35,* 90–102.

Mioni, G., Stablum, F., McClintock, M. S., & Cantagallo, A. (2012). Time-based prospective memory in severe traumatic brain injury patients: The involvement of executive functions and time perception. *Journal of the International Neuropsychological Society, 18,* 697–705.

Perbal, S., Couillet, J., Azouvi, P., & Pouthas, V. (2003). Relationship between time estimation, memory, attention, and processing speed in patients with severe traumatic brain injury. *Neuropsychologia, 41,* 1599–1610.

Schmitter-Edgecombe, M., & Rueda, A. D. (2008). Time estimation and episodic memory following traumatic brain injury. *Journal of Clinical and Experimental Neuropsychology, 30,* 212–223.

Stuss, D. T. (2011). Traumatic brain injury: Relation to executive dysfunction and the frontal lobes. *Current Opinion in Neurology, 24,* 584–589.

Stuss, D. T., Stethem, L. L., Hugenholtz, H., Picton, T., Pivik, J., & Richard, M. T. (1989). Reaction time after head injury: Fatigue, divided and focused attention, and consistency of performance. *Journal of Neurology, Neurosurgery, and Psychiatry, 52,* 742–748.

19 Are Language and Reading Impairments Caused by Temporal Information Processing Problems?

Despite decades of research on this subject, it is difficult to provide a definitive answer to this question. There is some controversy as to whether a deficit in temporal information processing mechanisms is the main factor causing reading problems, or speech and language impairments (SLI). In fact, this question again shows the nuances needed in research and the difficulty of deciding when debates are needed during scientific work. In any case, as will be seen, the question is worth asking. But this time, the temporal processing of interest mainly affects judgments about the order of arrival of sensory stimuli or the ability to detect an interruption in a continuous signal, rather than explicit judgments about duration.

Speech and Language Impairments

We refer to SLI when a delay in the development of speech and language skills that cannot be attributed to impaired hearing or other developmental disorders such as general cognitive impairment. Such a disorder affects nearly 7% of children (Leonard, 1998).

The reasons that may explain why SLI occurs remain unclear, but a hypothesis, which has become classical, was raised nearly 50 years ago by Paula Tallal. According to Tallal, the skills needed to process temporal information are at the root of these impairments (see Tallal, 2003; Tallal, Galaburda, Llinas, & von Euler, 1993). In fact, it must be understood that the acquisition of language originally consists in correctly perceiving the sounds of speech. This perception becomes possible only when the stream of words can be segmented into significant units. This is a difficult task, considering the rapid rhythm of succession of phonemes in speech.

As early as 1973, Tallal and Piercy had shown that, compared to children with no language impairment, those with one have a much greater difficulty in determining the temporal order of nonverbal auditory stimuli when the duration between these stimuli is 150 ms or less. Similar observations have also focused on the use of syllables that follow each other rapidly (Tallal & Piercy, 1974, 1975). In a large study involving over 160 variables known to be related to a language disorder, 98% of children in the study were correctly classified as having or not having a disorder, based on six variables, each involving temporal processing skills (Tallal, Stark, & Mellits, 1985). A longitudinal study has even shown that the capabilities to process information rapidly in the auditory mode in early childhood allow the identification of children at risk of developing language impairments (Benasich & Tallal, 2002).

If the basic problem depends on temporal processing skills, the deficits associated with this processing should not be limited to the sole use of auditory signals. Thus, children aged six to nine with specific language impairment were compared to children in a control group on two temporal order judgment tasks. In one task, both stimuli were visual and the children had to indicate which one, the one on the left or the one on the right, appeared first; in the other task, they had to indicate whether a sound or light had appeared first. Children with specific language impairment had more difficulty doing each of these two tasks (Grondin et al., 2007). The same children, who had scores comparable to that of children of the control group for nonverbal IQ, were also worse (more variability) in producing series of one-second intervals. Also, the visual test alone was sufficient to predict whether a child belongs to one or the other of the groups (with vs. without impairment) under study with a 78% accuracy rate.

All the results reported previously suggest that the hypothesis of a temporal processing deficit as a causal factor of specific language impairments is viable. However, some authors oppose this interpretation (Catts, Adlof, Hogan, & Weismer, 2005; Mody, Studdert-Kennedy, & Brady, 1997). In particular, Bishop, Carlyon, Deeks, and Bishop (1999) report that many children with specific language impairment do not show any temporal information-processing deficits; moreover, some children with a temporal information-processing deficit do not have specific language impairment.

Reading Impairments

The repercussions of temporal information processing problems is not be limited to oral language, but also extend to learning to read (Farmer & Klein, 1995). Oral language requires a temporal organization of acoustic elements that define distinct phonological units, in addition to the acquisition of the succession of intonations, pauses, and changes in intensities and frequencies that determine the prosody (the rhythm of language). Ultimately, the inability to correctly perceive the phonemes causing the problem of processing temporal information would hinder the learning of reading. If it is not possible to establish a coherent classification of the sounds of speech and the words they compose, it becomes difficult to associate these sounds with the graphemes that correspond to them.

Tallal's developmental studies of temporal information processing were not limited to language impairments. Tallal was also interested in the role of temporal processing in children with learning difficulties in reading. A reading disability is diagnosed as such when the reading ability is significantly worse than that normally expected of a child of a given age, taking into consideration their sensory and intellectual skills and the teaching received. This disorder is often called dyslexia, or developmental dyslexia (Ramus, 2003); it is not a mere delay in learning. Tallal (1980) found that compared to children having no problem, those with a reading learning disability also find it difficult to perceive the order of arrival of stimuli separated by 8 to 305 ms.

In a study of children with different levels of reading efficiency, the hypothesis of a temporal processing deficit was tested using gap detection, temporal order judgment, interval discrimination, and interval reproduction (Plourde, Gamache, Laflamme, & Grondin, 2017). For each of the tasks in this study, children were tested under conditions where the stimuli were auditory and under conditions where the stimuli were visual. There was a significant positive correlation between reading skills and each task used in the study, and this holds true for both sensory modality conditions. In other words, the temporal deficits in children with reading difficulties were global and went beyond the processing within a given sensory modality. Finally, among the tasks used in this study, it is with the gap detection of a visual signal that one can most effectively predict the child's reading skills.

The possibility of observing differences between children with a reading disability and those with normal development could depend on the length of the intervals under study. In the article by Plourde et al. (2017), the intervals to be reproduced lasted 1 or 1.7 s and differences were observed. When longer intervals are under study, there is apparently no difference between groups in the reproduction (Gooch et al., 2011; Moll, Göbel, Gooch, Landerl, & Snowling, 2016) or production tasks (McGee, Brodeur, Symons, Andrade, & Fahie, 2004). In Gooch et al. (2011), intervals to be reproduced lasted 2 to 10 s; in the same study though, the authors observed differences in the ability to discriminate intervals defined by continuous sounds ranging from 400 to 1200 ms.

Phonological awareness is at the heart of the link between temporal processing and reading skills in general. Phonological awareness is the ability to consciously access and use phonological representations. When learning to read, this phonological awareness makes it possible to match phonological and orthographic codes. Malenfant et al. (2012) have shown, in a study of eight-year-old children with normal development, that phonological awareness is a mediator of the link between temporal processing and reading understanding. In fact, the link between the temporal order judgments between two auditory stimuli and reading passes mainly via phonological awareness, whereas the link between temporal order judgments involving a sound and a light and reading is more direct. Such results support the view that reading requires the contribution of two pathways, a phonological one related to hearing, and an orthographic one related to the visual modality.

Conclusion

There is no doubt that children with a specific language or reading impairment will often have difficulty performing tasks involving time resolution.

The question of whether SLI or reading disorder are caused by a deficiency of the temporal information processing mechanisms (detecting a discontinuity in a stimulus, determining the order of arrival of two auditory stimuli, two visual stimuli, or two stimuli, one visual and the other auditory) remains tricky. Temporal processing, however, would be at the heart of the development of the phonological awareness, which is itself necessary for learning to read. But beyond the question of temporal processing, an important question is whether language and reading disorders are different manifestations of the same underlying problem (a general disorder of language development), if they partly share the same cause (phonological processing for example), or if they are distinct, with different causes, even if they sometimes occur in the same individual (Bishop & Snowling, 2004).

References

Benasich, A. A., & Tallal, P. (2002). Infant discrimination of rapid auditory cues predicts later language impairment. *Behavioural Brain Research, 136*, 31–49.

Bishop, D. V. M., Carlyon, R. P., Deeks, J. M., & Bishop, S. J. (1999). Auditory temporal processing impairment: Neither necessary nor sufficient for causing language impairment in children. *Journal of Speech, Language and Hearing Research, 42*, 1295–1310.

Bishop, D. V. M., & Snowling, M. J. (2004). Developmental dyslexia and specific language impairment: Same or different? *Psychological Bulletin, 130*, 858–886.

Catts, H. W., Adlof, S. M., Hogan, T., & Weismer, S. E. (2005). Are specific language impairment and dyslexia distinct disorders? *Journal of Speech, Language and Hearing Research, 48*, 1378–1396.

Farmer, M. E., & Klein, R. M. (1995). The evidence for a temporal processing deficit linked to dyslexia: A review. *Psychonomic Bulletin & Review, 2*, 460–493.

Gooch, D., Snowling, M., & Hulme, C. (2011). Time perception, phonological skills and executive function in children with dyslexia and/or ADHD symptoms. *Journal of Child Psychology and Psychiatry, 52*, 195–203.

Grondin, S., Dionne, G., Malenfant, N., Plourde, M., Cloutier, M., & Jean, C. (2007). Temporal processing skills of children with and without specific language impairment. *Canadian Journal of Speech Language Pathology and Audiology, 31*, 38–46.

Leonard, L. B. (1998). *Children with specific language impairment*. Cambridge, MA: The MIT Press.

Malenfant, N., Grondin, S., Boivin, M., Forget-Dubois, N., Robaey, P., & Dionne, G. (2012). The contribution of temporal processing skills to reading comprehension in 8-year-olds: Evidence for a mediation effect of phonological awareness. *Child Development, 83*, 1332–1346.

McGee, R., Brodeur, D., Symons, D., Andrade, B., & Fahie, C. (2004). Time perception: Does it distinguish ADHD and RD children in a clinical sample? *Journal of Abnormal Child Psychology, 32*(5), 481–490.

Mody, M., Studdert-Kennedy, M., & Brady, S. (1997). Speech perception deficits in poor readers: Auditory processing or phonological coding? *Journal of Experimental Child Psychology, 64*(2), 199–231.

Moll, K., Göbel, S. M., Gooch, D., Landerl, K., & Snowling, M. J. (2016). Cognitive risk factors for specific learning disorder: Processing speed, temporal processing, and working memory. *Journal of Learning Disabilities, 49*, 272–281.

Plourde, M., Gamache, P.-L., Laflamme, V., & Grondin, S. (2017). Using time-processing skills to predict reading abilities in elementary school children. *Timing & Time Perception, 5*, 35–60.

Ramus, F. (2003). Developmental dyslexia: Specific, phonological deficit or general sensorimotor dysfunction? *Current Opinion in Neurobiology, 13*, 212–218.

Tallal, P. (1980). Auditory temporal perception, phonics, and reading disabilities in children. *Brain and Language, 9*, 182–198.

Tallal, P. (2003). Language learning disabilities: Integrating research approaches. *Current Directions in Psychological Science, 12*, 206–211.

Tallal, P., Galaburda, A., Llinas, R. R., & von Euler, C. (Eds.). (1993). *Annals of the New York academy of sciences, vol. 682: Temporal information processing in the nervous system: Special reference to dyslexia and dysphasia.* New York: New York Academy of Sciences.

Tallal, P., & Piercy, M. (1973). Developmental aphasia: Impaired rate of nonverbal processing as a function of sensory modality. *Neuropsychologia, 11*, 389–398.

Tallal, P., & Piercy, M. (1974). Developmental aphasia: Rate of auditory processing and selective impairment of consonant perception. *Neuropsychologia, 12*, 83–93.

Tallal, P., & Piercy, M. (1975). Developmental aphasia: The perception of brief vowels and extended stop consonants. *Neuropsychologia, 13*, 69–74.

Tallal, P., Stark, R. E., & Mellits, E. D. (1985). Identification of language-impaired children on the basis of rapid perception and production skills. *Brain and Language, 25*(2), 314–322.

20 Can Time and Rhythm Be Useful in Physical Rehabilitation?

The virtues of music have long been known to create social cohesion (see Chapter 22) and contribute to individual well-being. What we are now realizing more and more is the full potential of rehabilitation offered by music, especially when motor functions need to be restored. In fact, the rhythmic aspect is at the heart of this potential, of the exploitation of what allows brain plasticity. And in parallel with the possibilities offered by rhythm, time estimation can also be used in some forms of training aimed at physical rehabilitation.

Rhythmic Training

The efficiency of rhythm in rehabilitation is based on audition (Rossignol & Melvill Jones, 1976; Thaut & Abiru, 2010). It is the rhythmic auditory stimulations that will be most likely to contribute to motor rehabilitation, because of the close relationship between the auditory and motor areas of the brain. For example, in a task where participants have to synchronize finger taps (motor task) with a more or less varying tempo, the magnitude of the neural responses at the primary auditory cortex is related to the magnitude of these tempo variations (Tecchio, Salustri, Thaut, Pasqualetti, & Rossini, 2000). Such observations indicate that this part of the brain is at the source of the motor adaptations required to maintain synchronization.

The positive influence that rhythmic activity can have on motor skills has been applied to situations where a pathology causes problems to a motor component. For example, Parkinson's disease can greatly affect locomotion ability. Thus, training in rhythmic auditory stimulation has been given to people suffering from this disease. Such training involves knowing the initial speed of the gait of each participant in order to synchronize the auditory stimulation to the rhythm of the gait for eventually increasing this rhythm slightly. This increase not only increases the rate of walking, but also the length of the stride (McIntosh, Brown, Rice, & Thaut, 1997). Training of this kind, if continued for a few weeks, reduces the variability of muscle and leg activity and thus stabilizes gait (Miller, Thaut, McIntosh, & Rice, 1996).

The effectiveness of rhythmic auditory stimulation for improving the walk of Parkinson's patients seems now well established. However, this same type of training also seems to benefit people who have suffered a stroke. Among the problems consecutive to a stroke, there are of course those related to walking. Rhythmic training allows for observing improvements in different gait parameters, such as step frequency and stride length (Thaut, McIntosh, & Rice, 1997; see Abiru, Mihara, & Yoshii, 2009). It also allows improving the effectiveness of the swinging of the arms that accompanies the gait (Ford, Wagenaar, & Newell, 2007).

In fact, the potential of rhythm training in rehabilitation is not limited to cases of Parkinson's disease or stroke. For example, in addition to the case of stuttering described next, there is an improvement with rhythmic training of the attentional abilities of 6 to 12-year-old boys with attention deficits (see Shaffer et al., 2001). This training consists of a task requiring the synchronization of a series of continuous hand taps with a metronome, after which a series of feedback is provided to the participant revealing how far the taps were from the reference rhythm. Such training has improved not only attention, but also reading skills and motor control.

The Case of Stuttering

We know that people with a stuttering disorder have a deficit in many tasks that require temporal information processing. In particular, there is an overestimation of long intervals by stutterers when the interval to be estimated includes a verbal component, such as reading aloud or conversing with an experimenter (Ezrati-Vinacour, & Levin, 2001). In fact, the weaker the verbal fluency of stuttering people is, the longer their temporal estimations are (Barasch, Guitar, McAuley, & Absher, 2000).

Besides, stuttering people have more difficulty than non-stutterers in discriminating short time intervals and rhythmic sequences (Wieland, McAuley, Dilley, & Chang, 2015) and have difficulty in synchronizing finger taps with a rhythm dictated by a metronome (Falk, Müller, & Dalla Bella, 2015). Olander, Smith, and Zelaznik (2010) even argue that child stutterers having the most difficulty in a motor synchronization task are the most likely to have their disorder persisting during adulthood. In fact, the stuttering disorder could be the result of coordination problems between breathing, phonation and articulation, lack of synchronism between language and motor planning, or difficulty in generating temporal sequences (Park & Logan, 2015).

Given the importance that temporal processing and rhythm production appear to have in stuttering, one would expect a reduction in the disorder if interventions such as the induction of rhythm were made to improve verbal fluency. In this regard, different techniques have been put forward, among which we note reciting with someone (in chorus) or reading aloud with simultaneous listening of a recording where the same text is read. Such an approach reduces stuttering (Freeman & Armson, 1998), just as the use of a metronome improves the fluidity of speech (Etchell, Johnson, & Sowman, 2014), but this improvement does not necessarily allow to reach the level of comfort observed with non-stutterers (Boutsen, Brutten, & Watts, 2000).

With recent advances in neuroscience, there is growing evidence that the cortical and subcortical structures responsible for processing temporal information of stuttering people are at the root of the stuttering problem (Chang, Chow, Wieland, & McAuley, 2016; Etchell et al., 2014). The problem could be in the connection between the putamen and the supplementary motor area (Chang et al., 2016). For their part, based on an investigation using functional magnetic resonance imaging, Toyomura, Fujii, and Kuriki (2011) report that, in a task involving speech without the aid of a metronome, the activation of basal ganglia is higher in non-stuttering than in stuttering people, but there is no difference between groups in a condition where non-stutterers benefit from the rhythmic support that a metronome provides. Finally, with this support, there is an increase in the activation of the superior temporal gyrus in stutterers.

Temporal Equivalence

Another form of time perception can be used in the field of physical rehabilitation. In fact, mental training, and more specifically motor imaging, is used to remedy motor problems, whether it is walking or complex motor activity such as writing (Malouin, Jackson, & Richards, 2013).

Imagining an action or doing it physically requires much of the same neural networks. Mental imagery may not be as effective as physical training, but it is far more effective than doing nothing. Thus, mental imagery offers a way to undertake physical rehabilitation before physical training is possible; this allows one to take a step ahead in a physical rehabilitation program (Pascual-Leone et al., 1995). In fact, the addition of mental imagery to such a program reduces the number of physical repetitions and, as a result, reduces physical fatigue resulting from physical training.

A good indicator of the level of accuracy of motor imaging is the use of chronometry. When using mental imagery in a clinical setting, it is recommended to compare the duration of the actual movement with that of the mental performance of a movement. With good temporal equivalence, we can ensure that a patient has the right temporal representation of the task.

Note that mental imagery is also widely used in the field of sports performance and is a very popular research avenue (Moran, Guillot, Macintyre, & Collet, 2012). In particular, athletes are expected to accurately reproduce the duration normally taken by a sports action performed physically. For example, the temporal equivalence between mental imagery and the physical performance of expert divers is higher than that of mid-level divers (Reed, 2002). In the latter, the visualization time is slower than the actual execution time.

Conclusion

Clearly, time and rhythm can be very helpful when accidents, injuries, or illnesses interfere with the good functioning of the motor system. Thus, rhythmic training makes it possible to improve the various parameters used to evaluate the effectiveness of the gait. The integration of motor imagery, particularly with consideration of temporal equivalence, can help to increase the effectiveness of physical rehabilitation. Rhythmic training also allows stuttering people to speak more fluently. Finally, outside the sphere of rehabilitation, temporal equivalence offers a key to intervene in another avenue of motor skills, that of sports performance.

References

Abiru, M., Mihara, B., & Yoshii, F. (2009). Approach to therapy: Neurologic disease and music therapy. *Annual Review of Neurology, 25,* 66–74.

Barasch, C. T., Guitar, B., McAuley, R. J., & Absher, R. G. (2000). Disfluency and time perception. *Journal of Speech, Language and Hearing Research, 43*(6), 1429–1439.

Boutsen, F. R., Brutten, G. J., & Watts, C. R. (2000). Timing and intensity variability in the metronomic speech of stuttering and nonstuttering speakers. *Journal of Speech, Language, and Hearing Research, 43,* 513–520.

Chang, S. E., Chow, H. M., Wieland, E. A., & McAuley, J. D. (2016). Relation between functional connectivity and rhythm discrimination in children who do and do not stutter. *NeuroImage: Clinical, 12,* 442–450.

Etchell, A. C., Johnson, B. W., & Sowman, P. F. (2014). Beta oscillations, timing, and stuttering. *Frontiers in Human Neuroscience, 8,* 1036. doi:10.3389/fnhum.2014.01036.

Ezrati-Vinacour, R., & Levin, I. (2001). Time estimation by adults who stutter. *Journal of Speech, Language, and Hearing Research, 44,* 144–155.

Falk, S., Müller, T., & Dalla Bella, S. (2015). Non-verbal sensorimotor timing deficits in children and adolescent who stutter. *Frontiers in Psychology, 6.* doi:10.3389/fpsyg.2015.00847.

Ford, M., Wagenaar, R., & Newell, K. (2007). The effects of auditory rhythms and instruction on walking patterns in individuals post stroke. *Gait and Posture, 26,* 150–155.

Freeman, K., & Armson, J. (1998). Extent and stability of stuttering reduction during choral reading. *Journal of Speech-Language Pathology and Audiology, 22,* 188–202.

Malouin, F., Jackson, P. L., & Richards, C. L. (2013). Towards the integration of mental practice in rehabilitation programs: A critical review. *Frontiers in Human Neurosciences, 7,* 576. doi:10.3389/fnhum.2013.00576.

McIntosh, G. C., Brown, S. H., Rice, R. R., & Thaut, M. H. (1997). Rhythmic auditory-motor facilitation of gait patterns in patients with Parkinson's disease. *Journal of Neurology, Neurosurgery, and Psychiatry, 62,* 22–26.

Miller, R. A., Thaut, M. H., McIntosh, G. C., & Rice, R. R. (1996). Components of EMG symmetry and variability in parkinsonian and healthy elderly gait. *Electroencephalography and Clinical Neurophysiology, 101,* 1–7.

Moran, A., Guillot, A., Macintyre, T., & Collet, C. (2012). Re-imagining motor imagery: Building bridges between cognitive neuroscience and sport psychology. *British Journal of Psychology, 103,* 224–247.

Olander, L., Smith, A., & Zelaznik, H. N. (2010). Evidence that a motor timing deficit is a factor in the development of stuttering. *Journal of Speech, Language, and Hearing Research, 53*(4), 876–886.

Park, J., & Logan, K. J. (2015). The role of temporal speech cues in facilitating the fluency of adults who stutter. *Journal of Fluency Disorders, 46,* 41–55.

Pascual-Leone, A., Nguyet, D., Cohen, L. G., Brasil-Neto, J. P., Cammarota, A., & Hallett, M. (1995). Modulation of muscle responses evoked by transcranial magnetic stimulation during the acquisition of new fine motor skills. *Journal of Neurophysiology, 74,* 1037–1045.

Reed, C. L. (2002). Chronometric comparisons of imagery to action: Visualizing versus physically performing springboard dives. *Memory & Cognition, 30,* 1169–1178.

Rossignol, S., & Melvill Jones, G. (1976). Audio-spinal influences in man studied by the H-reflex and its possible role in rhythmic movement synchronization to sound. *Electroencephalography and Clinical Neurophysiology, 41,* 83–92.

Shaffer, R. J., Jacokes, L. E., Cassily, J. F., Greenspan, S. I., Tuchman, R., F., & Stemmer, P. J. (2001). Effect of interactive metronome training on children with ADHD. *American Journal of Occupational Therapy, 55,* 155–162.

Tecchio, F., Salustri, C., Thaut, M. H., Pasqualetti, P., & Rossini, P. M. (2000). Conscious and preconscious adaptation to rhythmic auditory stimuli: A magnetoencephalographic study of human brain responses. *Experimental Brain Research, 135,* 222–230.

Thaut, M. H., & Abiru, M. (2010). Rhythmic auditory stimulation in rehabilitation. *Music Perception, 27,* 263–269.

Thaut, M. H., McIntosh, G. C., & Rice, R. R. (1997). Rhythmic facilitation of gait training in hemiparetic stroke rehabilitation. *Journal of Neurological Sciences, 151,* 207–212.

Toyomura, A., Fujii, T., & Kuriki, S. (2011). Effect of external auditory pacing on the neural activity of stuttering speakers. *NeuroImage, 57,* 1507–1516.

Wieland, E. A., McAuley, J. D., Dilley, L. C., & Chang, S.-E. (2015). Evidence for a rhythm perception deficit in children who stutter. *Brain and Language, 144,* 26–34.

Part 3
Personal and Social Time

21 Are Musicians Better at Perceiving Time?

In Chapter 8, we learned that it is possible to reduce, with a training lasting 60 to 90 minutes, the variability of nonmusicians in a task involving continuous production of short time intervals (Madison, Karampela, Ullén, & Holm, 2013). However, the authors of this study report that the level of production after such training is comparable to that achieved by musicians in other studies using a similar method. Part of the difference between musicians and nonmusicians observed in some studies of temporal judgments may not be due to long musical training. Nevertheless, there are many studies that provide strong support for the idea that musicians are better than other people when performing a task requiring skills for processing temporal information. Moreover, the fact that a classical test for assessing musical aptitude, the Seashore Measures of Musical Talents (Seashore, Lewis, & Saetveit, 1956), includes elements specific to duration, is certainly indicative of the importance given to temporal processing in music. In addition to assessing the ability to distinguish tone, timbre and loudness, the Seashore allows you to evaluate tonal memory and, above all, sensitivity to rhythm and duration.

Some Facts

The superiority of musicians, when compared to nonmusicians, has been demonstrated in tasks with a motor component, such as the production or reproduction of time sequences (Drake, Penel, & Bigand, 2000). For example, when typing at the same time as the sound of a metronome, the asynchrony between this sound and the tap is much smaller among musicians than among nonmusicians (Aschersleben, 2002). In fact, nonmusicians tend to anticipate, to tap a little too early, which is not the case for musicians (Repp, 2005).

There is also a big difference between musicians and nonmusicians when it is necessary to reproduce long intervals (from 6 to 24 s) in conditions where a strategy can be used to hold time. Whether counting or singing (*Au clair de la lune*) at a personal rate, the musicians arrive much closer to the target, and have much less variability over the tests than nonmusicians (Grondin & Killeen, 2009). This difference between these two groups is hardly surprising considering the importance of counting in music. Furthermore, from 6 to 24 s, the coefficient of variation remains about the same for nonmusicians, whereas for musicians it is significantly lower at 24 than at 6 s.

Finally, musical training could even allow better estimation of the duration of a song (Panagiotidi & Samartzi, 2013). At the end of an experiment with teenagers (12 to 15 years old), these authors report that nonmusicians are much more likely than musicians to overestimate the duration of sad songs and to underestimate the length of happy songs.

Resistance to Certain Effects and Difficulty Levels

Musical training seems to be able to reduce the scope of some of the robust effects of time distortion encountered in the literature. Among these effects, there is one known as Vierordt's law which consists in a tendency, in a given distribution of intervals, to underestimate the long intervals and to overestimate the shortest ones (see Chapter 2). In one of their experiments, Aagten-Murphy, Cappagli, and Burr (2014) asked their participants to reproduce intervals that ranged around central values of 671, 847, or 1023 ms. Three methods of reproduction were used: holding the spacebar for the duration of the interval to be reproduced, hitting the bar twice to indicate the beginning and the end, or hitting the bar once, at the moment when should arrive the third of three signals so that the interval between the second and third signals is of the same length as that between the first two signals. With each of these three methods, the regression effect was robust in nonmusicians while musicians' reproductions remained close to the target range.

Nazari, Ebneabbasi, Jalalkamali, and Grondin (2018) tested the relative vulnerability of musicians and nonmusicians to the classic oddball effect. When identical stimuli are presented successively, there is a reaction to the presentation of a different stimulus. Notably, if the discordant stimulus differs from others because of its duration, this different stimulus is generally perceived to be longer than the others (Tse, Intriligator, Rivest, & Cavanagh, 2004). Such a discrepancy effect has long been known in the field of electroencephalography as mismatch negativity (MMN, see Chapter 12). For the same experimental conditions, the impression that the duration of the discordant stimulus is longer is manifested in nonmusicians, but not in musicians (Nazari et al., 2018). This difference between the groups is probably due to the fact that the efficiency of temporal processing by the musicians protects them against this oddball effect. In fact, the MMN is modulated by the musical training. In an experiment where a sound arrives every 150 ms, if a sound suddenly arrives much too early (50 ms too early), there is an MMN among musicians and nonmusicians. However, if the sound arrives 20 ms too early, there is a MMN in the musicians, but not in the nonmusicians who apparently cannot detect this temporal change (Rüsseler, Altenmüller, Nager, Kohlmetz, & Münte, 2001). Musical training would therefore be accompanied by a change in neural activity. In short, for difficult tasks, nonmusicians do not show any effect of MMN, and for tasks too easy that lead to an oddball effect among nonmusicians, musicians do not show any sign of this effect.

Another study shows that the difficulty level of a task can modulate the magnitude of the differences between the groups of musicians and nonmusicians. Take for instance the following condition where very distinct sequences (different tempos) of a given musical extract are presented: a standard tempo and a comparison tempo (constant stimulus method), with a short pause between the two presentations. For this task where the tempos must be discriminated, the musicians are better than the nonmusicians (Grondin & Laforest, 2004). If the tempo, after the presentation of the standard, begins to vary slowly before reaching the value of the comparison tempos, the task becomes much more difficult for the nonmusicians, but not for the musicians; the difference in sensitivity between the groups then becomes even more obvious. In fact, we know that, unlike nonmusicians, musicians are able to detect very subtle time changes occurring within cycles of rhythmical patterns (Jones & Yee, 1997).

Finally, other studies show that the difficulty level of the task could be decisive in detecting differences between the groups of musicians and nonmusicians. For example, Yamada and Tsumura (1998) report that the difference between pianists and novices, relative to the temporal variability in the execution of motions on a piano keyboard or on an aluminium keyboard, only appears when these motions become complex (multiple finger tapping, in opposition to single finger tapping).

Generalization of the Competence

The superiority of musicians over nonmusicians was observed by Rammsayer and Altenmüller (2006) in a series of temporal tasks in the auditory modality. In particular, this difference is manifested in a task involving rhythm and in three tasks dealing with the discrimination of duration. However, the temporal generalization tasks used in their study do not reveal any differences between musicians and nonmusicians. Later, Rammsayer, Buttkus, and Altenmüller (2012) asked 40 musicians and 40 people without musical experience to perform a series of temporal tasks: rhythm perception, temporal fusion, duration discrimination (standard of 50 ms and 1 s) and temporal generalization (standard of 75 ms and 1 s). To delimit time, all these tasks included the use of auditory stimuli during some experimental sessions and of visual stimuli in other sessions. In all cases, except for temporal generalization, there is a superiority of audition over vision. This superiority of audition over vision for temporal performance is not surprising (see Chapter 7). Indeed, in this study by Rammsayer and his collaborators (2012), the most important observation is that in all cases, except for generalization, musicians perform better than nonmusicians. In other words, the superiority of the musicians for the processing of temporal information is not limited to audition which, obviously, is at the heart of musical activity. It extends to the visual modality. Such an observation, supported by subsequent statistical analysis (principal component analysis), led the authors to assume that there is an internal mechanism for general timing, a mechanism independent of task and sensory modality. This conclusion is consistent with the fact that, in a study on reducing the effect of Vierordt's law, Aagten-Murphy et al. (2014) report that the benefits of musical training are not limited to the reproduction of intervals delimited by sounds, but extend to the conditions where the intervals are delimited by visual stimuli.

Some studies, however, encourage some caution about the effects of music training. In a study with 17 musicians and 22 nonmusicians, Güçlü, Sevinc, and Canbeyli (2011) report that, for interval discrimination (standards at 0.5 s and 3 s), the results are better in auditory modality than in the tactile modality; but more importantly, their results indicate that the superiority of musicians over nonmusicians seems to be limited to the auditory modality. Moreover, in a study on the judgment of the arrival moment of the last of a series of six stimuli, auditory or tactile, Lim, Bradshaw, Nicholls, and Altenmüller (2003) report that there are no differences between musicians and nonmusicians.

Conclusion

Are musicians better than other people when performing a temporal task? In many tasks requiring a temporal judgment, it seems that yes, the musicians stand out for their excellence. This excellence may have been the result of a musical training where the temporal component must be mastered, as if it were possible to improve a temporal performance. But the question remains whether musicians have not just become musicians because of this ability to cope with temporal demands.

We know that the sensory-cognitive aspects of musical training generate a certain cerebral plasticity that improves not only the processing of music, but also that of other sounds (Habib & Besson, 2009; Kraus & Chandrasekaran, 2010). On such a basis, we can believe that the expertise of the musicians developed during their training would include as a secondary benefit a generalized capacity to process temporal information. But when we know that temporal information processing capabilities are closely linked to attention (see Chapter 9), we can also ask ourselves whether the benefits of training do not come basically from better attentional capabilities, or perhaps even from some motivational aspects when doing laboratory tasks as musicians (McAuley, Henry, Wedd, Pleskac, & Cesario, 2012).

Beyond the temporal question, that of musical talent remains mysterious. Some insist that practice alone can lead to expertise (Ericsson, Krampe, & Tesch-Romer, 1993), but other researchers argue the importance of a genetic factor in explaining musical performance (Hambrick & Tucker-Drob, 2015; Platz, Kopiez, Lehmann, & Wolf, 2014). Ullén, Hambrick, and Mosing (2016) propose instead a multifactorial model involving an interaction between genes and the environment.

References

Aagten-Murphy, D., Cappagli, G., & Burr, D. (2014). Musical training generalises across modalities and reveals efficient and adaptive mechanisms for reproducing temporal intervals. *Acta Psychologica, 147,* 25–33.

Aschersleben, G. (2002). Temporal control of movements in sensorimotor synchronization. *Brain and Cognition, 48,* 66–79.

Drake, C., Penel, A., & Bigand, E. (2000). Tapping in time with mechanically and expressively performed music. *Music Perception, 18,* 1–25.

Ericsson, K. A., Krampe, R. T., & Tesch-Romer, C. (1993). The role of deliberate practice in the acquisition of expert performance. *Psychological Review, 100,* 363–406.

Grondin, S., & Killeen, P. R. (2009). Tracking time with song and count: Different Weber functions for musicians and nonmusicians. *Attention, Perception & Psychophysics, 71,* 1649–1654.

Grondin, S., & Laforest, M. (2004). Discriminating the tempo variations of a musical excerpt. *Acoustical Science and Technology, 25,* 159–162.

Güçlü, B., Sevinc, E., & Canbeyli, R. (2011). Duration discrimination by musicians and nonmusicians. *Psychological Reports, 108,* 675–687.

Habib, M., & Besson, M. (2009). What do music training and musical experience teach us about brain plasticity? *Music Perception, 26,* 279–285.

Hambrick, D. Z., & Tucker-Drob, E. M. (2015). The genetics of music accomplishment: Evidence for gene: Environment correlation and interaction. *Psychonomic Bulletin & Review, 22,* 112–120.

Jones, M. R., & Yee, W. (1997). Sensitivity to time change: The role of context and skill. *Journal of Experimental Psychology: Human Perception and Performance, 23,* 693–709.

Kraus, N., & Chandrasekaran, B. (2010). Music training for the development of auditory skills. *Nature Reviews Neuroscience, 11,* 599–605.

Lim, V. K., Bradshaw, J. L., Nicholls, M., & Altenmüller, E. (2003). Perceptual differences in sequential stimuli across patients with musician's and writer's cramp. *Movement Disorder, 11,* 1286–1293.

Madison, G., Karampela, O., Ullén, F., & Holm, L. (2013). Effects of practice on variability in an isochronous serial interval production task: Asymptotical levels of tapping variability after training are similar to those of musicians. *Acta Psychologica, 143,* 119–128.

McAuley, J. D., Henry, M. J., Wedd, A., Pleskac, T. J., & Cesario, J. (2012). Effects of musicality and motivational orientation on auditory category learning: A test of a regulatory-fit hypothesis. *Memory & Cognition, 40,* 231–251.

Nazari, M. A., Ebneabbasi, A., Jalalkamali, H., & Grondin, S. (2018). Time dilation caused by oddball serial position and pitch deviancy: A comparison of musicians and nonmusicians. *Music Perception, 35,* 425–436.

Panagiotidi, M., & Samartzi, S. (2013). Time estimation: Musical training and emotional content of stimuli. *Psychology of Music, 41,* 620–629.

Platz, F., Kopiez, R., Lehmann, A. C., & Wolf, A. (2014). The influence of deliberate practice on musical achievement: A meta-analysis. *Frontiers in Psychology, 5.* doi:10.3389/fpsyg.2014.00646.

Rammsayer, T. H., & Altenmüller, E. (2006). Temporal information processing in musicians and nonmusicians. *Music Perception, 24,* 37–48.

Rammsayer, T. H., Buttkus, F., & Altenmüller, E. (2012). Musicians do better than nonmusicians in both auditory and visual timing tasks. *Music Perception, 30,* 85–96.

Repp, B. H. (2005). Sensorimotor synchronization: A review of the tapping literature. *Psychonomic Bulletin & Review, 12,* 969–992.

Rüsseler, J., Altenmüller, E., Nager, W., Kohlmetz, C., & Münte, T. F. (2001). Event-related brain potentials to sound omissions differ in musicians and non-musicians. *Neuroscience Letters, 308,* 33–36.

Seashore, C., Lewis, D., & Saetveit, J. (1956). *Seashore measures of musical talents*. New York: Psychological Corporation.

Tse, P. U., Intriligator, J., Rivest, J., & Cavanagh, P. (2004). Attention and the subjective expansion of time. *Perception & Psychophysics, 66,* 1171–1189.

Ullén, F., Hambrick, D. Z., & Mosing, M. A. (2016). Rethinking expertise: A multifactorial gene: Environment interaction model of expert performance. *Psychological Bulletin, 142,* 427–446.

Yamada, M., & Tsumura, T. (1998). Do piano lessons improve basic temporal controllability of maintaining a uniform tempo? *Journal of the Acoustical Society of Japan, 19,* 121–131.

22 What Place Does Synchronization Have in Relationships Between People?

The way of communicating between people involves different implicit rules. There is of course the posture, the eye contact, and the gestures, which send a message to the other person on the inclination to enter in contact or not. Once two people are in contact, a certain rhythmicity is set in between them. This rhythmicity is a way of varying the flow of the speech, to adopt that of the other; or a way of exchanging moments of silence and speech. In fact, getting in touch is partly aiming to synchronize in order to be predictable for the other.

Synchronization of Gestures

There is a need for synchronization between people in many spheres of activity. Of course, the members of an orchestra have to play together, at the right moment; this synchronism is essential to the success of the group. In fact, temporal coordination, that is to say the exact moment when an instrument must arrive during the interpretation of a piece of music, is crucial. If this temporal coordination is slightly offset, so that it can be detected by a third person, that person will be able to use this information to get an idea of the quality of the coalition among the group members (Hagen & Bryant, 2003).

On a smaller scale, it is known that clapping hands synchronously with another person helps to generate a stronger sense of affiliation; such a feeling cannot be generated by the synchronization with only the sound of a metronome (Hove & Risen, 2009). This coordination between two people is particularly related to the spatial proximity between them (Wu, Chapman, Walker, Bischof, & Kingstone, 2013). Besides, if children are singing and dancing together, they will be more likely to help each other later if an incident occurs while playing (Kirschner & Tomasello, 2010). In fact, at all times, singing and dancing has helped to improve the coordination of group efforts (McNeill, 1995).

Thus, during the social interactions between two people, each one modifies their actions according to the movements of the other person. Everyone participates in this continual adaptation and everyone contributes, sometimes as a model, sometimes in the role of the imitator. In principle, such activity requires synchronization of oscillatory processes of the brain. The possibility of spontaneously imitating the movements of the hands of another person interacting with another person would depend on the emergence of the synchronization network between the brains of these people. This activity, which makes social interaction possible, would imply the alpha-mu band between the right centroparietal regions (Dumas, Nadel, Soussignan, Martinerie, & Garnero, 2010).

Speech Pace

Linguistic communication is made of synchronizations, whether it is the respiratory rhythm or the postural oscillations. People sometimes go so far as to adopt what the other person is saying and their way of using words (see Koole & Tschacher, 2016). This synchronization effect is stronger in positive relationships. For example, when there is shared trust between students and teachers, there is a synchronicity of movements; similarly, the synchrony between the members of a couple is greater when marital satisfaction is high rather than low. And if a mother speaks more slowly to her child, the child will decrease their speech production rate (Guitar & Marchinkoski, 2001). In fact, we tend to synchronize with those with whom we want to develop positive relationships.

What must be synchronized is also the way of exchanging speech, of taking or waiting for one's turn, in everyday life. Transitions are made freely, usually very quickly, in less than 200 ms. That is to say that the next speaker is already preparing his answer before the speaker has finished his intervention. To understand how transitions can be so fast, Magyari, De Ruiter, and Levinson (2017) did the following experiment. Pre-recorded questions accompanied the presentation of images on a screen to participants. The participants, who had to answer these questions, began their answer during the question for the trials where it was possible to guess the length of the last word of the question. Participants also sought to predict when the time would come to respond. They based this prediction on the length of the words expected and on the probability that their turn to speak is about to arrive, given the duration of all previous tests.

The speech pace can even reveal the approximate age of a person. You can guess age quite well by looking at a face, and you can guess it, admittedly a little less well, based on the voice, because of changes in some of the physical characteristics of the voice. But, based on the pace alone, we can know that a person is a little older if this person speaks more slowly and younger if the pace is fast. If we hear extracts from a natural way of speaking collected from young, old, or middle-aged adults, but accelerate or decelerate the pace a bit, the estimation of age will be affected. The acceleration gives the impression that the person is younger than when a normal pace is presented, whereas with the deceleration, one gives a higher age (Skoog Waller, Eriksson, & Sörqvist, 2015). This effect is somewhat stronger when the speakers are elderly, suggesting that the speech pace is an important clue to guessing the age of older people.

The convergence of the pace of speech indicates an eventual good cooperation between two people. Manson, Bryant, Gervais, and Kline (2013) let three people of the same sex talk to each other for 10 minutes before inviting them to play a game (prisoner's dilemma) with each of the other two people. Even when participants felt they had the same speech style, it did not really predict the level of future cooperation during the game. However, those who had a speech pace that converged during the conversation were more likely to cooperate well. Such a convergence of the execution in time, by the training of a coupling of independent oscillators, would thus favor prosocial behaviors.

Finally, note that there are theoretical works aimed at modeling interactions between people (Prepin & Pelachaud, 2011a, 2011b). One of the avenues studied, using simulations, touches the link between the level of synchrony and the level of shared understanding. When the understanding of what is said between two people who interact is high (more than 85%), the synchrony is great, but on the other hand, when their shared understanding is weak, they get out of sync (Prepin & Pelachaud, 2011b). These authors recall that the synchronization/desynchronization dynamic is proceeding rapidly. Also, the resistance to desynchronization and the ability to resynchronize depend on the sensitivity of these people to nonverbal behaviors.

In Therapy

There are therapeutic alliances between a client and a therapist. Some researchers believe that synchrony contributes to these, synchrony being the temporal coordination of client and therapist activities. For example, the synchronization of movements by the client and the therapist is associated with the alliance and, ultimately, with the success of the therapy. This synchrony also contributes to the establishment of a common language and emotional co-regulation between the client and the therapist (Koole & Tschacher, 2016).

Communication between therapist and client, during psychotherapy, includes linguistic elements such as semantics and syntax, extralinguistic elements such as gaze and eye contact, posture, gestures, and physical proximity, as well as paralinguistic elements like prosody, intonations, and speech pace. This last case is of particular interest to us since it touches the unfolding in time.

As reported by Tonti and Gelo (2016), the rate of speech seems crucial in the therapeutic relationship. For example, they cite a study by Spivack (1996) that measured the number of words uttered on average per 10-second interval by a client and a therapist during a long psychoanalytic treatment. What was analyzed was how much the pace of the client at a given moment influenced the pace of the therapist, and how much of the pace of the therapist influenced the patient's pace. This synchronization seems linked to the success of the therapeutic intervention. Besides, Rocco (2005; in Tonti & Gelo, 2016) measured, for two therapies, the number of syllables per second pronounced by a client and his therapist during three sessions. In each case, there was a correlation between the rate of the client's speech and that of the therapist's speech, but this correlation was higher in the case of the therapy that worked best. For their part, Tonti and Gelo (2016) report that a reduction in speech rate (here measured in terms of words per second) is associated with emotional and cognitive regulation, the latter being recognized as a necessary component of the change process of the client.

Conclusion

People engaged in rhythmic activities most often tend to influence each other. They synchronize their activities, which has the effect of increasing the cohesion between them. In fact, people feel a greater affiliation with those with whom there is greater coordination.

The pace of speech is particularly crucial in social interactions. Everyone has already noted the impertinence of the one who never stops talking, who takes all the place, or the other who continually interrupts the speaker. In contrast, the adoption of the speech pace contributes to the cohesion between two people and would even be at the heart of success in the therapeutic alliance between client and therapist.

References

Dumas, G., Nadel, J., Soussignan, R., Martinerie, J., & Garnero, L. (2010). Inter-brain synchronization during social Interaction. *PLoS One*, 5(8), e12166.
Guitar, B., & Marchinkoski, L. (2001). Influence of mothers' slower speech on their children's speech rate. *Journal of Speech, Language, and Hearing Research*, 44, 853–861.
Hagen, E. H., & Bryant, G. A. (2003). Music and dance as a coalition signaling system. *Human Nature*, 14, 21–51.
Hove, M. J., & Risen, J. L. (2009). It's all in the timing: Interpersonal synchrony increases affiliation. *Social Cognition*, 27, 949–960.
Kirschner, S., & Tomasello, M. (2010). Joint music making promotes prosocial behavior in 4-year-old children. *Evolution and Human Behavior*, 31, 354–364.
Koole, S. L., & Tschacher, W. (2016). Synchrony in psychotherapy: A review and an integrative framework for the therapeutic alliance. *Frontiers in Psychology*, 7, 862. doi:10.3389/fpsyg.2016.00862.
Magyari, L., De Ruiter, J. P., & Levinson, S. C. (2017). Temporal preparation for speaking in question-answer sequences. *Frontiers in Psychology*, 8, 211. doi:10.3389/fpsyg.2017.00211.
Manson, J. H., Bryant, G. A., Gervais, M. M., & Kline, M. A. (2013). Convergence of speech rate in conversation predicts cooperation. *Evolution and Human Behavior*, 34, 419–426.
McNeill, W. H. (1995). *Keeping together in time: Dance and drill in human history*. Cambridge, MA: Harvard University Press.
Prepin, K., & Pelachaud, C. (2011a). Effect of time delays on agents' interaction dynamics. *Proceedings of 10th International Conference on Autonomous Agents and Multiagent Systems (AAMAS)*, Taipei, Taiwan, 1055–1062.

Prepin, K., & Pelachaud, C. (2011b). Shared understanding and synchrony emergence: Synchrony as an indice of the exchange of meaning between dialog partners. *Proceedings of the 3rd International Conference on Agents and Artificial Intelligence (ICAART)*, Rome, Italy, Vol. 2, 25–34.

Rocco, D. (2005). Analisi degli aspetti paraverbali in una psicoterapia dinamica breve: il metodo dell'Attività Referenziale e l'analisi della Speech Rate [Analysis of paraverbal aspects during a brief dynamic psychotherapy: The method of the referential activity and the analysis of speech rhythm]. *Ricerca in Psicoterapia*, 8, 127–147.

Skoog Waller, S., Eriksson, M., & Sörqvist, P. (2015). Can you hear my age? Influences of speech rate and speech spontaneity on estimation of speaker age. *Frontiers in Psychology*, 6, 978. doi:10.3389/fpsyg.2015.00978.

Spivack, N. (1996). *Measuring mutual influence in the analytic discourse*. Garden City, NY: Adelphi University.

Tonti, M., & Gelo, O. C. G. (2016). Rate of speech and emotional-cognitive regulation in the psychotherapeutic process: A pilot study. *Research in Psychotherapy: Psychopathology, Process and Outcome*, 19, 102–112.

Wu, D. W.-L., Chapman, C. S., Walker, E., Bischof, W. F., & Kingstone, A. (2013). Isolating the perceptual from the social: Tapping in shared space results in improved synchrony. *Journal of Experimental Psychology: Human Perception & Performance*, 39, 1218–1223.

23 How Does Emotion Affect Time Perception?

Sometimes the circumstances of life create very strong emotions that plunge us into particular states of mind or body states. We have the impression that time is somehow suspended. If we are to estimate the length of the period during which we find ourselves in such states, it may be that this estimate does not correspond exactly to the actual duration. For example, Loftus (1975) recalls that, in a court murder case, one defendant said that only two seconds elapsed between the grabbing of a gun and the first shot, whereas one witness said that five minutes had passed. These temporal estimations, tinged with the emotional burden of tragic events, were crucial because a short delay would indicate that the accused might have been under the influence of fear, while a longer delay suggests that other factors were likely at stake.

In this chapter, we will attempt to describe what is known about the link between perceived duration and emotion, first by approaching it from the angle of long intervals and retrospective judgments on duration, then by focusing on the impact of certain emotion-related stimuli in the immediate estimation of duration.

Retrospective Judgments

As discussed in Chapter 1, retrospective judgments are used when assessing a time span during which it was not known that such an assessment would have to be made. However, despite the importance of the question, there is little research on the influence of emotion on the retrospective estimation of the duration of an event, and what is known does not allow us to draw clear conclusions.

In a study by Hornik (1992), participants had to attend a 12-minute class and then read for seven minutes. The duration of these two activities would eventually have to be estimated retrospectively. Between these two tasks, however, mood was manipulated, or by Velten's technique of reading a series of statements likely to induce a positive or negative mood, or by short movies with happy or sad content. Hornik reports that the happy state leads to a significant underestimation of the duration and that the state of sadness tends to create an overestimation of the duration. In other words, whether the participants were in the altered state (reading) or not (taking a course) at the time of the activity, the duration of which would have to be estimated, the results were the same. It is the state at the moment of making the judgment that seems to influence the temporal estimation.

In another study, where this time music was used to vary the emotional state, Kellaris and Kent (1992) observed that the 2.5-minute intervals judged retrospectively were overestimated when they were filled by a major-tone piece (positive valence). In contrast, Glicksohn and Cohen (2000) found no difference with their schizophrenic participants, between positive and negative conditions when mood was manipulated by music; in each condition, however, there was an underestimation of the duration.

Otherwise, in a study comparing the effect of a joyful vs. sad emotion induced by music on retrospective temporal judgments, Bisson, Tobin, and Grondin (2009) ask participants to listen to pieces of music for 3, 5, or 7 minutes. The study also included an emotionally neutral condition (a cognitive task). They observed that, as measured with three time estimation methods, the duration of the cognitive task was systematically underestimated (was considered shorter than it actually was), which was not the case for musical pieces. The duration of the happy pieces seemed longer than the same duration spent doing a cognitive task and, with the method of verbal estimation, the happy musical pieces seemed longer than the sad pieces.

In fact, reported in the context of ecological validity, the question of retrospective judgments brings up a supplementary question: What is the influence of the delay between the event whose duration must be estimated and the moment of making the temporal estimation? In retrospective time studies, people are most often asked to estimate the time immediately after the end of the period to be estimated. However, it turns out that this delay causes certain temporal distortions. When there is a delay in making this estimate, people tend to overestimate the duration, compared to conditions where the estimate is made immediately (Vitulli & Crimmins, 1998; Vitulli & Shepard, 1996; Zakay & Fallach, 1984). Notably, in a study in which a 30-second bank robbery simulation was shown on video, participants estimated that, 48 hours after viewing the video, the simulation lasted about 150 seconds (Loftus, Schooler, Boone, & Kline, 1987).

In another study, participants watched short videos for 15 minutes that generated joy, sadness, or left one neutral (Grondin, Laflamme, Bisson, & Désautels, 2014). The retrospective verbal estimate of this 15-minute duration occurred immediately after the presentation of the videos, a week later or a month later. The results show that the duration is strongly overestimated after a week or a month, but not when the estimate is made immediately after viewing. Finally, there was no difference in temporal estimation as a function of the emotional state generated by the videos. Although retrospective judgments are based on memory content and that memory capacity can be modulated by emotional content, retrospective judgments do not appear to undergo systematic transformation as a function of the emotional state of a person at the moment of occurrence of the event whose duration must be estimated.

Prospective Judgments

A research domain linking temporal perception and emotions has recently proved fruitful, thanks to the many studies from the team at Blaise-Pascal University in Clermont-Ferrand, France. This work deals with prospective judgments of short time intervals and most often involves the use of the temporal bisection method (see Droit-Volet & Gil, 2009; Droit-Volet, Fayolle, Lamotte, & Gil, 2013).

Typically, in a bisection task involving emotion-related stimuli, neutral images whose duration of presentation delineates the shortest and the longest of a series of intervals are followed by the presentation of faces showing an emotional facial expression. Compared to neutral images, the presentation duration of faces expressing fear, anger, or joy is perceived as longer (Droit-Volet, Brunot, & Niedenthal, 2004; Effron, Niedenthal, Gil, & Droit-Volet, 2006), but that of faces expressing shame is underestimated (Grondin, Laflamme, Bienvenue, Labonté, & Roy, 2015). The effect is particularly strong with angry faces (Effron et al., 2006; Tipples, 2008), but may not manifest with this facial expression when a generalization or temporal reproduction task is used (Gil & Droit-Volet, 2011). We can also observe that the duration is perceived as being longer when images provoking disgust (images of mutilations) are presented, compared to the presentation of neutral images or facial expressions of disgust (Grondin, Laflamme, & Gontier, 2014). Somewhat along the same line, women suffering from anorexia overestimate the duration of food pictures in comparison to neutral ones, because of the emotional reaction caused by food; also, compared to women with bulimia nervosa, women diagnosed with anorexia perceive the duration of joyful food pictures as longer, and tended to overestimate the duration of the disgusting ones (Gagnon, Bégin, Laflamme, & Grondin, 2018).

Some factors are likely to influence perceived duration during the presentation of faces. The presentation of elderly faces leads to a duration perceived as being shorter than the presentation of faces of young people (Chambon, Gil, Niedenthal, & Droit-Volet, 2005). In addition, compared to male faces, the duration of female faces is overestimated by men (Grondin et al., 2015). In addition, based on a task involving the reproduction of 133 to 2100-ms intervals, Arantes, Berg, and Wearden (2013) report that women will estimate that the duration is longer if they are presented with attractive men's faces rather than presented with the faces of unattractive men or women's faces.

The color of the faces presented briefly also affects the perceived duration of these presentations. Compared to the duration of the presentation of objects, the duration of presentation of faces of black people is perceived by white participants as being longer, an effect which is weaker when faces of white persons are presented (Moskowitz, Olcaysoy, Okten, & Gooch, 2015). As well, this effect is more apparent among those who are concerned about the occurrence of a prejudice bias. This work is interesting because it allows us to understand, for example, that a policeman called to make a decision quickly will probably not experience exactly the same speed of time depending on whether the person in his presence is black or white; this may even explain why the duration of white doctor interventions is shorter for black patients than for white patients (Cooper et al., 2012).

Most of the increases in perceived duration are explained by the authors by an increase in the physiological arousal caused by the images. This increase is argued to affect the pulse rate of the internal clock (see Chapter 4). According to Angrilli, Cherubini, Pavese, and Manfredini (1997), the effect of the level of arousal depends on the valence of the images used. In their experiment, which includes the reproduction of intervals of two to six seconds, they observe that, when the level of physiological arousal is high, a negative valence (for example fear) leads to a longer perceived duration than positive valence (for instance joy). Conversely, if the level of physiological arousal is low, a negative valence leads to a perceived duration being shorter than a positive valence.

The effect of emotion on time perception can also be demonstrated on the basis of auditory stimuli. For example, Schirmer, Ng, Escoffier, and Penney (2016) report that the intonation with which the syllable "ah" is pronounced is reflected in the perceived duration. The duration is underestimated if the syllable is pronounced in a tone of disgust rather than a tone of surprise. Voyer and Reuangrith (2015) report that the duration of a word uttered with an intonation expressing anger or joy is perceived as being shorter than if the word is pronounced in a neutral manner. The authors also note that the underestimation is greater (perceived duration as being shorter) with an intonation of anger rather than joy. They explain the underestimation by the fact that these emotional intonations capture the attention, thus diverting it from the processing of temporal information. Also, the emotional content of spoken words has an influence on the perceived duration (Mioni, Laflamme, Grassi, & Grondin, 2018), as can the content of words presented on screen and used to delimit time (Tipples, 2010). Moreover, in a bisection task involving short intervals, the mere fact of waiting for the arrival of an aversive stimulus, in this case, an unpleasant sound, results in an increase in the perceived duration of the interval (Droit-Volet, Mermillod, Cocenas-Silva, & Gil, 2010). Finally, in a time bisection task, a music deemed pleasant seems shorter than an unpleasant music (Droit-Volet, Ramos, Bueno, & Bigand, 2013).

Conclusion

The influence of emotion on retrospective judgments does not seem as important as that of a cognitive task or delay before recalling the duration. In the latter two cases, this influence may cause a significant overestimation of the duration. With prospective judgments, it is known that the increase in physiological arousal associated with the sight of a facial expression of joy, anger, or fear makes the duration seem longer. Also, this effect of physiological arousal would depend on the valence of the emotion.

References

Angrilli, A., Cherubini, P., Pavese, A., & Manfredini, S. (1997). The influence of affective factors on time perception. *Perception & Psychophysics, 59,* 972–982.

Arantes, J., Berg, M. E., & Wearden, J. H. (2013). Females' duration estimates of briefly-viewed male, but not female' photographs depend on attractiveness photographs depend on attractiveness. *Evolutionary Psychology, 11,* 104–119.

Bisson, N., Tobin, S., & Grondin, S. (2009). Remembering the duration of joyful and sad musical excerpts. *NeuroQuantology, 7,* 46–57.

Chambon, M., Gil, S., Niedenthal, P. M., & Droit-Volet, S. (2005). Psychologie sociale & perception du temps: l'estimation temporelle des stimuli sociaux & émotionnels. *Psychologie française, 50,* 167–180.

Cooper, L. A., Roter, D. L., Carson, K. A., Beach, M. C., Sabin, J. A., Greenwald, A. G., & Inui, T. S. (2012). The associations of clinicians' implicit attitudes about race with medical visit communication and patient ratings of interpersonal care. *American Journal of Public Health, 102,* 979–987.

Droit-Volet, S., Brunot, S., & Niedenthal, P. M. (2004). Perception of the duration of emotional events. *Cognition & Emotion, 18,* 849–858.

Droit-Volet, S., Fayolle, S., Lamotte, M., & Gil, S. (2013). Time, emotion and the embodiment of timing. *Timing & Time Perception, 1,* 99–126.

Droit-Volet, S., & Gil, S. (2009). The time-emotion paradox. *Philosophical Transactions of the Royal Society of London: Series B, Biological Sciences, 364,* 1943–1953.

Droit-Volet, S., Mermillod, M., Cocenas-Silva, R., & Gil, S. (2010). The effect of expectancy of a threatening event on time perception in human adults. *Emotion, 10,* 908–914.

Droit-Volet, S., Ramos, D., Bueno, J. L. O., & Bigand, E. (2013). Music, emotion, and time perception: The influence of subjective emotional valence and arousal? *Frontiers in Psychology: Emotion Science, 4,* 417. doi:10.3389/fpsyg.2013.00417.

Effron, D. A., Niedenthal, P. M., Gil, S., & Droit-Volet, S. (2006). Embodied temporal perception of emotion. *Emotion, 6,* 1–9.

Gagnon, C., Bégin, C., Laflamme, V., & Grondin, S. (2018). Temporal processing of joyful and disgusting food pictures by women with an eating disorder. *Frontiers in Human Neuroscience, 12,* 129.

Gil, S., & Droit-Volet, S. (2011). "Time flies in the presence of angry faces"... depending on the temporal task used! *Acta Psychologica, 136,* 354–362.

Glicksohn, J., & Cohen, Y. (2000). Can music alleviate cognitive dysfunction in schizophrenia? *Psychopathology, 33,* 43–47.

Grondin, S., Laflamme, V., Bienvenue, P., Labonté, K., & Roy, M.-L. (2015). Sex effect in the temporal perception of faces expressing anger and shame. *International Journal of Comparative Psychology, 28.*

Grondin, S., Laflamme, V., Bisson, N., & Désautels, F. (2014). The delay before recall changes the remembered duration of 15-min video sequences. *Applied Cognitive Psychology, 28,* 677–684.

Grondin, S., Laflamme, V., & Gontier, É. (2014). Effect on perceived duration and sensitivity to time when observing disgusted faces and disgusting mutilation pictures. *Attention, Perception & Psychophysics, 26,* 847–862.

Hornik, J. (1992). Time estimation and orientation mediated by transient mood. *Journal of Socio-Economics, 21,* 209–227.

Kellaris, J. J., & Kent, R. J. (1992). The influence of music on consumers' temporal perceptions: Does time fly when you're having fun? *Journal of Consumer Psychology, 1,* 365–376.

Loftus, E. F. (1975). Reconstructing memory: The incredible eyewitness. *Jurimetrics Journal, 15,* 188–193.

Loftus, E. F., Schooler, J. W., Boone, S. M., & Kline, D. (1987). Time went by so slowly: Overestimation of event duration by males and females. *Applied Cognitive Psychology, 1,* 3–13.

Mioni, G., Laflamme, V., Grassi, M., & Grondin, S. (2018). The effect of emotional spoken words on time perception depends on the gender of the speaker. *Timing & Time Perception, 6,* 1–13.

Moskowitz, G., Olcaysoy Okten, I., & Gooch, C. (2015). On race and time. *Psychological Science, 26,* 1783–1794.

Schirmer, A., Ng, T., Escoffier, N., & Penney, T. B. (2016). Emotional voices distort time: Behavioral and neural correlates. *Timing and Time Perception, 4,* 79–98.

Tipples, J. (2008). Negative emotionality influences the effects of emotion on time perception. *Emotion, 8,* 127–131.

Tipples, J. (2010). Time flies when we read taboo words. *Psychonomic Bulletin & Review, 17,* 563–568.

Vitulli, W., & Crimmins, K. (1998). Immediate versus remote judgements: Delay of response and rate of stimulus presentation in time estimation. *Perceptual and Motor Skills, 86,* 19–22.

Vitulli, W., & Shepard, H. (1996). Time estimation: Effects of cognitive task, presentation rate, and delay. *Perceptual and Motor Skills, 83,* 1387–1394.

Voyer, D., & Reuangrith, E. (2015). Perceptual asymmetries in a time estimation task with emotional sounds. *Laterality: Asymmetries of Body, Brain and Cognition, 20,* 211–231.

Zakay, D., & Fallach, E. (1984). Immediate and remote time estimation: A comparison. *Acta Psychologica, 57,* 69–81.

24 What Knowledge Do Children Have of Time?

In a study of four-day-old infants, researchers measured the average length of breaks between non-nutritive sucking periods. Then, they made the infant hear the mother's voice or a foreign voice, depending on whether the break between periods was lengthened or shortened. In this study, the child learned that it is somehow possible to hear the mother's voice by changing the length of the breaks (De Casper & Fifer, 1980). The study shows not only that the newborn recognizes the mother's voice, but also that it is possible to control the environment by playing with duration.

When reading the title question of the chapter, the answer given in the previous paragraph is probably far from what a normal reader had imagined. In fact, wondering about the beginnings and development of children's "time knowledge" is likely to take us down many roads (see Friedman, 1982). At this time, only a few avenues of the ontogeny of psychological time will be explored, ignoring in particular a literature showing the baby's ability to establish temporal relationships between events in general (see Friedman, 2008) and between stimuli of different sensory modalities (Lewkowitz, 2000).

Piagetian Approach

The numerous empirical works and texts of Jean Piaget shed light on the development of knowledge and cognitive processes in children. In particular, his work on time in children is a classic research avenue in the field (Piaget, 1946). This approach has highlighted the fact that development occurs in successive stages. Also, a central question in Piaget is how the child manages to figure out the relations between time, space, and speed.

In the Piagetian perspective of the study of time, development extends from four years to about nine years. Before age four, that is to say before the mastery of certain language skills, the child has only an intuitive knowledge of time which is limited to an organization of sensory-motor patterns. Each action has its own time, no conscious time link being made between events or actions.

It is only later, after about four years, that the child develops the ability to make logical operations about time, this development being spread over three stages. In the first stage, the child can grasp the sequence and order of events and the increase of their duration, but only if this applies to a single series of events. If two small cars move and stop at the same time, but one stops further than the other because of its speed, the child in stage one will say, in his confusion, about the car that stopped further, that it stopped later. The child does not judge the duration in itself; the child is caught by the distance traveled.

In the second stage, the child is still not able to consider some aspects of a situation and instead focuses on one aspect. Nevertheless, now able to consider the temporal order, the child can admit the simultaneity of the stops of the cars (to resume the previous example) but will still have difficulty to admit that the durations are equal. They oscillate between the idea that what goes faster must take longer and the idea that going faster means taking less time. An adult understands the second attitude and will find even absurd the following "reasoning" that will guide the child: After having posited that the faster we go, the further we go and the further we go, the longer it takes, the child concludes that the faster we go, the more time it takes. At this point, the child still has what is called preoperational thinking (usually up to seven years old).

The child reaches, at some point between seven and twelve years, the operational thought. Quite often, around eight or nine years old, they reach the third stage of the construction of the notion of time. It will be possible to understand that when two things begin and end at the same time, they have the same duration. Similarly, if two events start at the same time and one ends before the other, they will not have the same duration. Thanks to the introspection and a certain reversibility of the operations, the child now manages to separate duration, space, and speed; in fact, according to Piaget, the child is intuitively guided by what speed and space reveal. Eventually, they manage to extract the duration from its container.

The exact age of acquisition of this notion of time may in fact depend on the tests used to evaluate it. By using the understanding of works of art, for example, would lead to believe that this notion can be reached before eight or nine years (Actis Grosso & Zavagno, 2008).

Temporal Estimations

The use of traditional temporal estimation or time conditioning tasks sheds a different light on the assessment of children's temporal skills and the age at which they are acquired (see Droit-Volet, Provasi, Delgado, & Clément, 2005; Friedman, 2008; Macar, 1980; Pouthas, Macar, Lejeune, Richelle, & Jacquet, 1986).

It is possible to teach duration to children between five and six years old in a sequence of five images as follows: a bowl full on a table presented for four seconds, a child at table in front of the bowl for a second, the child who drinks the content of the bowl for one second, the child in front of the empty bowl for one second, and the empty bowl on the table for four seconds (Macar & Grondin, 1988). In a learning phase, the child learns to press a rubber bulb during the presentation of the images, and to release when the image is that of the child drinking. In the test phase, the child must press the bulb, without the images, so as to fall on the third image. During this test phase, the child sometimes relaxes a little too early, but according to certain experimental conditions (resistance offered by the bulb in the learning and testing phases), the child gets the right image about 20% of the time. It is with a more flexible bulb, allowing to put more sensory cues at the disposal of the child, that the best results occur. The study shows that young children learn not only the duration, but also the importance that kinesthetic cues can have in learning it.

Goldstone and Goldfarb (1966; Pouthas et al., 1986) report that it is only at age eight that children are able to estimate, in much the same way as adults, time intervals of 0.2 to 2 s when they are required to compare the time interval presented to them with their representation of a second. However, if the temporal reproduction method is used, six-year-olds have results that are comparable to those of adults if the intervals to be reproduced are less than one second (Fraisse, 1948). However, with long intervals (5 or 20 seconds), children experience much more difficulty at age six than at age eight.

More recently, the ability of three- and five-year-olds to properly order time intervals has been established with generalization tasks involving intervals around 400 ms or around 4 s (Droit-Volet, 2002), and with bisection tasks involving intervals of 1 to 4 s and 2 to 8 s (Droit-Volet & Wearden, 2001). Of course, at this age, children do not have the same level of performance as adults, but at age eight they get close to it. Moreover, with a bisection task, it can be noted that children aged three, five, and eight, as we saw for adults in the previous chapter, feel that the duration is longer when the interval is delimited by the image of a female face expressing anger only when it is delimited by a feminine face that is neutral in terms of emotional expression (Gil, Niedenthal, & Droit-Volet, 2007).

Temporal Representations on a Larger Scale

Friedman (2008) makes an interesting summary of the different facets of the children's temporal abilities. He notes that, depending on the language, children arrive to correctly use verb tenses to describe past or future events at around three years old. They still make a lot of mistakes at this age in their use of adverbs like "yesterday" or "this afternoon". It is rather towards four years old that they manage to wisely use terms like "before" and "after", or "yesterday" and "tomorrow".

Bill Friedman has extensively studied the abilities of children to deal with the order of events on a daily basis and their ability to remember the order of occurrence of ancient events. If it is a matter of recognizing the order in which past events have occurred, the child is able to identify events that occurred the day before or the week before, but has difficulties, even up to nine years old, to know which of two events (his birthday or Christmas, for example) occurred before or after the other if they occurred several months ago. In fact, this ability to order past events depends on the distance between events; it is easier to order if one event happened recently and another one much longer ago. Also, the ability to correctly locate these events over time (see Chapter 28) requires mastery of the concepts related to the annual cycle as revealed for example by the ability to order the months of the year (Friedman, 1992).

Moreover, for a series of events they can attend, very young children are able to get a fair representation of the sequence of events. For example, three-year-olds will be able to correctly describe a sequence related to an activity in the kitchen: for cookies, put the pieces of chocolate in the dough, place the cookies in the oven, remove them from the oven, put them on the table (see Hudson, Fivush, & Kuebli, 1992). Similarly, at age four or five, they can report in an orderly fashion over time when events such as waking up, lunch, dinner, and bedtime occur, and can even rebuild the opposite sequence at the age of six (Friedman, 1990). However, they need more time to master sequences that fit into much longer cycles. Thus, around six and seven years old, the child becomes able to put in order a set of cards that represent seasons (Friedman, 1977); at around age seven, he can correctly enumerate, in order, the days of the week and, at about eight, the months of the year (Friedman, 1986). It is necessary to wait until the middle of adolescence so that the capacity to go, in the reverse order, from one day to another or from one month to another is well integrated.

Conclusion

As can be seen, adaptation to the temporal demands of life has many faces. In each case, it is difficult to determine with precision and certainty at what age certain skills can be taken for granted. For time, as for other cognitive abilities, the concepts develop and consolidate most often over a long period. A full understanding of the notion of time is long in coming, but the ability to recognize temporal relationships between events happens very early.

References

Actis Grosso, R., & Zavagno, D. (2008). The representation of time course events in visual arts and the development of the concept of time in children: A preliminary study. *Spatial Vision, 21*, 315–336.

De Casper, A. J., & Fifer, W. P. (1980). Of human bonding: Newborns prefer their mothers' voices. *Science, 208*, 1174–1176.

Droit-Volet, S. (2002). Scalar timing in temporal generalization in children with short and long stimulus durations. *Quarterly Journal of Experimental Psychology, 55A*, 1193–1209.

Droit-Volet, S., Provasi, J., Delgado, M., & Clément, A. (2005). Le développement des capacités de jugement des durées chez l'enfant. *Psychologie française, 50*, 145–166.

Droit-Volet, S., & Wearden, J. (2001). Temporal bisection in children. *Journal of Experimental Child Psychology, 80*, 142–159.

Fraisse, P. (1948). Étude comparée de la perception & de l'estimation de la durée chez les enfants & chez les adultes, *Enfance, 2*, 199–211.

Friedman, W. J. (1977). The development of children's understanding of cyclic aspects of time. *Child Development, 48*, 1593–1599.

Friedman, W. J. (Ed.). (1982). *The developmental psychology of time*. New York: Academic Press.

Friedman, W. J. (1986). The development of children's knowledge of temporal structure. *Child Development, 57*, 1386–1400.

Friedman, W. J. (1990). Children's representations of the pattern of daily activities. *Child Development, 61*, 1399–1412.

Friedman, W. J. (1992). Children's time memory: The development of a differentiated past. *Cognitive Development, 7*, 171–187.

Friedman, W. J. (2008). Developmental perspectives on the psychology of time. In S. Grondin (Ed.), *Psychology of time* (pp. 345–366). Bingley, UK: Emerald Group Publishing.

Gil, S., Niedenthal, P. M., & Droit-Volet, S. (2007). Anger and time perception in children. *Emotion, 7*, 219–225.

Goldstone, S., & Goldfarb, J. L. (1966). The perception of time by children. In A. H. Kidd & J. L. Rivoire (Eds.), *Perceptual development in children* (pp. 445–486). New York: International University Press.

Hudson, J. A., Fivush, R., & Kuebli, J. (1992). Scripts and episodes: The development of event memory. *Applied Cognitive Psychology, 6*, 483–505.

Lewkowitz, D. J. (2000). The development of intersensory temporal perception: An epigenetic systems/limitations. *Psychological Bulletin, 126*, 281–308.

Macar, F. (1980). *Le temps: Perspectives psychophysiologiques*. Bruxelles: Mardaga.

Macar, F., & Grondin, S. (1988). Temporal regulation as a function of muscular parameters in 5-year-old children. *Journal of Experimental Child Psychology, 45*, 159–174.

Piaget, J. (1946). *Le développement de la notion de temps chez l'enfant*. Paris: Presses universitaires de France.

Pouthas, V., Macar, F., Lejeune, H., Richelle, M., & Jacquet, A. Y. (1986). Les conduites temporelles chez le jeune enfant (lacunes & perspectives de recherche). *L'Année psychologique, 86*, 103–121.

25 Does Time Perception Differ According to Sex?

In different areas of research in cognitive psychology, there are some differences in performance levels related to the sex of participants. These differences are often small, but they do exist. For example, women are better than men in tasks related to episodic memory, that is recalling and recognizing words and facts (Herlitz, Airaksinen, & Nordstroem, 1999; Herlitz, Nilsson, & Bäckman, 1997), but men are more proficient in space skills or visuospatial working memory (Halpern, 2000; Voyer, Voyer, & Bryden, 1995, Voyer, Voyer, & Saint-Aubin, 2017). Similarly, for time-related tasks, there appear to be differences in gender-related outcomes, but the understanding of them requires some methodological nuances.

Prospective Judgments

As early as 1904, McDougall reported that women tend, under various experimental conditions, to overestimate time intervals lasting a quarter of a minute to a minute and a half, much more than men. Although the differences for prospective judgments are often thinner than those reported by McDougall, it emerges from the meta-analysis of Block, Hancock, and Zakay (2000), conducted on this issue almost a century later, that, compared to men, women actually tend to make verbal estimations of duration that are higher.

Block and his collaborators explain these differences between men and women for verbal estimation by the ability of women to pay more attention to time during the interval to be estimated. In the terms of an internal clock, more attention to time means accumulating more pulses. Block and his collaborators also conclude that the women's productions of a target interval are shorter than that of men, because women, by their better attention to time, accumulate more quickly the number of pulses necessary to reach the target duration. However, these results are modulated by different factors. The sex effect appears to increase with the increase of participants' age and with the number of trials required in an experiment (Block et al., 2000). In addition, it is not possible to draw the same conclusions with the reproduction method, as this method generally does not allow to show such gender differences.[1] The results for the prospective judgments obtained with the verbal estimation and the reproduction of intervals (up to 16 s) have recently been corroborated by those of Grondin and Laflamme (2015) for intervals of 16 s and less. Also, Espinoza-Fernandez, Miro, Cano, and Buela-Casal (2003) report, for very long intervals (one and five minutes), a larger under-production by women than by men.

Recently, Glicksohn and Hadad (2012) also observed sexual differences in an interval production task, with women producing shorter intervals than men. These authors, however, interpret their results in terms of speed of the internal clock, that of women being greater, according to them. These authors also bring a significant nuance to their analysis. These shorter interval productions for women occur when the dependent variable used is the ratio of production to target, the ratio being smaller for women than for men. On the other hand, if we use the absolute value of the difference between the production and the target, or the absolute value of the difference between the production and the target divided by the target, the sexual differences are not clearly apparent.

Finally, there is no difference between the sexes for time interval discrimination of less than 100 ms (Rammsayer, 1998) or for the reproduction of intervals lasting 1 to 5 s (Rammsayer & Rammstedt, 2000). However, in the latter case, the variability of the reproductions can be explained quite well on the basis of two personality factors (openness to experience and impulsivity) for men, but not for women.

Retrospective Judgments

In the case of retrospective judgments, studies are less numerous, but the general picture that can be drawn from them is a little clearer. Again, the ratio of production to target is higher for women than for men (Block et al., 2000). This effect depends in fact this time on the number of events and the complexity of the stimuli occurring during the interval to be estimated, and on the delay between the presentation of the target duration and the moment when this duration must be judged.

Block and colleagues (2000) attribute this difference to the superiority of women over men for episodic memory (Herlitz et al., 1997, 1999). They are better for remembering the events and the contextual changes that occur during the period whose duration is to be estimated, and the duration in retrospective judgments depends on the number of events and the complexity of these changes. Moreover, it is not excluded that men forget the information contained during this period more quickly than women, which would explain the increase in sexual differences when the delay between the presentation of the target duration and the moment when the duration is judged is increased.

Emotions

One way to highlight a sexual effect on temporal perception is to look at the influence of certain factors that may not affect men and women in the same way. For example, Giovannelli et al. (2016) report the results of a study in which intervals between 510 and 690 ms had to be reproduced in a context where there are pleasant, unpleasant, or neutral smells. In the condition of unpleasant odors, women's reproductions were less accurate and much longer than those of men, this effect being even greater when the intensity of odors was increased.

We have seen in Chapter 23 that the emotion expressed by a face, when the presentation of the latter delimits a duration to be estimated, has an influence on the perceived duration. For example, in a time bisection task, the duration of presentation of faces expressing anger is judged to be longer than the duration of presentation of faces expressing shame (Grondin, Laflamme, Bienvenue, Labonté, & Roy, 2015). However, this kind of effect depends on the sex of the face presented and the sex of the participant. Women overestimate the duration of presentation of angry faces, compared to the condition of shameful faces, but only when it comes to male faces. Compared to the same duration resulting from the presentation of female faces, men for their part judged the duration resulting from the presentation of male faces as shorter (Grondin et al., 2015). The results obtained by Kliegl, Limbrecht-Ecklundt, Dürr, Traue, and Huckauf (2015), also using a temporal bisection task, even make it possible to generalize this statement: the duration of presentation of the faces of the opposite sex seems longer than the duration of presentation of faces of the same sex.

In another study involving the use of a bisection task, where the intervals were delineated by words with positive, neutral, or negative emotional content and pronounced by a male or female, the data reveal that men generally find that the intervals are long more often than women (Mioni, Laflamme, Grassi, & Grondin, 2018). Note that, in the same study, compared to the condition with women's voices, the duration of words uttered with a man's voice is more overestimated when the words have a negative meaning. Also, when a sound is spoken with a voice of surprise or disgust, women, and not men, judge the duration of this sound to be shorter than the duration of a neutrally pronounced sound (Schirmer, Ng, Escoffier, & Penney, 2016). Finally, note that women more than men tend to overestimate the duration of a sound whose intensity increases compared to a sound whose intensity decreases (Grassi, 2010).

Conclusion

When we consider the task of verbal estimation, women overestimate duration more than men, under the conditions of both prospective and retrospective judgments. Even if this difference between men and women could depend on greater efficiency of women to pay attention to time or to use episodic memory, it is not excluded that this effect also results from a difference in use of chronometric units (Grondin et al., 2015). For the prospective judgments, the results obtained with the production of intervals corroborate those obtained with the verbal estimation, which is not the case with the use of interval reproduction.

Otherwise, it should be noted that one way to bring out sexual differences in the perception of time is to manipulate certain factors, such as the reading of emotional facial expressions, which may not affect men and women in the same way. Finally, it should be noted that the current state of knowledge about sexual differences for the perception of time does not clearly explain how the hormonal or genetic differences that distinguish men and women would affect the timing mechanisms in order to explain the observed differences (Williams, 2012).

Note

1. Some results, such as those of Eisler and Eisler (1992), nevertheless show that there appear to be differences even with the use of the reproduction method.

References

Block, R. A., Hancock, P. A., & Zakay, D. (2000). Sex differences in duration judgments: A meta-analytic review. *Memory and Cognition, 28*, 1333–1346.

Eisler, H., & Eisler, A. (1992). Time perception: Effects of sex and sound intensity on scales of subjective duration. *Scandinavian Journal of Psychology, 33*, 339–358.

Espinoza-Fernandez, L., Miro, E., Cano, M., & Buela-Casal, G. (2003). Age-related changes and gender differences in time estimation. *Acta Psychologica, 112*, 221–232.

Giovannelli, F., Giganti, F., Saviozzi, A., Rebai, M., Marzi, T., Righi, S., . . . Viggianni, M. P. (2016). Gender differences in time perception during olfactory stimulation. *Journal of Sensory Studies, 31*, 61–69.

Glicksohn, J., & Hadad, Y. (2012). Sex differences in time production revisited. *Journal of Individual Differences, 33*, 35–42.

Grassi, M. (2010). Sex difference in subjective duration of looming and receding sounds. *Perception, 39*, 1424–1426.

Grondin, S., & Laflamme, V. (2015). Stevens's law for time: A direct comparison of prospective and retrospective judgments. *Attention, Perception, & Psychophysics, 77*, 1044–1051.

Grondin, S., Laflamme, V., Bienvenue, P., Labonté, K., & Roy, M.-L. (2015). Sex effect in the temporal perception of faces expressing anger and shame. *International Journal of Comparative Psychology, 28*.

Halpern, D. F. (2000). *Sex differences in cognitive abilities* (3rd ed.). Mahwah, NJ: Lawrence Erlbaum.

Herlitz, A., Airaksinen, E., & Nordstroem, E. (1999). Sex differences in episodic memory: The impact of verbal and visuospatial ability. *Neuropsychology, 13*, 590–597.

Herlitz, A., Nilsson, L.-G., & Bäckman, L. (1997). Gender differences in episodic memory. *Memory & Cognition, 25*, 801–811.

Kliegl, K. M., Limbrecht-Ecklundt, K., Dürr, L., Traue, H. C., & Huckauf, A. (2015). The complex duration perception of emotional faces: Effects of face direction. *Frontiers in Psychology, 6*, 262. doi:10.3389/fpsyg.2015.00262.

MacDougall, R. (1904). Sex differences in the sense of time. *Science, 9*, 707–708.

Mioni, G., Laflamme, V., Grassi, M., & Grondin, S. (2018). The effect of emotional spoken words on time perception depends on the gender of the speaker. *Timing & Time Perception, 6*, 1–13.

Rammsayer, T. H. (1998). Temporal information processing in male and female subjects. *Studia Psychologica, 40*, 149–164.

Rammsayer, T. H., & Rammstedt, B. (2000). Sex-related differences in time estimation: The role of personality. *Personality and Individual Differences, 29*, 301–312.

Schirmer, A., Ng, T., Escoffier, N., & Penney, T. B. (2016). Emotional voices distort time: Behavioral and neural correlates. *Timing and Time Perception, 4*, 79–98.

Voyer, D., Voyer, S. D., & Bryden, M. P. (1995). Magnitude of sex differences in spatial abilities: A meta-analysis and consideration of critical variables. *Psychological Bulletin, 117*, 250–270.

Voyer, D., Voyer, S. D., & Saint-Aubin, J. (2017). Sex differences in visual-spatial working memory: A meta-analysis. *Psychonomic Bulletin & Review, 24*, 307–334.

Williams, C. L. (2012). Sex differences in counting and timing. *Frontiers in Integrative Neuroscience, 5*, 88. doi:10.3389/fnint.2011.00088.

26 How Do People Differ in Their Relationship to Time?

We have all known people who are more or less organized, for whom deadlines do not seem to weigh heavily or cause any concern; or otherwise known people for whom time is a permanent concern, but who have a life set to the metronome for everything to work. One wonders if one should envy or pity those people who are careless of time or those who are stuck in time. Obviously, we differ from each other in many facets of time, but, as we will see, we still share certain cultural traits.

Assessment of Individual Differences

One way to see how we differ in our relationship to time is to look at the temporal dimensions that researchers have tried to evaluate over the years. Questionnaires for investigating individual differences include the *Temporal Personality Inventory* (TPI: Francis-Smythe & Robertson, 1999a, 1999b). This scale includes 43 questions and assesses the behaviors, cognitions, and emotions of five dimensions of temporal personality: awareness of free time, punctuality, planning, polychronicity, and impatience. These are traits, that is, predispositions to be or act in a certain way. In its French version, validated with 1267 people, the scale has eight dimensions (Bisson, Grondin, & Francis-Smythe, 2015). In the French version, in addition to the awareness of free time to refer to the fact that a person may or may not prefer having a schedule and deadlines even during free time, punctuality is sort of split into two dimensions, respect of timelines and social temporal beliefs; there is a distinction between planning and use of time at work, and planning and use of time at home (but not on vacation). There is also a distinction between polychronicity, which is the inclination of a person to perform several tasks simultaneously, and proximity of the results, which designates the fact that a person can have a greater or lesser preference for tasks whose results can be seen quickly. Finally, the impatience dimension refers to the fact that someone perceives him or herself as someone who encourages others to hurry, both at home and at work.

Some of these temporal dimensions are closely related to more general dimensions of personality as measured by a frequently used questionnaire, the NEO-FFI (Bisson et al., 2015). Thus, the neuroticism factor, which refers to the sensitivity to aversive stimuli (perceived as threatening and painful) is strongly correlated with impatience, but inversely correlated with respect for deadlines. Polychronicity is strongly correlated with extraversion (see also Conte & Jacobs, 2003), whereas agreeableness is inversely correlated with impatience (see also Settles et al., 2012). Finally, it is not surprising to learn that the conscientiousness dimension of NEO-FFI is very closely linked to the respect of deadlines (Bisson et al., 2015).

Another classic questionnaire in the field of psychological time is that of Zimbardo and Boyd (1999: the *Zimbardo Time Perspective Inventory*—ZTPI). This questionnaire has in fact been validated in many countries (Sircova et al., 2014), including France (Apostolidis & Fieulaine, 2004). The ZTPI requires participants to respond to a series of statements on a five-point Likert type scale in order to assess five dimensions. Thus, individuals have, to varying degrees, a generally negative or aversive view of the past (1: past negative), a sentimental and positive attitude towards the past (2: positive past), an attitude of helplessness and hopelessness to life (3: present fatalistic), an attitude of risk-taking, oriented towards pleasure and the present moment, without reflection on the future consequences (4: present hedonistic) and, finally, a general inclination towards the future (5: future-oriented). The inventory now includes another dimension, transcendental future, meaning that people plan during their lives as a function of their faith, believing that there is a better life after death (Zimbardo, Sword, & Sword, 2012).

Some links can be established between the ZTPI and the TPI. In a study conducted in French, high TPI scores related to planning (at home or at work), as well as those related to adherence to deadlines, are very closely linked to high scores on the "future" dimension of the ZTPI (Bisson et al., 2015). Moreover, it is interesting to note negative correlations between the consciousness of time on vacation (TPI) and the dimension "present hedonistic" (ZTPI), and between the respect of deadlines (TPI) and the dimension "past negative" (ZTPI). However, this last dimension is positively correlated with impatience (TPI). Finally, note that in the ZTPI, a high score on the "past negative" dimension is closely related to a high score on the *Beck Depression Inventory* and a high score on the anxiety trait, but is inversely correlated with self-esteem; in addition, a high score in the "future-oriented" dimension is closely related to being conscientious, and a high score in the "present hedonistic" dimension is closely related to a high score on the search for sensation or novelty (Boyd & Zimbardo, 2005).

There are many other questionnaires designed to identify aspects of the temporal organization of people, especially in the area of time management. This area of study could be defined as follows: "Time management is the self-controlled attempt to use time in a subjectively efficient way to achieve outcomes through setting and prioritizing goals, planning and scheduling tasks, and monitoring progress both against the schedule and of task completion, in an iterative process, in order to accommodate changing goals and priorities" (Francis-Smythe, 2006, p. 145).

150 *Personal and Social Time*

Among the self-administered questionnaires used in the area of time management are the *Time Structure Questionnaire* (TSQ: Bond & Feather, 1988), the *Time Management Behavior Scale* (TMBS: Macan, Shahani, Dipboye, & Phillips, 1990), and the *Time Management Questionnaire* (TMQ: Britton & Tesser, 1991). These questionnaires make it possible to highlight different aspects of the temporal organization of individuals. The TSQ includes assessment of routine and planning as well as persistence, the TMBS is about the control that people think they have about their time, and the TMQ is about short-term and long-term planning and the impression of using time constructively.

Cultural Differences

Despite the many dimensions that can distinguish people from one another in relation to time, there are often within a society common ways to act as a function of time. The value and meaning given to time may however differ considerably from one society to another.

Studies have focused on the pace of life in different countries. Levine (1988, 1996) studied the question using the following indicators: the precision of clocks in banks, the average walking speed to cover one hundred feet (about 30 meters) and the time required to go to post a package. The countries compared were England, the United States, Indonesia, Italy, Japan, and Taiwan. It has been found that there is some stability between these indices. For example, it is in Japan that clocks are the most accurate, that the walking pace is fastest, and that packages are delivered the fastest. People from Indonesia are last or penultimate in all three categories. Obviously, the relationship to time differs in these two countries, the pace of life being faster in Japan.

In a study on the pace of life involving 31 countries and based on the same three indicators, Levine and Norenzayan (1999) found that this pace is faster in Japan and in Western European countries, and slower in developing countries. The pace is actually generally faster in countries with an individualistic culture, those that have a thriving economy, and those where the climate is colder. These authors also point out that places where the pace of life is faster attract people likely to support such a pace. Moreover, it is interesting to note the following paradox. This accelerated pace of life is usually accompanied by a higher level of feeling of well-being, but also, on the other hand, by a higher rate of unhealthy behavior, such as smoking, and by a higher rate of coronary heart disease.

Countries were also compared on the tendency to favor a short-term orientation rather than a long-term orientation. Western countries, where individualistic values are important, are characterized by short-term orientation and planning, as opposed to long-term orientation, as is the case in Taiwan or China, where there is respect for traditions and the need to fulfill one's social obligations (see Sircova et al., 2015).

That being said, one can still read some stability across the different countries for the preference for certain dimensions of the time perspective as measured by the ZTPI. First, these dimensions do not seem to differ according to cultures (Sircova et al., 2015). Also, the more positive directions towards the future, or the present, are gaining popularity in most countries. In China, on the other hand, there is an inclination for the present fatalistic and past negative.

Conclusion

The relation to time is a vast field of study that goes beyond the strict framework of social psychology. Time being crucial in social organization, it is not surprising to see that the question has interested researchers in the field of management. In psychology, interest has been focused on differences in time traits, such as those measured by the TPI and ZTPI. Beyond the individual differences in the ways of being in time and dealing with it, our relationship to time is also partly a reflection of the cultural context in which we are immersed; the social environment determines a certain lifestyle, imposes a certain pace on life.

References

Apostolidis, T., & Fieulaine, N. (2004). Validation française de l'échelle de temporalité: The Zimbardo time perspective inventory (ZTPI). *European Review of Applied Psychology, 54*, 207–217.

Bisson, N., Grondin, S., & Francis-Smythe, J. (2015). Validation de la version française du Time Personality Indicator. *L'Année psychologique/Topics in Cognitive Psychology, 115*, 561–590.

Bond, M. J., & Feather, N. T. (1988). Some correlates of structure and purpose in the use of time. *Journal of Personality and Social Psychology, 55*, 321–329.

Boyd, J. N., & Zimbardo, P. G. (2005). Time perspective, health and risk taking. In A. Strahman & J. Joireman (Eds.), *Understanding behavior in the context of time: Theory, research and applications* (pp. 85–107). Mahwah, NJ: Lawrence Erlbaum.

Britton, B. K., & Tesser, A. (1991). Effects of time management practices of college grades. *Journal of Educational Psychology, 83*, 405–410.

Conte, J. M., & Jacobs, R. R. (2003). Validity evidence linking polychronicity and big five personality dimensions to absence, lateness, and supervisory performance ratings. *Human Performance, 16*, 107–129.

Francis-Smythe, J. A. (2006). Time management. In J. Glicksohn & M. S. Myslobodsky (Eds.), *Timing the future: The case for a time-based prospective memory* (pp. 143–170). River Edge: World Scientific Publishing.

Francis-Smythe, J. A., & Robertson, I. T. (1999a). On the relationship between time management and time estimation. *British Journal of Psychology, 90*, 333–347.

Francis-Smythe, J. A., & Robertson, I. T. (1999b). Time-related individual differences. *Time and Society, 8*, 273–292.

Levine, R. V. (1988). The pace of life across cultures. In J. E. McGrath (Ed.), *The social psychology of time: New perspectives* (pp. 39–62). Newbury Park, CA: Sage.

Levine, R. V. (1996). Cultural differences in the pace of life. In H. Helfriech (Ed.), *Time and mind* (pp. 119–142). Seattle, WA: Hogrefe & Huber Publishers.

Levine, R. V., & Norenzayan, A. (1999). The pace of life in 31 countries. *Journal of Cross-Cultural Psychology, 30*, 178–205.

Macan, T. M., Shahani, C., Dipboye, R. L., & Phillips, A. P. (1990). College students' time management: Correlations with academic performance and stress. *Journal of Educational Psychology, 82*, 760–768.

Settles, R. E., Fischer, S., Cyders, M. A., Combs, J. L., Gunn, R. L., & Smith, G. T. (2012). Negative urgency: A personality predictor of externalizing behavior characterized by neuroticism, low conscientiousness, and disagreeableness. *Journal of Abnormal Psychology, 121*, 160–172.

Sircova, A., van de Vijver, F. J. R., Osin, E., Milfont, T. L., Fieulaine, N., Kislali-Erginbilgic, A., . . . 54 members of the International Time Perspective Research Project Time Perspective Profiles of Cultures. (2015). Time perspective profiles of cultures. In M. Stolarski, N. Fieulaine, & W. van Beek (Eds.), *Time perspective theory: Review, research and application* (pp. 169–187). Suisse: Springer and Cham.

Sircova, A., van de Vijver, F. J. R., Osin, E., Milfont, T. L., Fieulaine, N., Kislali-Erginbilgic, A., & Zimbardo, P. G. (2014). A global look at time: A 24-country study of the equivalence of the Zimbardo Time Perspective Inventory. *Sage Open, 4*(1). doi:10.1177/2158244013515686.

Zimbardo, P., & Boyd, J. (1999). Putting time in perspective: A valid, reliable individual-differences metric. *Journal of Personality and Social Psychology, 77*, 1271–1288.

Zimbardo, P., Sword, R., & Sword, R. (2012). *The time cure*. San Francisco, CA: Jossey-Bass.

27 Do We Correctly Estimate the Time It Takes to Do a Task?

It is sometimes said that if you want a task to be done, you have to ask someone very busy to do it! Apparently, busy people have so little time that they have to be efficient and do things without waiting. These people probably know how to manage their time. But this ability to manage time efficiently, without procrastination, requires at least a good estimate of the time required to complete a task. So, to estimate the time that a task will take, it is still necessary to know this task. This knowledge might include the need to remember how much time performing a similar task had taken, or normally takes.

Retrospective Judgments

We have seen in Chapter 23 that emotion can influence retrospective judgments on duration. However, even in more neutral contexts, the memory of the duration of events or activities can be highly imprecise. In other words, our estimate of how long a task will take is sometimes based on uncertain grounds. Block and Zakay (1997) recall that retrospective judgments leave room for much variability.

Participants had to complete five cognitive tasks, such as giving the names of animals or plants in alphabetical order or calculate from 500,000 by subtracting from 3 each time. Each task was performed during one of five durations ranging from 2 to 8 minutes (Grondin & Plourde, 2007). In general, the 50 participants in this study tended to overestimate short intervals and to underestimate long intervals, a result consistent with Vierordt's law (see Chapter 2; Roy & Christenfeld, 2008). In the same study, participants were also asked for each task to indicate the minimum duration and the maximum duration that they seemed to have had. The results indicate that the actual duration falls in the estimated window only in 77 of the 250 cases. There was even one participant who could not notice that the tasks had had different durations. Moreover, when asked to make a judgment on the duration of the entire experiment, only 10 of the 50 participants managed to establish a window covering the actual duration. In other words, people are sometimes very bad at estimating the duration of a past activity.

That being said, the following caveat must be made before concluding that retrospective temporal judgments are necessarily bad. As discussed in Chapter 23, the duration of activities or events judged retrospectively tends to be overestimated if the estimate is made after a certain period rather than immediately after the period to be estimated. In addition, retrospective time estimations are sometimes no more imprecise than prospective time estimations; at least that has been observed with video game players in a gaming environment (Tobin, Bisson, & Grondin, 2010).

Otherwise, the duration of events likely to occur on a daily basis is better retained when the duration of these events remains stable (Yarmey, 2000). If this duration varies, changes over time, it becomes more difficult to remember it correctly. Thus, we remember better, by dint of use, the duration of a normal cycle of machine washing or the time it takes for a ball to cross a bowling alley than the usual duration of a conversation with friends or colleagues, the duration of a transaction at an ATM or the waiting time at the restaurant before service. Finally, it should be noted that in the Yarmey study, tasks lasting 2.5 minutes or less tend to be significantly overestimated.

Other researchers wanted to know the accuracy of the memory of the duration of public events. It turned out that estimation errors can sometimes be very large. For example, in a study conducted in 1990, the median value of estimates of the reign of Pope John Paul I (which began in August 1978) was 90 days, whereas the reign lasted only 33 days. In contrast, the median value of the same participants' estimates of the duration of the hostage crisis at the US embassy in Iran (started in November 1979) was 28 days, while the actual duration was 442 days (Burt & Kemp, 1991). This last example is more reflective of a general result of this study: participants most often tend to underestimate the duration of the events they need to remember. These estimations are also the result of a process of reconstruction in memory. In other words, estimating the duration of an event is not only an estimate of the event itself, but also a consideration of the duration of the events of the same category (Burt, 1993; Burt & Kemp, 1991). It is therefore difficult to judge the duration of the reign of a given pope without taking into consideration our knowledge of the supposed duration of the reign of the popes in general.

Planning Fallacy

There are many reports of an effect called *planning fallacy*, where people tend to believe that they will be able to accomplish a task faster than it will happen. Thus, people underestimate the time required to do a task and this effect does not diminish as the deadline approaches (Tversky & Kahneman, 1974). According to Kahneman and Tversky (1973), this effect would be caused by the tendency of people to consider certain specific aspects of the task and how it will be completed, rather than relying on the duration that the performance of similar tasks required.

The planning error could also be explained by the difficulty to consider each sub-component of a task and making a clear plan of what to do (see Francis-Smythe, 2006). The mistake may occur if we cannot properly unpack, or properly operationalize everything that needs to be done. Intentions must result in the implementation of what needs to be done, where it should be done and when. Besides, although we need to look at cognitive processes to understand planning error, motivational factors should not be discounted (Francis-Smythe & Robertson, 1999).

In their literature review, Roy, Christenfeld, and McKenzie (2005) report a strong tendency to underestimate the duration of future activities or events. This seems all the more true when the activities or events in question last more than five minutes. These authors attribute this effect to the imperfect recollection of the time required for a similar task previously completed. In fact, the effect of past task-related experience on the temporal prediction of this task is well documented (Thomas, Handley, & Newstead, 2007). Notably, receiving feedback over time (Roy, Mitten, & Christenfeld, 2008) or receiving a minimum of work-related training (Roy & Christenfeld, 2007; Thomas, Newstead, & Handley, 2003) allows to improve the prediction. In short, "knowledge about the duration of the task" (Tobin & Grondin, 2012) seems to play an important role in the quality of the temporal prediction relative to this task.

One factor that can influence this knowledge about the duration of the task is the level of expertise in performing this task. Participants in experimental studies on the effect of training on duration usually practice for only a few hours or weeks (see Chapter 8). However, some people, in a natural context, undergo very long training. This is the case, for example, for athletes or high-level musicians (experts) who are subjected, mostly on a daily basis, to trainings that sometimes last several years. It turns out that such training allows the acquisition of a fine knowledge of the duration of the task. Notably, Tobin and Grondin (2015) have observed that, for a 5-km run, expert runners are more accurate than novices not only to estimate the duration of a race that has just ended, but also to predict the running time of a race to come.

The tendency to underestimate the time that a task will take seems even greater in the field of engineering and management of large projects where the durations at stake are much longer. In this particular area, Halkjelsvik and Jørgensen (2012) recall the necessity to distinguish predicting the number of hours needed to make a project from predicting when the task will be accomplished (i.e. the delivery date of the project). In order to reduce the inaccuracy of time estimations, these authors recommend taking into account data from previous projects and looking at the shifts in orientation that occurred between what was planned to what the final product became. They also recommend the use of experienced estimators and group estimates, which allows grouping pieces of information and defining precisely the activities necessary for the success of the project. Similarly, Halkjelsvik and Jørgensen propose making the estimators responsible by making the precision of the estimate an evaluation criterion. In addition, the same authors advise against using an estimation based on uncertainty where minimum and maximum values must be determined; better just ask how long the project will take.

Finally, an overestimation, rather than an underestimation, of the time required to complete a task could have certain consequences, according to the extensions given to Parkinson's law. Developed in the field of administration, this law stipulates that the more time one has to do a job, the more work will be done in order to ensure that the time allocated to it is fully occupied (Parkinson, 1958). In other words, if you have a lot of time to do a task, it is likely to become more complex. There would therefore be a possible gain in efficiency when the duration of a task is underestimated.

Conclusion

When we think that the construction of the Sydney Opera House took 16 years, rather than the predicted 6 years, we see how crucial it is, on a large scale, to correctly predict the time it takes to do something. In fact, in general, one would tend to underestimate the duration of a complete task. This would be partly due to the difficulty of correctly recalling the duration of past activities or events, or to the negligence or difficulty in taking these durations into consideration.

References

Block, R. A., & Zakay, D. (1997). Prospective and retrospective duration judgments: A meta-analytic review. *Psychonomic Bulletin & Review, 4*, 184–197.

Burt, C. D. B. (1993). The effect of actual event duration and event memory on the reconstruction of duration information. *Applied Cognitive Psychology, 7*, 63–73.

Burt, C. D. B., & Kemp, S. (1991). Retrospective duration estimation of public events. *Memory and Cognition, 19*, 252–262.

Francis-Smythe, J. A. (2006). Time management. In J. Glicksohn & M. S. Myslobodsky (Eds.), *Timing the future: The case for a time-based prospective memory* (pp. 143–170). River Edge: World Scientific Publishing.

Francis-Smythe, J. A., & Robertson, I. T. (1999). On the relationship between time management and time estimation. *British Journal of Psychology, 90*, 333–347.

Grondin, S., & Plourde, M. (2007). Judging multi-minute intervals retrospectively. *Quarterly Journal of Experimental Psychology, 60*, 1303–1312.

Halkjelsvik, T., & Jørgensen, M. (2012). From origami to software development: A review of studies on judgment-based predictions of performance time. *Psychological Bulletin, 138*, 238–271.

Kahneman, D., & Tversky, A. (1973). On the psychology of prediction. *Psychological Review, 80*, 237–251.

Parkinson, C. N. (1958). *Parkinson's law or the pursuit of progress*. London, UK: John Murray.

Roy, M. M., & Christenfeld, N. J. S. (2007). Bias in memory predicts bias in estimation of future task duration. *Memory & Cognition, 35*, 557–564.

Roy, M. M., & Christenfeld, N. J. S. (2008). Effect of the task length on remembered and predicted duration. *Psychonomic Bulletin & Review, 15,* 202–207.

Roy, M. M., Christenfeld, N. J. S., & McKenzie, C. R. M. (2005). Underestimation of future duration: Memory incorrectly used or memory bias. *Psychological Bulletin, 131,* 738–756.

Roy, M. M., Mitten, S. T., & Christenfeld, N. J. S. (2008). Correcting memory improves accuracy of predicted task duration. *Journal of Experimental Psychology: Applied, 14,* 266–275.

Thomas, K. E., Handley, S. J., & Newstead, S. E. (2007). The role of prior task experience in temporal misestimating. *Quarterly Journal of Experimental Psychology, 60,* 230–240.

Thomas, K. E., Newstead, S. E., & Handley, S. J. (2003). Exploring the time prediction process: The effects of task experience and complexity on prediction accuracy. *Applied Cognitive Psychology, 17,* 655–673.

Tobin, S., Bisson, N., & Grondin, S. (2010). An ecological approach to prospective and retrospective timing of long durations: A study involving gamers. *PLoS One, 5*(2), e9271.

Tobin, S., & Grondin, S. (2012). Time perception is enhanced by task duration knowledge: Evidence from experienced swimmers. *Memory & Cognition, 40,* 1339–1351.

Tobin, S., & Grondin, S. (2015). Prior task experience affects temporal prediction and estimation. *Frontiers in Psychology: Perception Science, 6,* 916. doi:10.3389/fpsyg.2015.00916.

Tversky, A., & Kahneman, D. (1974). Judgment under uncertainty: Heuristics and biases. *Science, 185,* 1123–1131.

Yarmey, A. D. (2000). Retrospective duration estimations for variant and invariant events in field situations. *Applied Cognitive Psychology, 14,* 45–57.

28 How Do We Remember When an Event Occurred?

We have seen in the preceding chapter that it is rather difficult to remember how long an event or an activity had lasted. Similarly, it can be difficult to identify when exactly, or how long ago, an event has occurred, and this includes the chronology of events in one's own life. The question is difficult, because there does not seem to be any temporal stamping on our numerous memories, or direct temporal path, when we navigate in our memory of the past events, to trace the moment of their occurrence.

As Friedman (1993) has rightly pointed out, the quest for understanding the mechanisms by which psychology researchers can trace the date of an event in memory may resemble that of archaeologists attempting to trace back to the origin of certain artifacts. Archaeologists must attempt to establish the age of a given object, to see whether or not this object belongs to the level of technological development of the presumed era, and to determine whether something in this object makes it possible to situate it chronologically with respect to other objects.

Theoretical Proposals

There are several hypotheses related to the memory of time. In the wake of the analogy with archeology, Friedman (1993) proposes three categories of explanations: one based on the distance between the event and the present, one based on the place where the event took place and the information left at the time of encoding, and one based on the moment of occurrence relative to other events.

In distance-based interpretations, information about when a memory occurred is a process functioning between the moments of encoding and remembering. Among these explanations, there is one stipulating that the ability to remember depends on the strength of the trace that an event leaves in memory. The stronger this trace, the more recent this event would seem. In fact, some researchers rather report that it is not the trace in itself that matters, but the number of proposals about an event. Thus, if one can remember several details about the event, it will appear more lively, more recent. This kind of theoretical interpretation is based on the idea that memories are tinged in some way by the passage of time in order to leave clues in order to identify the age of said memories.

There are other distance-based interpretations of the memory of time. One of these states that the representations of events are stored in memory according to their chronological order of occurrence. The older a trace is, the farther away it is from the psychological present (Murdock, 1974), which brings us back to the hypothesis described in the previous paragraph. Other researchers argue instead that the context in which is found an event that one wants to identify temporally proves decisive. If components of the context at the time of encoding the event are also present at the time of the recall, this will help to give the impression that the event is more recent (Glenberg, Bradley, Kraus, & Renzaglia, 1983).

The previous interpretations were based on what happens to the information between the time of the encoding and the moment of the recall. Other interpretations rely instead on the information gathered at the time of encoding or of reconstructing memory. One of these, the time tagging, states that there would be an assignment, a marking, some specific temporal information that would be done automatically at the time of encoding events (Glenberg, 1987). Another interpretation states that, when an event occurs, there is rather an encoding of the general context, an association with control elements, that is, markers of some sort occurring at different times through elements to remember. Without self-repetition of these elements, the temporal information about the order of the elements ends up being lost, as well as the order of the control elements that are displaced on the timeline (Estes, 1985). Friedman (1993) calls this interpretation encoding perturbation. Finally, another interpretation of the way of remembering time consists in positing that it is a process of reconstruction in memory which also relies on contextual associations, the contexts here being the knowledge of temporal references which are social, natural or personal.

Finally, a third category of interpretations is based on the moment of occurrence relative to other events. For example, it could be linking the moment when we visited a country with another moment (another year, for example) when we visited another country. The memory of time thus depends on an associative chain (Lewandowsky & Murdock, 1989). This memory could also depend on the coding of a new element with an older element already stored. By finding the old element when the new one arrives, their relative order would be automatically encoded. It is not so much here to understand how one does to know when an event has occurred, but rather in what order events happen.

Some Facts

Often, the interpretations described in the preceding paragraphs follow an investigation involving a specific method. In fact, two types of studies have been used to enrich knowledge in the field of spotting past events (Block &

Zakay, 2008). In laboratory studies, lists of words are taught to participants and they are asked, for example, what was the relative position of these words, without necessarily informing them in advance that the temporal aspect (order or time of appearance) is important. The other type of study deals with autobiographical (or everyday) memory. Participants must, for example, fill in a daily diary where the moments of the events are recorded, after which, several weeks, months or years later, they can be questioned about this information.

In a laboratory study, participants had to pay attention to a list of 50 words, without knowing that they had to worry about their order. Later, the same words were presented in random order and participants were asked to report their approximate time position in the previous presentation. These participants located more precisely the words that first appeared in the initial list than the words located further down the list (Hintzman & Block, 1971). This kind of result is not compatible with an interpretation that the judgments of the temporal position depend on the gradual decline of the trace in memory left by the words, the oldest being supposed to have less strength than the most recent ones. Such results also suggest that temporal encoding is circumstantial, automatic, effortless. In fact, other studies of this kind indicate that temporal encoding is based on information specific to a certain context and not on a continuous and absolute time scale (Hintzman, Block, & Summers, 1973).

Autobiographical studies reveal some precision in the chronological recall of events, but sometimes also some biases. For example, participants may sometimes clearly remember that events may have occurred at a specific time of day, but cannot remember the day, month, or year in which they occurred (Friedman & Wilkins, 1985). The memory of the age of an event would therefore not be based on a specific time tagging, but on the basis of contextual associations. Besides, data collected from children reveal that they can remember the order of arrival of an event that occurred a week ago, as opposed to an event that happened seven weeks ago, without remembering day, month, or season information (Friedman, 1991; Friedman & Kemp, 1998). In other words, children seem able to order events without contextual associations, as if there was a process based on distance, on a subjective impression, itself made possible by the strength of a trace left in memory by each event (see Block & Zakay, 2008).

Finally, it should be noted in general that people tend to believe that old events did not occur so long ago (Loftus & Marburger, 1983), and recent events sometimes tend to be remembered as being older than they are really (Kemp, 1996). Such bias occurs in recalling news, recalling personal events, and even recalling historical facts, that is, facts that occurred before the participant's birth (Kemp, 1988, 1994).

Memory Encoding Troubles

People may have problems in correctly situating past events in the right time and may even lose their time references relative to days, years and even decades. These people may, however, have no trouble doing certain temporal tasks involving short intervals (less than a minute for example) like those often described in this book.

To understand a little what can happen, it must be remembered that there are two major categories of disorders of the functioning of memory. Sometimes people are unable to remember facts that happened more than a minute ago. If you talk to a very old person one day, you will find that the ability to remember recent information, a skill that is taken for granted, is a specific skill. Seniors tend to repeat the same questions after a few minutes of conversation, often unable to correctly encode the answer. They may have trouble recording new information but will be able to remember fairly accurately events from a distant past. This inability to retain new information is called anterograde amnesia. In contrast, people may no longer be able to recall very old memories. This is called retrograde amnesia. What is interesting about retrograde amnesia is that a person could very well remember what the concept of marriage is, but not remember his own.

Damage to a brain structure called the hippocampus, in the medial temporal lobe, will cause anterograde amnesia. However, memories are not stored in the hippocampus, but rather in a network of neurons that includes parts of the temporal lobe around the hippocampus (Damasio, 2002). Temporal lobe damage will cause retrograde amnesia and an inability to remember when and where specific events occurred. Disorders such as Alzheimer's disease will cause irreversible loss of autobiographical memories (see El Haj & Kapogiannis, 2016). Finally, note that an injury to a part of the brain called the basal forebrain would not prevent some events from being remembered, but would make it impossible to remember when they occurred. In other words, this part of the brain would be assigned to identify chronological aspects related to events (Damasio, 2002).

Conclusion

The study of the mechanisms of memory is in itself a gigantic field of research of experimental psychology, but we will not go further in this field. However, remember that understanding the specific encoding of the temporal aspects of memories is a huge challenge for researchers. Given the different approaches (in laboratory or with autobiographical memories) to address the issue, it is not surprising that the theoretical interpretations of the question are numerous. The encoding and recalling of a correct chronology of events is crucial to having a full understanding of these events. One can realize it fully when these functions are defective.

References

Block, R. A., & Zakay, D. (2008). Timing and remembering the past, the present, and the future. In S. Grondin (Ed.), *Psychology of time*. Bingley, UK: Emerald Group Publishing.

Damasio, A. R. (2002). Remembering when. *Scientific American, 287*, 66–73.
El Haj, M., & Kapogiannis, D. (2016). Time distortions in Alzheimer's disease: A systematic review and theoretical integration. *npj Aging and Mechanisms of Disease, 2*, 16016. doi:10.1038/npjamd.2016.16.
Estes, W. K. (1985). Memory for temporal information. In J. A. Michon & J. Jackson (Eds.), *Time, mind, and behavior* (pp. 151–168). Berlin: Springer-Verlag.
Friedman, W. J. (1991). The development of children's memory for the time of past events. *Child Development, 62*, 139–155.
Friedman, W. J. (1993). Memory for the time of past events. *Psychological Bulletin, 113*, 44–66.
Friedman, W. J., & Kemp, S. (1998). The effects of elapsed time and retrieval on young children's judgments of the temporal distances of past events. *Cognitive Development, 13*, 335–367.
Friedman, W. J., & Wilkins, A. J. (1985). Scale effects in memory for the time of events. *Memory & Cognition, 13*, 168–175.
Glenberg, A. M. (1987). Temporal context and recency. In D. S. Gorfein & R. R. Hoffman (Eds.), *Memory and learning: The Ebbinghaus centennial conference* (pp. 173–190). Hillsdale, NJ: Lawrence Erlbaum.
Glenberg, A. M., Bradley, M. M., Kraus, T. A., & Renzaglia, G. J. (1983). Studies of the long-term recency effect: Support for the contextually guided retrieval hypothesis. *Journal of Experimental Psychology: Learning, Memory, and Cognition, 9*, 231–255.
Hintzman, D. L., & Block, R. A. (1971). Repetition and memory: Evidence for a multiple-trace hypothesis. *Journal of Experimental Psychology, 88*, 297–306.
Hintzman, D. L., Block, R. A., & Summers, J. J. (1973). Contextual associations and memory for serial position. *Journal of Experimental Psychology, 97*, 220–229.
Kemp, S. (1988). Dating recent and historical events. *Applied Cognitive Psychology, 2*, 181–188.
Kemp, S. (1994). Bias in dating news and historical events. *Acta Psychologica, 86*, 69–87.
Kemp, S. (1996). Association as a cause of dating bias. *Memory, 4*, 131–143.
Lewandowsky, S., & Murdock, B. B. (1989). Memory for serial order. *Psychological Review, 96*, 25–57.
Loftus, E. F., & Marburger, W. (1983). Since the eruption of Mt. St. Helens, has anyone beaten you up? Improving the accuracy of retrospective reports with landmark events. *Memory & Cognition, 11*, 114–120.
Murdock, B. B. (1974). *Human memory: Theory and data*. Potomac, MD: Lawrence Erlbaum.

29 Why Does Time Seem to Go Faster as We Get Older?

Because it refers to a fundamental intuition or, say, a powerful feeling that pops up from time to time within most of us, this simple question seems most appropriate. However, what this question suggests is that time actually seems to go faster as we get older. It would probably be more prudent to ask a similar question, but without starting with "why". So, does time really seem to go faster as we get older? It depends on what the idea of the passage of time refers to. If you ask an elderly person at some point in the middle of the day if they feel that time is passing quickly, it is far from clear that the answer will be "yes"; rather, the answer may be "no" if that person has nothing to do when the question is asked. There are many differences between the immediate passage of time (and the reading of the time that is passing by) and the impressions left by the experiences of the past, more or less distant, relative to the flow of temporal extents (months, years). In other words, it is possible to receive, for one question, two opposite answers: time passes slowly today (time seems long), but life passes quickly (time passes quickly).

If you have, dear reader, if only once, felt that time is now passing faster than before, then the answer to the question about the speed of passage of time with aging becomes "yes, time seems to go faster as you get older". This answer draws some of its relevance from the fact that it is extremely unlikely that you experienced the opposite impression, that is, time seems to go slower as we get older. Therefore, it is reasonable to consider that the phenomenon is true; the impression of temporal acceleration[1] is real. Starting from the assertion that there is such an impression of acceleration, then the question as to why it is so becomes legitimate again and takes all its meaning. And there are actually several hypotheses for explaining why such an impression may occur.

Some Classical Interpretations or Hypotheses

The perhaps most classic interpretation of the impression of temporal acceleration could be described as the ratio theory. Each time segment—day, week, month, or year—represents an ever-smaller portion of our life as we get older. For example, one year at 10 years old represents 10% of one's life, but at age 50, one year represents only 2%. This change in ratio over the years could be at the heart of the impression that time seems to pass more quickly as one gets older. In other words, it is not a period in itself that counts, but this period in contrast to the rest of our life. According to Lemlich (1975, p. 275), "the subjective duration of an interval of real time varies inversely with the square-root of the total real time (age)". A smaller proportion would then be interpreted as a faster passage of time. This ratio theory, however, does not reveal how such an interpretation would be possible, that is to say what psychological mechanism leads to this interpretation, or generates this impression.

Another hypothesis for explaining the impression of temporal acceleration is the number of memorable events that occur at different times in life. More specifically, this number decreases over the years. During childhood, many new events occur, almost on a daily basis, and enrich the repertoire in memory. As we get older, more and more events are stored and it becomes less and less likely that we are exposed to novelty. Also, there is a greater proportion of things that are done on a routine basis. However, we know that time is perceived as shorter when it is filled with more routine activities (Avni-Babad & Ritov, 2003). The thinking underlying this memory-based hypothesis is therefore that the temporal impression depends on the number of events that could be recalled for a given period of time and that the recall possibility depends on the importance and significance of the events occurring.

This hypothesis could be related to a classical discovery in the field of time perception. When someone does not know that it will be necessary to make a judgment about time, but is suddenly asked to estimate the duration of an event or of an activity (a retrospective judgment on duration; see Chapter 27), the duration is estimated to be longer if more events are recalled (Block & Zakay, 1997). If, as we get older, it becomes more and more difficult to access or retrieve events that have occurred over a period of time, this difficulty in retrieving and recalling these events or information would give the impression that the period was shorter than it really was; as a result, time would then be interpreted as having passed more quickly.

Other functions modified with age may affect the relation to time. The slowing down of the pace of biological processes, in general, could be translated into an impression that external time (i.e. calendar time, which remains unchanged) is accelerating (Draaisma, 2004). As an example of a slowdown, we know that when people of different ages are asked to do a series of spontaneous finger taps, the rate adopted varies according to age. Older people tap more slowly than children or young adults (McAuley, Jones, Holub, Johnston, & Miller, 2006). Moreover, among the other functions that age modifies, there is attention which, incidentally, determines perceived duration under conditions of prospective judgments over time: time is perceived as longer when we allocate more attention to time (see Chapter 9). However, we also know that aging is accompanied by a decline in attentional resources (Craik & Hay, 1999). Therefore, in this perspective, with aging, a given time interval is perceived as shorter due to a lack of attentional resources.

The following two hypotheses may be even more interesting. Basically, they do not apply to aging problems, but are associated with the fact that time itself might seem to pass more or less quickly. There is literature on the memory of past events revealing a phenomenon called forward telescoping. This phenomenon is the tendency to underestimate how long past events, whether public news or personal events, have occurred (see the previous chapter). If someone feels the impression that an event has occurred much longer ago than it seems to be, it may seem like time is passing quickly. It is difficult to say whether this impression increases with aging. However, as we get older, there is more and more room for such an impression, as the number of much older events increases and the magnitude of the error of underestimation that could be made also increases. Together, these potential factors could compete and lead to the impression that time seems to go faster as we get older.

Another hypothesis is linked to the temporal pressure exerted by the need to perform several tasks in daily life. People often underestimate the time required to complete a task (see Chapter 27). As a result, they often find themselves in situations where they run out of time. Failure to complete as many tasks or activities as expected creates the impression that time has passed quickly. Children usually have fewer responsibilities than adults; children—hopefully— have more time for themselves than adults, more room for maneuver on a daily basis. Seen from this "time-pressure" angle, the impression that time seems to pass quickly would be stronger when there is more to do. This should probably correspond to the period of life, in their thirties, when people try to establish themselves professionally and try to create a family, to take care of young children.

Study of Temporal Acceleration

There are not many empirical demonstrations that show that there is a phenomenon like temporal acceleration, probably because it is difficult to make such demonstrations. If people are asked to compare their real impression of the speed of the passage of time with the impression they had during childhood, the impression of acceleration will appear (Gallant, Fidler, & Dawson, 1991; Lemlich, 1975). However, the few cross-sectional studies assessing age differences for time-course impressions tend to indicate that young adults and older adults do not differ much. The surveys are based on questions such as the following (see Friedman & Janssen, 2010, p. 240), where participants are asked to respond on a five-point scale ranging from "very slowly" (-2) to "very fast" (2):

1. How fast does time usually pass for you?
2. How fast do you expect the next hour to pass?
3. How fast did the previous week pass for you?
4. How fast did the previous month pass for you?
5. How fast did the previous year pass for you?
6. How fast did the previous 10 years pass to you?

Although at all ages time seems to pass quickly for most people, only the question related to the previous 10 years, among those reported previously, shows significant age differences. Older people are those who find that the last 10 years have passed the fastest. Such results were reported for a group of 499 German or Austrian participants aged 14 to 94 (Wittmann & Lehnhoff, 2005), for a group of 868 Japanese participants aged 16 to 80 (Janssen, Naka, & Friedman, 2013), as well as for a group of 1865 mainly Dutch or New Zealander participants aged 16 to 80 (Friedman & Janssen, 2010). Janssen and colleagues (2013) also report that it was the participants who reported having experienced the most pressure 10 years ago who said that the last 10 years had passed the fastest. In fact, there is also a strong link between the current time pressure and the impression that recent periods have passed quickly (Janssen et al., 2013).

In another study involving 366 participants aged 20, 38, and 71, it was not the older participants who reported the strongest impression that time went faster, but people aged about 38 (Flaherty & Meer, 1994). This result is attributable to the fact that people of the middle age group are very busy. In fact, factors such as the quality of the activities and the level of engagement seem to determine the impression one has of the passage of time (Larson, 2004; Larson & von Eye, 2006).

Finally, in our own laboratory, we observed that the impression that time seems to be faster is more apparent in older participants than in adolescents (Gagnon-Harvey et al., 2019). Moreover, for adolescents, the impression that time passes quickly is tightly related to anxiety, with more anxiety resulting in a lower impression that time passes fast (Morin et al., 2019). In the study, the impression that time passes quickly was also closely related to higher scores on the present hedonistic and future-oriented components of the Zimbardo temporal perspective inventory (Chapter 26).

Conclusion and Ad Lib

From the moment a person has the impression that time passes faster with age, the phenomenon exists, if only for this one person. However, it is difficult to demonstrate experimentally, on the basis of a comparison between different age groups, that there is, as aging progresses, a continuity of the temporal acceleration. Having a lot of things to do (daily work and family demands) in middle age gives the impression that time passes quickly during this particular period of life.

Different hypotheses can be used to explain the impression of temporal acceleration. It could be a contrast effect between durations. At age 10, it is not possible to contrast last year with the last 20 years. As we get older, it becomes possible, for example, to contrast the last five years with the previous five, or even with the previous 10 or 20. It is not the percentage of our life represented by a given period, per se, that would be critical, but the possibility of contrasting it with longer periods. In short, this phenomenon of temporal acceleration would result from a certain form of successive contrast.

Finally, one can posit the following bold hypothesis. At some point in the last decades of life, it becomes impossible to maintain the illusion that we have eternity in front of us. The probability of dying increases and our time is increasingly counted. A wind of consciousness rises, and with it appears more and more clearly the evidence of being only passing. Faced with such an impression, failing to be able to resort to some emergency measure, there might be an unconscious will to slow down the normal pace of life: The impression of the greater speed of time would then come from our desire that this pace be slowed down. In other words, it is not the accumulation of past time that is critical, but the decrease in life expectancy.

Note

1. In this chapter we will call "temporal acceleration" the impression that time seems to pass more rapidly as we get older.

References

Avni-Babad, D., & Ritov, I. (2003). Routine and the perception of time. *Journal of Experimental Psychology: General, 132*, 543–550.

Block, R. A., & Zakay, D. (1997). Prospective and retrospective duration judgments: A meta-analytic review. *Psychonomic Bulletin & Review, 4*, 184–197.

Craik, F. I. M., & Hay, J. F. (1999). Aging and judgments of duration: Effects of task complexity and method of estimation. *Perception and Psychophysics, 61*, 549–560.

Draaisma, D. (2004). *Why life speeds up as you grow older* (How Memory Shapes Our Past). Cambridge: Cambridge University Press.

Flaherty, M. G., & Meer, M. D. (1994). How time flies: Age, memory, and temporal compression. *The Sociological Quarterly, 35*, 705–721.

Friedman, W. J., & Janssen, S. M. J. (2010). Aging and the speed of time. *Acta Psychologica, 134*, 130–141.

Gagnon-Harvey, A. A., Fortin-Guichard, D., Tétreault, É., Boutin, J.-P., & Grondin, S. (2019). Étude de la compression temporelle en fonction des caractéristiques individuelles (Study of temporal compression according to individual characteristics). Poster at *41st Annual Meeting of the Societé québécoise pour la recherche en psychologie*, Trois-Rivières, Canada.

Gallant, R., Fidler, T., & Dawson, K. A. (1991). Subjective time estimation and age. *Perceptual and Motor Skills, 72*, 1275–1280.

Janssen, S. M. J., Naka, M., & Friedman, W. J. (2013). Why does life appear to speed up as people get older? *Time & Society, 22*, 274–290.

Larson, E. (2004). The time of our lives: The experience of temporality in occupation. *Canadian Journal of Occupational Therapy, 71*, 24–35.

Larson, E., & von Eye, A. (2006). Predicting the perceived flow of time from qualities of activity and depth of engagement. *Ecological Psychology, 18*, 113–130.

Lemlich, R. (1975). Subjective acceleration of time with aging. *Perceptual and Motor Skills, 41*, 235–238.

McAuley, J. D., Jones, M. R., Holub, S., Johnston, H. M., & Miller, N. S. (2006). The time of our lives: Life span development of timing and event tracking. *Journal of Experimental Psychology: General, 135*, 348–367.

Morin, A., Bernier, M., Boutin, J.-P., & Grondin, S. (2019). Vitesse du passage du temps et caractéristiques individuelles des adolescents (Speed of passage of time and individual characteristics of adolescents). Poster at the *41st Annual Meeting of the Societé québécoise pour la recherche en psychologie*, Trois-Rivières, Canada.

Wittmann, M., & Lehnhoff, S. (2005). Age effects in perception of time. *Psychological Reports, 97*, 921–935.

Index

adaptation level 13
adjustment 7
affordance 69
Allan, L. G. 7, 24, 26, 67
Alzheimer's disease 161
anorexia 132, 134
anterograde amnesia 161
anxiety 96–99
attention 40, 56–59
attentional gate model 59
attention deficit hyperactivity disorder 86–89
auditory modality 17, 38, 44–46, 51
autistic spectrum disorder 82

basal ganglia 33, 35, 88, 100, 116
Beck Depression Inventory 149
bisection tasks 5, 7
Bisson, N. 3, 52, 133, 148–149, 154
Block, R. A. 4, 23, 56, 58, 143, 144, 153, 159–160, 164
Boltz, M. G. 3, 56
Brochard, R. 41
Brown, S. W. 3, 56–58, 63
Bueti, D. 33, 45–46

Cahoon, D. 56
Casini, L. 18, 32, 57–58, 83
categorization 7
caudate nucleus 33, 40
cerebellum 32–35
children 138–140
chronostasis 67
Church, R. M. 12
circadian rhythm 16
cognitive effects 68–71
comparison 5, 6, 7
Connors test 53
Coull, J. T. 58

Creelman, C. D. 24
cultural differences 150

Davalos, D. B. 32, 79
decision-making 102
Delevoye-Turrell, Y. 77
depressive state 91–93
difference threshold 6, 7, 8
d' index 7
discrimination task 5, 51, 106
dorsolateral prefrontal cortex (DLPFC) 32
double task 57
Drake, C. 12, 19, 38–39, 121
Droit-Volet, S. 26, 84, 134, 139–140
drugs 70
dynamic attending theory 40–41

Eisler, A. -H. 3, 11, 13, 19, 26, 44, 146
electroencephalography (EEG) 30, 33, 79, 122
emotion 132–135
encoding perturbation 159
entrainment model 41
expectancy 42

Fechner, Gustav 10
flash-lag 17
forward telescoping 165
Fraisse, P. 12, 19, 20, 140
Francis-Smythe, J. A. 148–149, 155
François, M. 24
Friedman, W. J. 138–141, 158–160, 164–166
frontal cortex 32
functional magnetic resonance imaging (fMRI) 30, 33, 39, 79, 87, 100, 116

Gamache, P.-L. 26, 45, 52, 57, 111
gap detection 111

generalization 5, 7
Getty, D. 12, 19
Gibbon, J. 13, 25–26
Giersch, A. 17, 77–78
Gil, S. 84, 134, 140
Goldstone, S. 44, 140
Grassi, M. 7, 135, 145
Grondin, S. 12, 20, 38, 45, 57, 63, 92, 134
Grube, M. 33, 39

Harrington, D. L. 30, 33–34
Hasuo, E. 7, 45, 47, 62, 68
Hellström, A. 13, 19, 26, 101, 106
hemineglect 33
Hicks, R. E. 3, 58
Hinton, S. C. 20, 32–33
hippocampus 161
Hoagland, H. 25
Hubbard, T. L. 17

imputed-velocity model 62
indifference interval 13, 18–19
insula/operculum 79
intermodality 45
internal clock model 23–26
Ivry, R. B. 34, 101

James, W. 20
Jones, C. R. G. 100–101
Jones, L. A. 26
Jones, M. R. 19, 40, 123

kappa effect 61–62, 64
Keele, S. W. 34
Kemp, S. 154–160
Killeen, P. R. 12, 25
Koch, G. 34–35
Kristofferson, A. B. 51
Kuroda, T. 7, 45, 47, 62–63, 68

Lalanne, L. 77–78
language impairment 109
Large, E. W. 40
Levine, R. V. 150
Libet, B. 17
Loftus, E. F. 132–133, 160
Lu, A. 69

Macar, F. 18, 32, 57–58, 139
Madison, G. 12, 50, 53, 121
magnetoencephalography (MEG) 30, 33
magnitude estimation 10
Maister, L. 83
Matthews, W. J. 44, 51, 63–64, 68, 88

McAuley, J. D. 19, 39, 124, 164
McDougall, J. A. 143
Meck, W. H. 33, 70
memory 20, 23, 26, 56, 160
Mento, G. 41
Merchant, H. 12, 31, 32, 35, 101–102
mindfulness 70
Minkowski, E. 77
Mioni, G. 4, 19, 25, 30, 46, 69, 92, 96, 102, 105–107, 145
mismatch negativity 79, 122
modality 31, 44–47
modulus 10
multiple-look hypothesis 38–39
music 121–124

Nagarajan, S. S. 51–52
Nakajima, Y. 62, 68
Nazari, M. A. 122
negative contingent variation (CNV) 32
NEO-FFI 148
noncentral timing 31

Oberfeld, D. 78, 91–93
oddball effect 122–123
Ogden, R. S. 26, 71
olivo-cerebellar network 40
Ornstein, R. E. 23
oscillator 40–41

pacemaker 23–24, 58, 70–71, 96
pacemaker-counter device 24–25
pace of life 150
parietal cortex 32–33
Parkinson's disease 100–103
Penney, T. B. 9, 24, 26, 32, 49, 135, 145
perceptual effects 67–68
Pfeuty, M. 32
phenomenal present 18
phonological awareness 111–112
physical magnitude 10–11
physical rehabilitation 114–116
Piaget, Jean 138–139
place theory 47
planning fallacy 154
point of subjective equality 6, 8
polychronicity 148–149
Poppël, E. 17, 20, 84
Pouthas, V. 32–33, 53, 105, 139–140
power function 11
premotor cortex 35, 40
preoperational thinking 139
production 4–5, 11
prospective judgments 3, 57, 134, 143
prospective memory 83, 85, 107

psychological moment 17–18
psychometric functions 6
psychophysics 5–6, 10–13
putamen 33, 40, 116

Rammsayer, T. H. 18–19, 24, 26, 34, 47, 51, 53, 101, 123, 144
ratio theory 163–164
Rattat, A. C. 26
reading impairments 110
reminder task 6
reproduction 4–5, 8
retrograde amnesia 161
retrospective judgment 3–4, 56, 132, 144, 153
return-trip effect 69
rhythm 38–42, 123
rhythmic training 114–115
rotor pursuit tracking task 57
Rousseau, R. 45, 57
roving standard 6
Roy, M. M. 69, 153, 155

scalar expectancy theory 25
scalar property 12
schizophrenia 77–80
Seashore Measures of Musical Talents 121
senses 44–47
sensitivity 84, 106
sex 143–145
signal detection theory 7
Simon effect 78
single stimulus procedure 7
Sircova, A. 149–150
social interactions 82, 127, 130
Sonuga-Barke, E. J. S. 88
space 61–64
speech 18, 34, 109, 128–130
sports 116–117
Staddon, J. E. R. 23
Stevens's law 10–11, 13
subcortical structures 33, 35
supplementary motor area (SMA) 32
synchronization 127–130

Tallal, P. 109–111
tau effect 61
Teki, S. 33–34, 39
temporal acceleration 163–167
temporal discounting 88–89
temporal displacement 17–18

temporal distorsions 67–71
temporal fusion 123
temporal orientation 92, 98
Temporal Personality Inventory 148
temporal pressure 70, 165
ten Hoopen, G. 38, 62, 68
thalamus 40, 79, 100
Thaut, M. H. 114–115
therapeutic alliances 129
Thomas, E. A. C. 58
Thomas, K. E. 155
Thomas's model 58
time conditioning 139
time management 82, 149–150
Time Management Behavior Scale 150
Time Management Questionnaire 150
time-shrinking illusion 67
Time Structure Questionnaire 150
Tipples, J. 134–135
Tobin, S. 3, 26, 52, 133, 154–155
transcranial magnetic stimulation (TMS or TMSr) 30, 32, 46
traumatic brain injury 105–107
Treisman, M. 24

Ulrich, R. 24, 26, 52–53, 68

van Noorden, L. P. A. 47
van Rijn, H. 31
van Wassenhove, V. 18
Velten's technique 132
verbal estimation 4–5, 10
Vicario, C. M. 68–69
Vicario, G. B. 17–18
Vierordt's law 13, 122, 124, 153

waiting effect 56
Walker, J. T. 45
Wearden, J. H. 12, 26, 44–45, 101
Weber, Ernst 11
Weber fraction 12–13
Weber's law 11–12, 14
Wiener, M. 32, 35
Wittmann, M. 70, 166

Yarrow, K. 67

Zakay, D. 56–57, 59, 69, 97, 133
Zelaznik, H. N. 34, 87, 115
Zimbardo Time Perspective Inventory 149

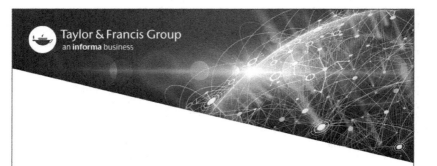

Taylor & Francis eBooks

www.taylorfrancis.com

A single destination for eBooks from Taylor & Francis with increased functionality and an improved user experience to meet the needs of our customers.

90,000+ eBooks of award-winning academic content in Humanities, Social Science, Science, Technology, Engineering, and Medical written by a global network of editors and authors.

TAYLOR & FRANCIS EBOOKS OFFERS:

A streamlined experience for our library customers

A single point of discovery for all of our eBook content

Improved search and discovery of content at both book and chapter level

REQUEST A FREE TRIAL
support@taylorfrancis.com